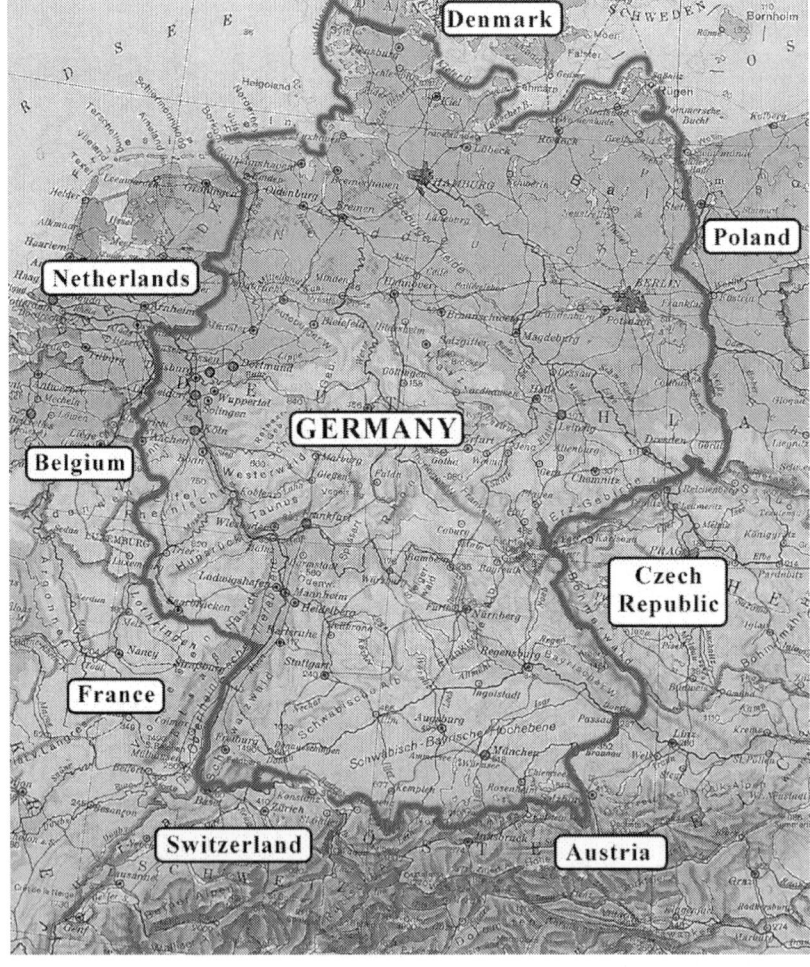

The Human Face
of
German History

World War II and What Came Before and After:

Stories of Survivors

The history of WWII told as experienced by 15 men and women

Waldtraut Wanninger

ISBN: 9798663520270
Imprint: Independently published

Production: Sirka Hummel
Maps and Cover Illustration: Sirka Hummel

Technical

My own remarks, explanations, important politic and social details are typed in the font "Times New Roman".

Direct quotations of interviews and memoirs are typed in "Lucinda Sans, Italic".

Footnotes *) are interspersed within the text as they occur.

The actual names of the interviewees have been changed for privacy. Only some of them decided to have their own names published.

To my children
Barbara, Andrea, Sirka, grandchildren Anika, Gwyneth, Mia, Sophie, Nathaniel; to my American friends who kept asking about the war, and to everybody else who is truly interested in what happened.

Timetable

1914:   WWI begins

1918:   WWI ends,
            The German Monarchy ends

1919:   Weimar Republic begins

1922/23:   German Inflation

1933:   Hitler becomes German Chancellor

1934:   The German President, Hindenburg, dies.
            Hitler assumes the office of President also

1939:   WWII begins

1945:   WWII ends

1961:   East Germany ("German Democratic Republic") builds the wall and
            fences against West Germany.

1989:   German Reunification

Index

Why this Book was Written

One summer my daughter Andrea and I were traveling in Germany. Driving along the *Autobahn* on a lazy Sunday afternoon, we were passing the exit to the city of Pforzheim and, without thinking, I said: "This was one of the most heavily destroyed small cities during the war in Germany." I did not feel any emotion. It was as if I had said, 'Pforzheim has one hundred thousand inhabitants' or something similarly insignificant.

But Andrea asked: "Why was it destroyed? Were there vital military plants there?" and after a short pause: "Why do you and Papa never talk about any of this? We don't know anything about the war, but we should. It's *our* history too." I had to agree with her and promised I would write it all down – soon.

But when I started to look at the events of more than 60 years earlier, I realized that, long ago, I had pushed all my experiences and emotions from that time down into the deepest recesses of my memory. They were still there, all scrambled up – untidy – unresolved, not thought-through or processed.

When I pulled them up, one by one, they started hurting again. And this made me angry; angry at the perpetrators on either side of the war, angry about the forced helplessness of people; and hateful toward anyone – any group – who had hurt others. It also made me angry at those still hurting, oppressing, torturing, and killing others today – despite knowing full well about the unspeakable cruelties committed in Europe during the war and before.

On a shelf in my kitchen I keep a can of pumpkin. When I am angry and need to let off steam, I open the door into the courtyard behind the kitchen, I grab the can and hurl it by all my might unto the ground. The pumpkin's weight and consistency of the mushy inside are perfect for this purpose. The can hits the cement slab hard; it does not bounce back; and it gets rather dented and scratched. This is extremely satisfying.

While my story was forming, de-forming, and re-forming inside my brain, my pumpkin can could become more and more mutilated and ugly. In other words: I made good progress in processing my memories.

I also realized that my experiences and those of my family were too limited to convey a full picture and feel for the events of the time. I needed to hear the experiences of more people of my own generation. I also needed to see the period through the eyes of those who had known a time *before* that turmoil, people whose view of life had been formed during times before. First, I asked friends my own age. Then I approached older relatives and friends for their life stories. And finally, I received memoirs written by people about even earlier years that had already passed away.

I also wanted to understand why all the things – mostly bad ones – had happened to me and to us all. What was the background? What was the reason?

I was born in 1933, the year Hitler came to power. I was eleven when the war ended, and about 15 when life slowly, very slowly, started to return to "normal". My whole childhood and early teens were spent in a world of pre-war, war, and post-war. Normal for me were oppression and fear, constant danger and shortage of everything. Not only I but many others had become so used of war and everything around had become normal life. I remember when I learned the Korea War had started and – for a few moments – I felt safe. I knew how to behave in war time.

Much later I started to collect the stories. For my interviewees, sharing their stories with me, very often became a release of feelings buried for many decades. Now they had an opportunity to talk about experiences never shared before with anyone, some of which had been too horrible to voice up until then. Sometimes we cried together; sometimes we laughed.

And I was touched by the many expressions of gratitude even in these darkest moments: gratitude for having been saved from deadly circumstances; and thankfulness for lifelong friendships that were made in the midst of conditions that seemed too terrible to bear.

I also heard about almost-magical moments like the following: Gertrud, a young anti-aircraft auxiliary in eastern Germany managed to avoid capture by the Soviet troops at the end of the war. But she still needed to get home to western Germany. For several days she, at night and very cautiously, moved westward. When she encountered two badly wounded German soldiers, also on their way west, the three of them decided to make their way together to the nearest border out of the Soviet occupation zone and into the British.

On their way they almost got too close to a Soviet military camp.

Some guards must have seen them and shot at them but luckily, they were not hurt. A heavily wooded mountainside seemed the safest route away from this danger. They crawled up the mountain, carrying their heavy backpacks. Through all this they were not even sure of the right direction anymore.

At the top of the mountain the dense forest gave way to a sunny meadow which at first seemed to all three of them a mirage, a hallucination caused by total exhaustion. But it was real. There in this meadow sat an old shepherd, knitting, and around him his sheep were peacefully grazing.

The shepherd could tell them that they had indeed come in the right direction. At the foot of the mountain flowed the river that formed the border between the Soviet and the British occupation zones. He could also describe to the fugitives the Soviet patrol routes and the times. And he knew the best spot from which to swim across the river and to – relative – safety.

Of the many people I interviewed, all but one had the same attitude about what they had gone through: some events had been almost indescribably terrible; nevertheless, they were grateful. One of them expressed it like this: "I am glad I lived those years. I think it made me what I am today. Of course, I do wish we did not have to go through that hell, all these hardships and dangers but in a way, it taught us things that we have carried on."

All these people had survived. Many have bad scars, physical and emotional. But they had made it. Millions did, of course, not make it. We remember, commemorate them with awe, and we deeply honor them.

In this book I want to tell the stories of people who did live through horrors and pain and loss and made it out alive. They managed to heal themselves up to a certain point. They built a new life of appreciation and all the small and large good things that later came their way.

Karl's Journey at age 11

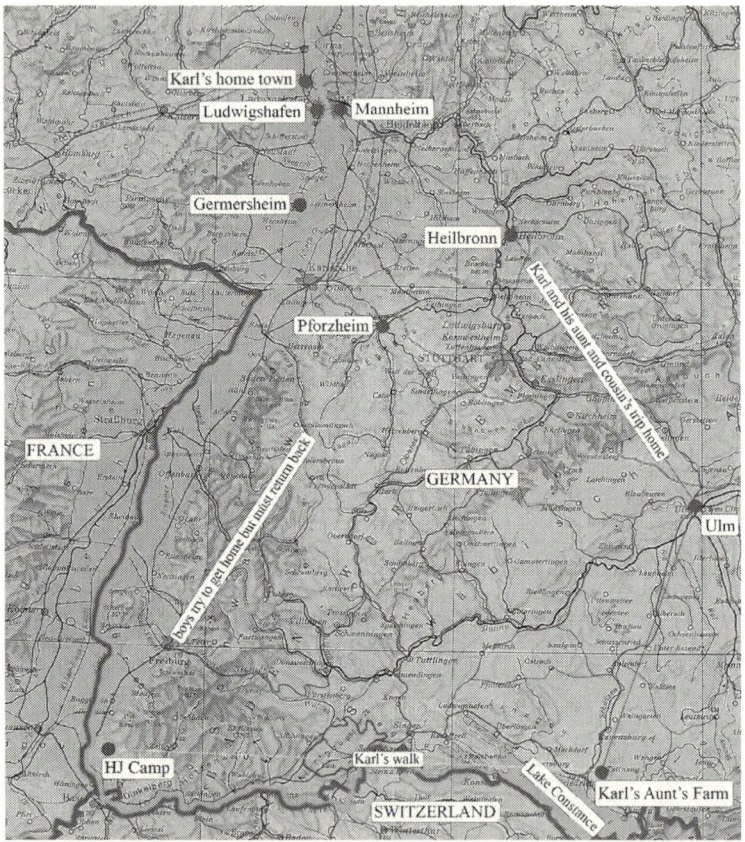

Karl's Journey at age 11 (born 1934)

Six years after the war I had finished the last grade of high school. We were 15 boys and girls who had, like I, lived through the "Third Reich", through the war and the, still dangerous and very poor, years after the war. We never ever spoke of these times.

But it seems that in school our subconscious still rebelled against the languages that had been enemy images for us during our earlier years. Our French teacher almost despaired about our (feigned!) inability to pronounce the language properly. We spent most of the English classes making fun of our (actually very nice) teacher. One of my classmates was planning to study these two languages and become an interpreter. She begged us to use proper accents as not to confuse her. I am happy to say that she reached her career goal despite our prejudices.

Fifty years later I flew to Germany to attend a reunion of my class. I think our memories of the dangerous times of our childhood and youth must have "mellowed" in the meantime. When I asked around for special experiences, Karl, readily, told me a story from his childhood. This is in his own words:

For a year or so I had been a member of the HJ Jungvolk)
and I must say, we always had a good time. (*)The "Jungvolk"
section of the HJ (=mandatory "Hitler Youth") comprised of the 10 -
14 year old boys.) In our small city it was rather apolitical**). I was
10 years old at the time.* * The "Hitler Jugend" (= "Hitler Youth") was
meant to be an educational tool to train young people into the NS-doctrine.
But very often (as in Karl's case) the leaders of these groups did not care
about political views. They conducted their groups very much like Boy Scout
troops.

*In early February of 1945 our group was invited to stay in
a Camp in the Black Forest. It turned out to be really nice. We lived
in a house, about 20 of us. In March we were supposed to go home
again. The trip from my hometown to the Black Forest had been
relatively easy. But on the way back home our train was shot at
repeatedly by enemy aircraft. We had to jump out and crouch
down, away from the tracks. They shot wherever they could, mostly
through the roofs of the passenger cars. It looked like they were
having fun. Luckily we were hiding well and not visible to them and
none of us got hurt.*

At one point the train could go no further because the train tracks were damaged and we had to walk. We marched for long distances. And one thing I will never forget: We walked through Pforzheim, the city of the goldsmiths. There had been a large bomb raid three weeks before. The whole city lay in ruins and there was the frightening smell of decay of human corpses! It was terrible! *)

*) At February 23, 1945, almost at the end of the war, Pforzheim was destroyed by explosive and incendiary bombs. 17,600 people, more than one third of the population, were killed, mostly burned by the phosphor fires that could not been extinguished.

We walked north for quite some distance until we found a bridge over the river Rhein that was still intact. We crossed over and marched on. In Germersheim people asked us where we were going. When we told them, they said: "You can't go on. The Americans are already there." Our leader said: "Then we will go back to the place in the Black Forest."

We did indeed make it back to Camp. We walked for long stretches. For part of the way we found a train, once a truck took us up.

Back at the Camp the time became very difficult because we did not know anything. I did not know what had happened to my parents and my sister. And we asked ourselves: 'The Americans, what kind of people are they?' We didn't know anything. We just knew the American bombers and the fighting planes; that we knew. But are they also ordinary people? How is something like this justifiable?

We did not have a bad time at Camp; actually it was even better than the first stay. This time we were distributed over several farms because the house where we had before stayed was not available anymore. At my farm I even got my socks darned and my cloths washed a few times. We hiked in the woods and slipped and slid around in the snow. It was nice. There were no bomb raids in the area. But when spring came, I could not stay there anymore. I think, not knowing about my family, not knowing where I belonged, was the worst.

As time went on, we realized that the end of the war was near. The leader of our Camp was a one-armed sergeant. One day I went to him and said: "Mr. Sergeant, I have an aunt near the Bodensee (=Lake Constance) and I want to go to her." At first he said: "I can not let you go." But I kept telling him that I could make it, and after some back and forth he said: "Bring me your backpack.

You may have it back tomorrow morning."When I came to him the next morning for my backpack, he had filled it with food. We also had maps at the Camp and I could look where exactly I wanted to go.

The Camp leader, this one-armed sergeant, knew, of course what might happen to his boys if they were found as a group, probably even the boys in their uniforms, by the American or the French army. They might be lucky and be looked at as children (that they were) or they might not. If one of the boys wanted to escape into the unknown and maybe to safety, he would help him.

Karl's story goes on:

First, I could take a train for a very short distance. It was rare to see a vehicle but when I did, I hitchhiked a bit; a child would be taken up easily. And then I walked and walked and walked. At night I slept in a ditch next to the road. After three or four days or so I was there. And then I was with my aunt.

But what now? First a few American troops came but they did not stay long. Then the French came and the whole area became part of the French occupation zone. And we still did not know anything yet. We tried to get a message to my family through the churches. We were told that this would work. We never got any message back but we were hoping that they had gotten ours and knew now that I was still alive. I had seen them last in February. Then suddenly, in August or September, one aunt of mine with her daughter, my cousin, appeared. They had somehow cheated their way through. They had obtained a permission to travel for part of the way. Since we were living on a farm, we had enough to eat, even some bacon and bread and sausage.

During that time farmers were a little better off than the people who had nothing but their small rations. Even though farmers had to hand over their products, except the rations for their family members, they all managed to keep a little more food than that. Therefore, it did not matter too much that Karl and later the newly arrived aunt and her daughter had no ration cards. They all could be fed at the farm.

But now the three of us tried to get home. There was a train to Ulm which we took. But after Ulm there were no passenger trains anymore. We walked around and around and finally found a soldier who told us about a freight train. (We gave him some of our food in return.) This train had only cattle wagons which was fine.

7

It went to Heilbronn but no further. From Heilbronn several reparation trains*) were leaving.*) The French occupation forces had forests cut down and the timber transported to France as part of the war reparations.

The open wagons were loaded high with timber. One was going to Mannheim and we climbed on. Up there we had to lie flat because there were many tunnels on the section between Heilbronn and Mannheim. In Mannheim we would have to cross the river Rhein towards my hometown. And there was a problem: my aunt and cousin had permits to cross the river which was the border between the American and the French occupation zone, but I had no papers.

The original bridge had been blown up, but the Americans had put up a pontoon bridge. On the Mannheim side of the bridge stood an American with some kind of squirt gun. Everybody had to strip and was then squirted with pesticide, everybody who came. Somehow I made it through. The guards must have thought, I was my aunt's child and not checked the traveling papers too closely. The French guards on the other side of the river did not even look at me.

From there we walked and walked and finally got home. There was great joy. The lost son had come back again. But of course, no calf was slaughtered; we did not even have any meat. Getting food in the city was not easy. We did have a little garden behind our house, but we were now six people. In the fall we would go to the potato fields that had been harvested, to dig for potatoes that had been missed. We also went to the fields where wheat or rye or barley or oats had been harvested and searched for ears of grain that had fallen down. Since most of the city people did this, one had to be early and diligent. What we had found, would be dried at home, the grains separated and ground in a hand crank coffee mill.

That's how far Karl recounted his "adventure" to me. Like most of my interviewees he only remembered what was important. Most of the details had gotten blurry, like: where did the boys sleep at the farms? In beds or in the straw in the barn? He could not remember. How many days did it take him to get to his aunt? Several. He walked long distances.

Afterwards he mused:

Why did I leave the Black Forest to go to my aunt at Lake Constance? Why did I not stay with the others? I don't know.

I just had to leave. And I did make it to Lake Constance. I was 11 years old and still a child but I was a grown-up nevertheless. I was totally on my own. This was an important experience and it has shaped me, left its mark on me, for all of my life. I knew now that I could do almost everything.

The End of the War

The end of WW II came to us, on the west side of the river Rhein, much earlier than to the rest of Germany.

I was 11 years old. My Aunt Lisa's and my, apartment was on the second floor of a private home. The house faced the street that ran, west-east, from our village to the next and the next, all the way towards east the river Rhein about 50 miles away. For weeks I had watched from a window as streams of people were fleeing the advancing Allied Forces. Most of them must have come from Alsace-Lorraine.

Alsace and Lorraine had changed hands between France and Germany quite often in the course of centuries. When Hitler had declared Alsace-Lorraine Germany again, he had been sent German "settlers" there who could get farms, larger than the ones they had at home. Now, as the Allied forces pushed eastward, all these people had to flee east, back into the "Reich". Most of these people were pulling small wagons or pushing carts with some of their belongings; a very few had horse-drawn wagons with people crowded on them. But there is one picture that will stay in my mind till the end of my life: A young woman was pushing a cart, and on this cart sat a little boy, maybe two or three years old, one small suitcase next to him. The woman was walking so slow that I could not imagine how she had managed the dip in the road a quarter mile before our house. And how would she ever reach the next village, two miles away? But she walked on, doggedly, just one slow step after the other. I knew for sure that she would never reach the river Rhein, which was at the time still believed by some to mean relative safety.

I watched all this from my window on the second floor, sitting behind the light curtain, somehow shielded from all this. Many years later I wondered, how I could have watched all this misery, feeling deep sorrow for this woman – and for so many others – and not have run down the stairs onto the street and brought her and her little boy inside, at least for a rest. I think that I knew even then deep down, that it would have been pointless. How could we have helped her? – and all the others? But she knew that she would not even have wanted to rest but go on and on.

On the evening of the 15th of March 1945 three German soldiers were billeted into our small apartment for the night. (They must have slept on the floor.) I remember the date because it was Aunt Lisa's birthday. The German soldiers said the plan was to give up the area west of the river Rhein but build up a defense line just across the river and from there push back the Allied forces.

One of the soldiers was a teacher, like my aunt, the other two were educated people also. They wanted to take my aunt and me in their truck the 50 miles to the river and then across to safety. After long and hard thinking, the next morning my aunt declined. Where would we stay? We would be within the mass of refugees that were already there. What would happen to us if the front did not stop at the river? (that indeed it did not). At least here we had a chance to be able to stay in our home or at least close by, and have our food stocks (mostly a couple of sacks of potatoes). Also her parents, my grandparents, lived in the next village. In the morning the soldiers gave us some of their "pilots' chocolate" (very dark coffee-chocolate to keep soldiers awake when necessary) and left.

A few days later the American troops came through our small town. But we were extremely lucky that there was no fighting. The Ortsgruppenleiter *) (a mayor with political = national-socialistic, authority) of our town had fled east a few days earlier. I saw him and his wife pass by our house. They walked behind a cart with a few suitcases on it, pushed by the town police man. I don't think that they got very far but at least they were gone. If he had stayed he would have been forced to order the tank traps (anti-tank obstacles) in the village to be closed. There was one right next to the house where we lived. Those were thick tree trunks, piled high in a square, and the inside filled with sand. Next to them lay long tree trunks that were supposed to be fitted into the structures and thereby block the road, at least temporary, to tanks. We knew that, if closed, the tanks would just ram their way through the houses to which the tank traps were attached.

Now our roads had not been blocked in this way and the American tanks were rolling by our house. After a while our elderly landlord and his lady and my aunt and I dared to stand by the front door which was opened just a slim slit to glance through. The tanks were moving very slowly, apparently always ready to fire at anything suspicious. I will never forget the scene as I saw one long gun barrel slowly move past my field of vision – and I screamed. I was certain that this barrel would turn in an instant and shoot us all. The person next to me immediately put his or her hand over my mouth. Luckily none of the soldiers inside the tank had apparently heard me.

The invasion into our town and at least the next village had gone peaceful, thank God. There was even a slightly funny turn in my grandparents' village. To my grandmother's terror, my grandfather, 70 years old, white hair and a veteran of WW I, stood outside their front door when the tanks came rolling through. One of the tanks stopped and the lid opened.

A soldier stuck his head out and asked him in very broken German: "'abben si Schießgewehr?" ('ave you shooting rifle?) My grandfather laughed and said no. The soldier pulled back his head, closed the lid, and the tank rolled on. Unfortunately, later on things did not go so peaceful in our area.

My husband's grandfather could have been hurt easily. In this rural town, the old man, around his 80, heard his doorbell ring and walked – slowly – towards the door. The allied soldiers were commanding houses for their own living. But they were impatient and so they simply shot out the lock. Grandpa immediately threw himself to the floor to be safe to more shots. He was not wounded.

I think most Germans realized fighting would be pointless and the war was lost anyway. My friend Victor told:

During these final days of the war some of the local officials all over Germany had the insane idea to follow their government's orders to mobilize every last man, no matter how old and frail, and every boy, often even younger than 14, for the totally hopeless defense of the country.

Victor and his mother, on their flight from the advancing armies, had been quartered at a farm in Bavaria. He remembered:

The war was drawing to an end. A stream of German soldiers passed by the farm. Then finally all was quiet. There were no people walking, no truck picking up milk from the farms, no farm machinery in the fields. It seemed, the whole world held its breath. Then one morning the sound of tanks was being heard in the distance. American tanks. But before them came a German military Volkswagen, a heavy machine gun mounted between the front seats, with three young teenagers, dressed in their Hitler-Youth uniforms. They wanted to set up a road block at the corner and an ambush right behind the farmhouse. The farmer gave them the gasoline they requested and something to drink. But he told them, a much better place to set up an ambush would be a third of a mile further down the road (and away from any houses). With that advice he saved his farm from sure destruction and the lives of the people within. The American tanks came; the boys fired their machine gun and were, naturally, mowed down by the tanks' cannons. Then the tanks moved on and for this village the war was over.

A former class mate of mine told me what happened to his physician-father:

The allied tanks drove through towns and villages, normally without any German resistance. At some settlement the tanks would stop a break or for a lunch break.

In the small town was the only physician, my father, elderly and therefore not drafted, who had treated sick people around the area. Private cars had long before been taken to the military. My father had received a small motor bicycle and a little gasoline so that he could visit patients.

During such a day my father had been called to a wounded man or someone very sick. The doctor drove with his paramedic riding pillion. When the two men saw the tanks they naturally stopped at the tanks and explained to the soldiers about their job (my father's English was very good). The soldiers told them to move the motor bicycle in front of one of the tanks and told the Germans to get out of the way. Then the tank rolled over the motor bicycle and they laughed at this great fun. I don't think that the sick person could have been treated after that.

Gertrud's life in Germany, in Poland and in East Germany

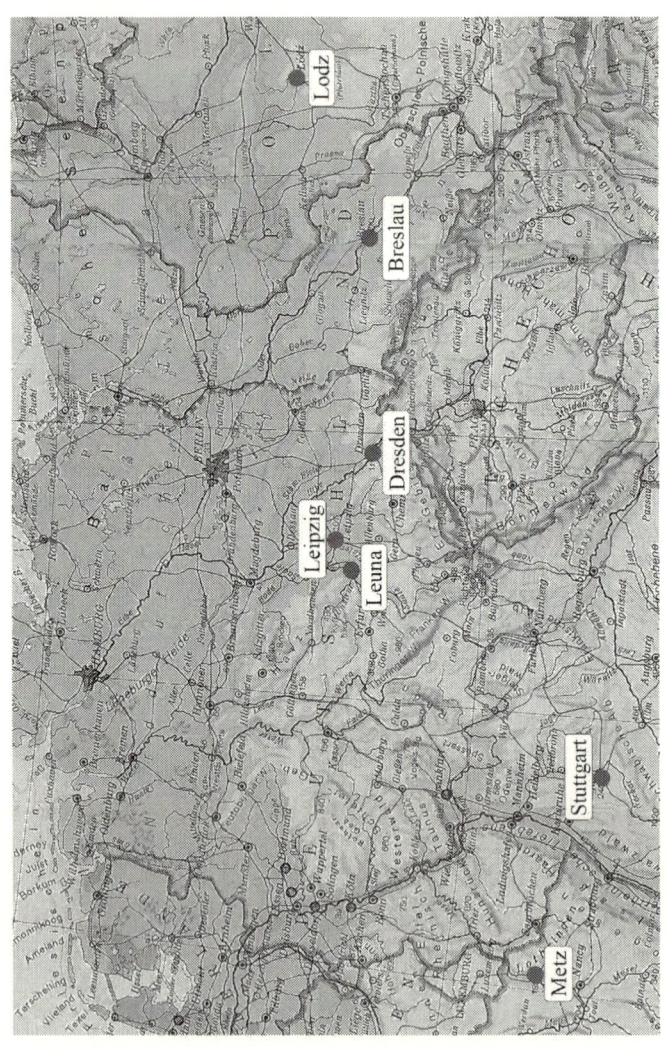

Gertrud's Life in Germany, in Poland and in East Germany (born 1921)

I met and acquired Gertrud as a distant cousin in 1961 via the simple act of getting married into the family. She was a slight woman, unassuming and modest. She was full of energy, but it was a controlled energy. She had a way of always being aware of other people's needs, moods and wishes. She appeared only a few years older than me, but had been born in 1921, which made her 12 years my senior. This made her old enough to have been actively involved in the events of Hitler's "Third Reich". When I met this lovely and caring woman, I had had no idea what she had been forced to do, how she had reacted to what she saw with her own eyes, how she survived, and, when after the terrible chaos and the war's aftermath, how she rebuilt a life for herself.

Gertrud was never meek or shy. She had something like a quietly energetic kindness around herself that was assertive and, at the same time, submitting to others' needs.

After Gertrud had retired at age 65 from her job as a librarian in Stuttgart, she spent a whole month with us in Florida. Our children, then young teenagers, loved her. I had been a little apprehensive because at the time our house was full of an odd assortment of pets. There was our big, feisty white tomcat that could and did open doors; a hamster who often managed to get out of its cage and would then explore the house, sometimes ending up in somebody's bed; the blue jay who had been brought to us with a broken wing; and a baby possum whose had been separated from its mother. Gertrud handled all this beautifully. We have a picture of her with the possum sitting on top of her head.

Several years later I asked her to tell me her life story. We were sitting in her cozy, sun filled living room in the retirement home in Stuttgart where she was living now, my little tape recorder on the coffee table between us. Even when I was concerned she would tire herself out, she kept on talking and talking. I was simply stunned. Before me, a life was enfolding that I had never suspected of quiet, sweet Gertrud. Here is her story:

Gertrud had been an energetic, inventive, and assertive girl, and she was always ready to stand up and speak out for what she thought was right. Her father had been a judge in a smallish city near Stuttgart in southwest Germany.

When Gertrud was about 5, her parents told her and her older brother, that in a few months a new baby would come into the family. Naturally, Gertrud wanted a little sister and her brother wanted a little brother. The parents suggested that the two children should present their wishes to God. And that's what they did every morning and evening. One Sunday morning they were at it again, Gertrud praying: "Dear God, give me a little sister" and her brother saying: "Dear God, give me a little brother." They got louder and louder, each one trying to out-pray the other. Finally Gertrud took the competition to a physical level and they both started to hit each other, all the while yelling their wishes to God. Their father heard them and came to break up the fight. He was a very kind and understanding man, and he told the children, it would not work that way and they should from now on just pray that the baby would be healthy. Obedient children that they were, they did so, and the baby-girl was indeed born healthy, so maybe Gertrud did have the louder voice.

When Hitler came to power 1933, Gertrud was 12, an age when she could perceive the situation around her, however with a childish naiveté. In the meantime her family had moved to the city of Stuttgart where the political and social issues were much more visible than in the countryside.

She remembers:

The whole population was, to a certain degree, impoverished. On top of it, the war reparations had to be paid, ensuing WWI. The Weimar Republic, as successor of the monarchy, had not done well. People were very dissatisfied and unhappy. Then came the big economic crisis in 1929/30 (with the bank crash in 1929) and even more people became jobless. In this situation Hitler only had to come and say: "We cancel the war reparations, we will give all of you work." and people naturally flocked to him.

During the earlier part of the century many youth groups had been created. There were various variations within the so-called "Jugendbewegung" (= youth movement). Some groups loved to go hiking, others made music, young farm women had their groups and many other. From England the concept of boy scouts and girl scouts arrived. When Hitler had come to power. all of these groups were given a national-socialistic name and imbued with a more or less national-socialistic mind set. Gertrud, then a young teenager, wanted to be part of such a group. The BDM*) Bund deutscher Mädchen = group of German girls, a National-Socialist institution just like the Hitler-Youth for boys) was something quite new and seemed interesting.

Gertrud tells about her girl's group:

It was quite lovely. On Sundays we went to church together; then we played in the woods. Sometimes we even went on hikes for a weekend and slept in barns on straw. My friends and I were lucky because we had found a nice circle. My parents were not too happy about it. They knew, of course, that the BDM was supposed to be a politic national-socialistic institution. My father had been forced to become a member of the NSDAP (= National Socialistic German Workers' Party) *because of his job. He often said: "If I knew a foreign language well enough to feed my family in a foreign country; that would be great. But I only know the grammar of a foreign language real well. And I don't even know the law anywhere. That won't help me in another country."*

Then came 1938. At the time I had to ride the tram each day clear across town to my high school. One morning, when we passed the Königstrasse [the main street in Stuttgart that traverses the business section of the city], *everything was covered with glass and there were SS and special police. I did not understand what was happening.*) *)* During the "Kristallnacht" ("the night of the broken glass", November 10, 1938") and after, Jewish businesses were vandalized and many Jews beaten and otherwise abused. *At school one of my classmates was terribly upset and in tears. I told her what she had seen and what she said that in her town (outside Stuttgart), it had been much, much worse. And she told me: "My father has been a party member* (NSDAP) *since 1925 because he was so excited that finally something would be done for Germany. This morning he happened to walk by where they beat up a Jewish physician and arrested him and he said to those men: 'This doctor has always cared for the poor of this town and you have probably been delivered by him for free because your parents had no money. How can you treat this man in this way?' And my classmate said: "My father is totally devastated. He had heard what Hitler had written in "Mein Kampf" and also others were saying about the Jews. Now he knows that they had really meant it all along and my father is inconsolable." And he said: "I don't know what to do. I can not quit the party, otherwise I and my family will be in a KZ*)."* *)KZ stands for **K**on**z**entrationslager = concentration camp. If somebody stood up against the government, most of the time not only he/she but also their whole family would be taken to a KZ.)

Does this statement answer the often asked question if the Germans knew about Concentration Camps? Yes and no. One knew of camps and feared them, but people had no idea what really went. The government keep them tightly secret.

I remember my first-grade teacher, a tall big man with a white beard and a frowning disposition. We were quite a large class, at least 40 children. In 1940 most male teachers had been drafted, therefore smaller classes had to be combined into larger ones. There were several poor children in our class, poor in worldly goods and poor in intelligence. They had to sit in the front part of the classroom while we "better" children sat in the back rows. Among the poor children were also a set of twins, a boy and a girl. They were dressed poorly, they had lice and they were shy and scared. One day the teacher said that their father had been in a Concentration Camp for some time because he had been "work-shy". He had been lately released and was now a model worker, industrious and conscientious. And wasn't this wonderful. I felt it was downright cruel and mean to tell this to the whole class. How could he be so unfeeling and to humiliate these twins in front of the whole class! Many years later one of my classmate still remembered this cruel and humiliated event.

This was when I heard the term "Concentration Camp". Gertrud and many others thought they must be prisons where people had to concentrate hard on their crimes and/or offences, and become better persons. The term "concentration camp" or "Dachau", the name of one of them, was talked about a scare tactic like: "Don't talk like this or you will be taken to taken to a concentration camp." Nobody knew what was happening there. Only after the war was over, the reality of the unbelievable terror of torture and killings at the camps became known. There many people could not believe that humans could act this way when they were told. I know that soldiers cried when they were told.

Now-a-days, living in a free country, would we know what goes on in our prisons, if there were no reports in the media about abuses in prisons? But during the Hitler era there was no free press in Germany; and "social media" was many decades away. This may sound naïve but that's the way it was. Also one must take into consideration that people were completely preoccupied on trying to survive during the war on a daily and hourly basis, physically, emotionally, and mentally.

As a child, Gertrud had seen the poverty and desperation around her and was now quite happy to see how Germany developed into a prosperous, orderly country, at least in the parts she could see. When she turned 18, she was automatically made a member of the NSDAP. She did not mind, it was the normal way of things and she really wanted to support the new Germany. She did, however, not attend many party meetings just because she was not interested.

But there were encounters with "ordered" anti-Semitism. Gertrud recalls:

> *I remember that one day I was riding in a streetcar when an old Jewish lady came in. (At that time they had to wear the yellow star most in cities.) I got up and offered her my seat. An SS-man was standing close by and he barked at me, demanding to know why I was getting up for this woman. I said to him: "Excuse me, but I was brought up to get up for old people and either I get up for all old people or for none of them." Then he was quiet.*

This could be called a little thing, of course. But when Gertrud told me about it, I was reminded of a young American woman who became our friend when we came to the US in 1964. This was the time when public buildings had separate bathrooms and even separate water fountains for "colored" and "white" people. White physicians who accepted black patients, had separate waiting rooms. This American friend of ours – she was the wife of a lawyer – made it a habit to take a black student with her into a "white" restaurant at least once a week. Gertrud's action in the street car had been a little more dangerous but, basically, the two young women had acted from the same principle. Did that change anything? Not really, I think. But sometimes we just have to do things because we feel they are right.

As time progressed, the Jews, especially in large cities, were in more and more danger. Gertrud explained:

> *In our neighborhood lived several Jewish families. When our parents realized that Jews were often harassed, they told us children, not to give out any information about them to anybody, should we be asked. One day I passed Mr. E., a Jewish man, on our street. He must have been in his thirties, I was probably fifteen. I greeted him but he did not answer my greeting. This did not bother me but after a few paces he came running after me and apologized profusely. I told him that he should not apologize. I understood perfectly that he had not noticed me at and he had been deep in thought.*

To understand this, one must know the "ritual" of greeting as it was practiced in Germany at the time (and still is to a certain degree). When people who knew each other – if ever so slightly – passed ones on the street, the lower one in rank (= age or social standing) would greet first. A man would draw his hat and bow slightly.

Among adults, the man would greet first to a woman, except when he had a very exalted position. When the 15-year old Gertrud passed the 30-year old man it was clear that she had to greet first. At the time, a 15-year old was still considered a child and disregarding a child's greeting (for whatever reason) was not a big thing. When Mr. E. realized that Gertrud had greeted him, he must have thought that, being in a rather precarious situation as a Jew, he had to be especially polite. Furthermore he most probably valued very highly his friendly relationship with Gertrud's family.

And then the war started. There are always complicated, and sometimes real silly, reasons to start a war. But my aunt kept saying: When a ruler senses, notices and realizes restlessness, agitation and discontent of the people with his style of rule, he starts a war because being at war automatically unites the people against the enemy and stand behind their ruler. The people's interests shifts from political and social issues and to the fates of the soldiers who are their sons, husbands and friends. And the people will have to survive themselves.

Around the beginning of the war every household was asked to tell how many people lived there so that the appropriate number of gasmasks could be distributed. Mr. M., the Ortsgruppenleiter, (the political mayor for our part of the city) had to check out every household. But he was a kind and considerate man. He came to my father and said he was sure it would upset our Jewish neighbors if he would come to their door in uniform (which he was ordered to do) What could he do? Finally the two men decided to have me put on my BDM uniform and go next door with the list. Our Jewish neighbor probably sensed that this list had other purposes too. He told me to ask Mr. M.(the Ortsgruppenleiter) to give him a little more time because he first wanted to talk to his Rabbi. A few days later they had fled as well as another neighborhood Jewish family. Mr. E., the young man I had greeted on the street, even came by our house before he fled to take leave of my mother. Unfortunately, he was caught in Amsterdam, as we learned later, and sent back. We do not know what happened to him.

Shortly before Gertrud's last year in high school was over, she was drafted into the Reichsarbeitsdienst ("country work service"), the mandatory work program for young people. All young people between the age 18 and 25 had to serve for 6, and later 12 months. The boys and girls worked at different tasks doing "community services", working at farms, at families, at business, building what needed to do.

Gertrud remembers:

We had been drafted into the Arbeitsdienst during the first weeks of winter when the temperature was -20°C (= -4°F). Everything had happened so fast that we were still walking around in our summer uniforms and I got my first really bad case of frostbites. That was terrible. We girls had been taken to a village in the hills country and were housed in an old villa. In our dorm we had triple bunk beds (three beds on top of each other). Above us, on the converted attic floor, was the local rescue station for people who had gotten lost in the mountains and/or had been injured.

Except for the extreme cold, it was actually a very nice and interesting time. It was so important that, as a young woman, one learned how hard the farmers had to work. I was very grateful for this experience. Early every morning we went to the farm to which we were assigned. While there was snow, we went on skis. When the snow was too high, a farmer from the village would come with a large sleigh to pick us up. But the farmers did not like to do this because it was actually too cold for the horses.

We did mostly the work that the men had done who had been drafted into the military. We had to muck out the stables, milk cows (I learned that after a while), help with the baking of bread and carry the loaves to the bake house, and just help with everything that came up. The winter was also butchering time. We helped with the processing of the meat for canning and smoking, and with making the sausages. All this food would have to last for most of the year. It was interesting work, even though I did not like the butchering as such.

When the war started in September 1939, Gertrud was 18 years old. How had she experienced that event?

I had not expected that there really would be a war. It started by German soldiers invaded Poland. We had heard reports of bloody fights between Polish-Germans and Poles in the corridor*) *)the Polish area located between German East Prussian and main Germany that Germany had later occupied. Nobody knew details about these fights and brutalities by Poles. The whole affair was probably exaggerated to stir up the Germans so they would dislike the Poles.*

Now Germany was at war but life had to go on. Gertrud had decided to become a librarian and to absolve her training in Leipzig (in the east of Germany) starting in the fall of 1941. During these early of the war, life was relatively secure in Germany.

My parents would have liked for me to spend a year at a school in a foreign country, especially since my mother had lived in France for a year as a young girl and my father had spent a long time in Switzerland. This was not possible now. But they said: "Even when there is a war, a young person needs to become independent and get to know a new environment." And my father said: "You will be surprised about all the interesting things that Leipzig has to offer. It will be especially great for a bookworm like you." And that was true. The music in Leipzig was fabulous, I heard Bach*) music all the time. (*)In Leipzig Sebastian Bach, the famous musician, lived, composed and founded the well known choir there from 1723 until his death in 1750.) *Friday evenings the Thomas Choir sang a Motet, on Saturday they performed parts of cantatas, with the students taking turns at conducting, and on Sunday the appropriate Sunday Cantata was performed in church. There were also great performances in the very beautiful university church. (This church was later destroyed by bombs as well as the university campus.) I really enjoyed Leipzig. And the nights were so quiet. Sometimes there were brief air raid alarms but the people were not at all prepared for real air raids.*

At home, in Stuttgart, every house had fire-beaters and pails of sand*) and gasmasks, but in Leipzig there was nothing. And then later they were so surprised when the city burned. *) fires from incendiary bombs could not be extinguished with water because of the phosphorus they contained but sand worked somehow.

I had a good time in Leipzig and the teaching was good too. I do not remember that it was politically stressed. The principal, who was very good, was of course had to be a member of the party, but so was I by this time too.

At that time Germans, especially young people, did not have a choice of where they would work – and often not even what kind of work it would be. Gertrud, with the first part of her studies finished, was sent to the city of Lodz in Poland to work as an intern at the library there. Throughout history Lodz and the area around it had been alternately German and Polish and Russian. When German troops pushed into Poland at the beginning of the war, Lodz was occupied too and it was supposed to be "Germanized". Its name was even changed – temporarily – to Litzmannstadt. Today Lodz is the second largest city in Poland (after Warsaw) with over 800,000 inhabitants. At the time when Gertrud was there, it was probably much smaller.

We were four German librarians all living in a little apartment above the library, together with the head librarian.

Three of us had come from the Reich*), one was Volksdeutsche*) (*)
Reichsdeutsche were German citizens living in Germany proper,
Volksdeutsche were ethnic Germans whose families had lived in another
country for a long time and most probably were citizen of that country.)

*My task was actually quite interesting. I had to compile
books on certain themes. I learned a lot about Polish cities and
their art treasures, and about Polish areas in the north where there
are cities with beautiful "art nouveau" architecture.*

*Shortly after my arrival in Lodz I received a letter saying
that since I now had been drafted, I had terminated my church
membership. I called and asked how they could know that I had
done this since I myself did not know anything about it. I was told
that this was automatic. When you are drafted into this area, your
church membership is automatically terminated. I told them I
would ask in Stuttgart, wrote a letter to my father and, after a few
weeks, received a letter back that I was still listed as a church
member. I called the appropriate office in Lodz and told them. And
then I actually went to church rather regularly, but I went to the
Russian church. There were many Russians in Lodz. The Russians
were very nice and they spoke German very well. I loved their
church services. Of course, I did not understand one word of the
service, but the music was beautiful.*

*The Germans treated the Russians much better than they
treated the Poles. The Russians were allowed to borrow books at
the library but the Poles were not. I felt so bad when I had to turn
Polish people away after having seen their identity cards. It was so
unfair. Many ethnic Germans spoke less German than many Poles
did. And there were no Polish books.*

*Poles were often humiliated. At that time many Poles had
been transported to Germany to work there instead of the German
men who were in the military. The families of these deported Poles
wanted to send them things. They did not have much to eat for
themselves but wanted to help their sons and daughters in the
Reich. They made up little packages but had to show everything,
publicly, at the post office. The controllers were sitting in a room
with the window down to the floor, and the people had to spread
out the contents of their little packages. It was terrible. I got to like
the Poles much better than my own compatriots.*

*My colleague at the library, the one who was Volksdeutsch
(ethnic German) once said to me: "It would have been so wonderful
if the Germans would not have come here. Things were going so
well. I attended the German school here together with many Poles.*

I have many friends among them, but now I am not allowed to have anything to do with them anymore. After all this is over, I will not be able to live here anymore and neither will my family. My father owns a factory but that will probably be gone by then. And all this is happening because you, Germans, came. We were so dumb and asked for the Germans to come here. And now look what they are doing."

There was not much to eat, everything was rationed and the rations were small. We four young librarians ate at a restaurant where we had to give our food ration stamps (together with money, of course). The Polish waiter there was very nice but as time progressed we noticed that he was becoming thinner and thinner. We decided to save some of our food for him but we had to ask him at least ten times until he finally accepted it. We saved bread for him, sometimes an apple and other things. We wrapped it in paper so that he could put it in his pocket and eat it later at home. We could not give him any of our food ration stamps because he would have been arrested for having German food ration stamps.

Then there was the Polish girl who worked at a neighboring house as a maid to two elderly and very grouchy ladies. She was very nice and friendly. She had passed her college entrance exam at the German school but now was not allowed to attend.

One day in winter – they had very cold winters there – I noticed that I could see her skin through her dress at a few places. I myself had two winter dresses so I said to her I wanted to give her one of mine because otherwise she would get sick. (She had about the same figure as I did.) She thanked me profusely but said she could not accept my dress because it would make her father very very sad if she would accept a gift from a German. I had to accept this and I admired her.

To get from our little peaceful street to the center of town we had to take the streetcar that went through the Jewish Ghetto. During this time there were about 20,000 people there in the area, where before, maybe 5,000 or at the most 10,000 had lived. These Jews were packed together so tightly. And they had to work like crazy. They had to make straw shoes and such things for the military, from morning into the night. And they had almost nothing to eat.

One day the ghetto was empty. You could see maybe one person every hour. I wanted to know what was happening. So, one day I went to a government office, or maybe it was the police. I don't remember.

And I said that I had had first aid training with the Red Cross and at the BDM. I had heard that from time to time a physician would go into the ghetto and I wanted to go with him to help. The official asked me why I wanted to do that. I said that I wanted to know what was going on there and what was happening that suddenly there was nobody to be seen anymore. The man said: "Let me tell you: you should be glad that you don't know, and don't you ever come back here, ever!"

One afternoon when I was alone in the library, an SS-man came in. I was 22 at the time, he probably 23. He looked totally devastated and he said: "I only came here so that I could get away." I asked where he was staying and he said: "I can not take it any longer. I have to be inhumane to people who have done nothing to me, just inhumane." I asked him why he had to do that and I said, I didn't think anybody could force him to act that way." But he said: "Yes, they can force me. You see I am an SS-man. When I was 17 years old, I joined the SS out of excitement. I thought that in doing this, I could really do something for my country. Now I have to be inhumane to people who have never done me any harm." When I asked him where he was stationed, he said he had to work with Jews. And he said: "You know, this would be no problem at all if I were alone. I could say to my boss: 'I will not participate anymore. They may shoot me; that would be perfectly alright with me.' But I am married and I have a small child. If I would kill myself, they would be after them and also after my parents, my siblings, probably even my wife's relatives. *) So I can't do that. And now I am thinking and brooding day and night how I could arrange an accident which would not look like suicide." And he said: "This is very difficult. There are no cars here. I have nothing but a revolver but if I point that at myself that won't work either. Somebody did that and then all his relatives got into the KZ." I never learned what happened to this young man. *) This system was called "Sippenhaft" (= liability of all the members of a family for the "crimes" of one member) and supposedly was an old Germanic rule.

I know another example. There was a fighter pilot, a famous one but I forgot his name. His plane crashed and there was a big funeral. It was even shown on the weekly newsreel (Wochenschau). The women of his family wore dark veils. Much later it was learned that the pilot had been against Hitler and his politics. A bomb had been placed into his plane and the plane went down.

Three days after the funeral the members of his family were taken to a KZ. The children, I think the youngest was 2, were taken to Italy to orphanages.

The mother and grandmother survived the KZ and after the war they traveled all over Italy, visiting all the orphanages. They thought that the children might remember the pet names by which they had been called at home. After a long, long search they really did find the children. I think there were two.

Gertrud's brother was in the army and was wounded. The field hospital where he was taken, was not too far away from where she worked and she was able to visit him there once.

When I visited my brother in the field hospital I learned something very mean and cruel. He pointed to another wounded soldier, who looked as if he was physically totally destroyed, and he said: "Look at that comrade. He was forced into the SS. He is a Russian-German. When they are drafted they don't have a choice where they will go. If they are above 1.78 or 1.80m (5'10" or 5'11") they are automatically put into the SS." He probably had the same problems as did the young SS-man who visited me in the library, and he probably had to go on too because he had to fear for his family.

After the war I had a teacher who had narrowly avoided the fate of being put into the SS. He had been born in Romania and – like many ethnic Germans (Volksdeutsche) – had come to Germany to study, but here he had been caught by the war. When he was drafted, he was told over and over to join the SS. (Luckily he was only of average height.) He had been warned by friends not to let himself be persuaded and he managed, probably due to his considerable charm and eloquence, to be allowed to join the air force instead.

There existed a different group SS that was not associated to the concentrated camps, the "Waffen-SS" (Weapon SS). They were like other soldiers but were looked at an elite troop who where used for special tasks. However, the ordinary soldiers kept saying that the Waffen-SS was not better than they were.

One time, probably after a short furlough in Stuttgart, Gertrud was traveling back to Lodz. She had a few hours to wait for her train connection in Breslau. She had heard that the train station was, architecturally, very beautiful and she wanted to explore it.

Suddenly I was standing there, looking at a large group of people, some of them lying on the floor, a few of them standing, but all of them only bones and yellowish skin. Around them were guardsmen too. I was totally frozen.

And then one guard told the ones who were standing that they should pick up the ones who were lying on the floor and make them stand too. But those who stood were just barely able to stand, and when they tried to pick up the others, they tumbled down. They also were clouted. At that point I saw that they were all wearing yellow Jewish stars. Finally they had everybody sorted out and then the guards saw me standing there, totally shocked and devastated, and I was told:

"Don't you ever, ever tell anybody what you have seen here." And I said: "Don't worry. This is the most terrible thing I have ever seen in my life. I wouldn't be able to put that into words." And they said: "Go away now or you will get slapped real good, and don't tell anybody what you have seen." – And I did not tell anybody because I just couldn't. Only after I had seen the movie "Shindler's List" a few years ago, was I able to talk about it. I have seen terrible things during the time I was in the service, people torn apart by bombs, 16-, 17-year old boys. That was terrible. But nothing was as terrible as what I had seen there in Breslau. It was so fiendishly, hellishly mean. I had not known before that something like this was possible.

When I heard about people being put in "protective custody" (Sicherheitsverwahrung), I thought it was just that. My father had a hard time explaining to me that this was actually prison and I believed it. But even he had no clue what really happened there. Even in Breslau I could not fathom why these Jewish people had assembled on that platform – just as I did not know but wanted to find out, why the Jews in the ghetto at Lodz had suddenly all left.

Gertrud stayed in Lodz for a year and then she had to go back to Leipzig to take her final exam at the library college. Already during her last months in Lodz she had not been well anymore. In Leipzig she became so weak that her classmates brought the study material to her because most of the time she could not attend classes. But she was determined to get through the exam.

During the last four weeks I could not even read anymore. A very sweet friend – she later died in an air raid in Dresden – came to me each day. We walked a little in the nearby park while she told me what had been taught that day and questioned me about earlier material. I made it to the exam, I did pass but I have no idea how I got home from the college. I just woke up in my bed.

During the next 9 months back in Stuttgart Gertrud slowly regained her health – and was ordered to report to two places in eastern

Poland. But each time after she had already packed her suitcase, she learned that the Russians were already there.

I should have gone to Austria, to the eastern part and actually close to Budapest. But the Russians were there too. Then I got a bad flu and could not report to the government employment center. There were no telephones at the time. The lady there told me that she would enlist me to the SS. I told her, I would do any work, join any part of the military but I did not want to join the SS. In the meantime a friend of mine, also a librarian, had been ordered to work in Metz (Lorraine)) Lorraine had been annexed into Germany. *at a library and they were short on people. She asked her boss to request me. I went back to the employment office and, after some negations, was allowed to go to Metz. But there the same nonsense started again: They wanted me in the SS. I asked what women could do there and was told that some did clerical work but they needed me for a mechanical repair shop, to repair engines and so on. I could say quite truthfully that I had absolutely no technical aptitude and skills. So the woman enlisted me to the FLAK**) and I realized that I couldn't come up with any arguments against that and so I had to go.* **) FLAK = **Fl**ieger-**A**bwehr-**K**anonen: Anti Airkraft Guns

I left the office and went back to Stuttgart, where I just had time to celebrate Christmas with my family and then, on December 31st, after spending a few hours in a bunker because of air raids, I went to Nürnberg for training. That same night Nürnberg had been badly bombed but also some planes had been shot down. One had to feel bad for the people who had died from bombs but also for the ones who had been shot down. We were trained on an instrument with which one calculated the flying altitude and the flight side angle of planes with the help of charts.

I was stationed near Leuna (in the eastern part of Germany) where the big brown-coal plant*) was and where gasoline was made from that coal. *)Brown coal, also called lignite, is somehow between peat and bituminous coal in texture. It is mostly found near the surface and can be won by opencast mining. *There were air raids all the time. The post had flight measurement devices (Flugmessgerät) near the canons. When they were broken or they were disturbed by the dropping of Allied planes of magnesium-"lametta" or so, the data were relayed to us and we had to calculate as quickly as possible and pass the data on directly to the canons. We were lucky because we were mostly sitting in the bunker but the others, 4 or 5 boys were standing at their flight measurement devices in the open. Those were boys, 16, 17, 18 years old and they saw directly how close the planes were.*

Sometimes we were called out so that we could at least push their heads down when they could not stand it any more for fear; the poor boys.

We also had Russian prisoners at our post. They sometimes came to us asking for food in the evening. But we did not have anything to give them. We got 2 or 3 slices of bread per day and a bowl of soup. Sometimes we might get a potato or two but it was mostly frozen. But we saw that the Russians always got a second bowl of soup with their bread. So one of us said to our commander: "Please give us that second bowl of soup and don't give it always to the Russians." But he said: "Come with us to the canons so that I can show you why they get a second bowl of soup." The canons, between 6 and 12, were distributed over a rather extended area and the ammunition too. The ground was all churned up by bombs. The only way to transport the ammunition to the canons was to carry them. The projectiles were huge and very heavy. Two men had to carry each one on their shoulders and that was actually too heavy for them but there was no other way to transport the ammunition. We accepted that the Russians did indeed need an extra bowl of soup and actually much more than that.

At a neighboring post I saw a young Russian who was supposed to be taken to a different camp because, as they said, he could not do hard work. I asked what had been his trade and they told me that he had been a tailor. I said to the leader of the post: "We don't have anybody who takes care of the uniform center (uniform store) and we desperately need somebody. Since you want to get rid of him anyway, why not give him to us." He came to us but we soon found out that he was so eager and anxious to help wherever he could. We had to tell everybody not to let him carry heavy loads. We tried to avoid him whenever he came running out of his workshop and when he was trying to carry something we told him: "Order, order!" and sent him back in.

The Russian prisoners were, of course, still here at the end of the war when first the Americans and then the Russians came. They were somewhere in town, as we were too. Our station was totally destroyed by now. When the prisoners saw us on the street, they pretended not to know us and none of them ever said anything against us to the authorities. This could have been dangerous for us.

I am afraid that they were later treated rather badly by the Russian officials because they had, however involuntary, cooperated with the Germans.

The Americans had come first. They stayed for a few weeks and then they left and the Russian occupation came to stay. I had been lucky to never have been taken prisoner. I stayed with a family in Zwenkau, a little town south of Leipzig. When I thought that the Allies had finally arranged between themselves as to who would occupy which area, I decided to make a push to get home to Stuttgart. I went to the (German) registration office to tell them that I was leaving the city but they warned me that it would be very difficult to get away across the border into the British occupied zone.

I knew that the trains were working again. It was strange, while the Americans had been here, nothing was repaired, but during the approximately 8 weeks of Russian occupation, the main train tracks had been repaired and trains were running again. I got on the train to Leipzig where I had to change trains to get near the border. There in Leipzig I met a soldier who was terribly wounded on his arms. The other wounds he had received were apparently somehow healed. He told me that he also wanted to get across the border in the Hartz mountains. And then we met another young soldier with the same destination. We three decided to stay together because it would be important to observe as much as possible so that one would not get into trouble at the border. We left the train at a little town near the border, stayed overnight at a refugee camp and set out the next morning. We asked for detailed directions, where the British were, where the border was and where the Russians were, so we should not run into them. We were told that the border ran along the small river Ilse to the British occupation zone.

We climbed up a rather steep mountain and then at the top it was like a dream. We all three did not know at first if we were hallucinating: There was a meadow and in this meadow a shepherd sat knitting socks and around him were his sheep. It seemed so unreal. But we asked him and he explained to us in detail where we should go down the mountain. There were, of course, no paths. We went between rocks and bushes. About 50 meters above the road that ran along the river we hid behind bushes to observe when the Russian guards were passing. One reason why each one of us had waited to make the push to go west, was to wait until the bushes in the mountains had started to get new leaves and thus provide better cover.

We soon recognized a pattern in the Russian guards' walking by and in the next break we rushed down the steep 50 meters, crossed the road and jumped into the river. The river was not very wide but it had become torrential during the spring snow melt, and it was strewn with large boulders.

As I jumped in, my foot got stuck between two rocks and I could not get loose again. Probably I had somehow sat down and my backpack had soaked itself full of water. I just could not get up. The one-arm soldier who had already crossed the river jumped back in and with his one arm he pulled me up. We just barely made it across and behind the first trees of the British side, before the Russians came again. It had become dark by then. We hung our blankets between the trees and slept as well as we could. It took us the whole day to make it into Goßlar where we were told about a train standing somewhere, which could take us into Göttingen. In the Russian occupation zone the train wagons had been ordinary 3rd class passenger cars but in the British zone they were open cattle cars.*) *)Probably more trains had been bombed and therewith destroyed in the west than in the east. *In Göttingen I found a train to Kassel, from Kassel to Marburg an der Lahn, and then somehow to Frankfurt. There we had to walk clear across the so terribly destroyed city, about 4 or 5 km, I with my wet heavy, backpack. Then there was a train to a suburb of Mannheim (because the station was not functional yet), from there to Heilbronn and finally to Stuttgart.*

I know about cattle cars. We had to ride them every day to school after the war. For the short ride, maybe 45 minutes, it was o.k. We stood or sat on the floor, staying away from the wide open gate. But Gertrud must have traveled several days and probably slept on the floor in one station or another. I did not ask her. But I asked her about food on the way and she said:

There was the Red Cross at some stations and every 6 or 7 hours one would get a little something.

When I asked Gertrud where she had gotten the money to pay for the trains, a whole new story came out. I had already wondered how she came to be with the family in Zwenkau. It turned out that a "colleague-comrade" of hers from the FLAK station was from Zwenkau and took Gertrud home with her. After they had somehow settled, Gertrud wanted to find some work, first, because she didn't want to be a burden to her friend's family and second, because the money she had earned with the military, was dwindling fast. Her friend's father had been a foreman in a factory but his, like most factories, had not started up again. However, her friend had been a secretary to an executive somewhere else before her FLAK service and managed to make her former boss find work for both girls as kitchen workers in a large canteen.

At this canteen was not much food, mostly stew with hardly anything in it. But I was allowed to scrape out the pots.

The cook had given me a container and each night I took that to a friend who lived about 6km away in Leipzig and who had been my classmate at the library college there. I had met her again, accidentally, on a harvested field of peas where we both were looking for some left over pea pods that the harvesters had missed. She was in terrible shape. She had had a severe case of dysentery and had lost all her hair in the process. Now she could walk again. During the approximately 3 months that I was in Zwenkau, I brought her the food that I could scrape out of the pots. It was not a comfortable walk because of the Russians who one met on the way. I myself have never had bad experiences with them but I know that in Zwenkau many husbands and fathers of women of any age attached ropes to them that would help them to climb out of any window, then cut the rope and run away.

There were Russian POWs, and there were Poles. The Polish women were sent as nurses into the barracks for infectious diseases. There was also the wife of a Polish general and she spoke German well. She knew nothing about her husband. I was rather sure that her husband had been killed by the Russians. Shortly after the war ended, large mass graves were found with Polish officers who had been murdered by the Russians. When I talked to her and told her that I had not heard anything from my parents and did not know if they were still alive, she said: "We just have to be patient and maybe someday something will come about."

You see, I have experienced many good things despite everything. I would not want to have missed this time. It is a curious thing that just when it is so very dark, there are these points of light. I have to say that without those points of light it would often not have been bearable. But this way, I must say, it was always alright, even if not always pretty.

Gertrud passed on at age 84. I had always admired her calm good sense and especially her acceptance of whatever came to her. She had spent her years after the war as a librarian in Stuttgart. She was fond of traveling she loved to hike, and she was interested in everything that came her way. She had no children (her fiancé died in the war) but her nieces and nephews and her godchildren (among them one of our daughters) were very important to her – and she to them. Strangely, I have never ever heard her say anything negative about anybody. Some might have been tempted to call her meek but she was never that. She had a very special presence, and she was a true lady. She was calm and kind and she radiated security; At the same time she was a bundle of energy, ready at any time. I feel that the world is a tiny bit better and lighter because of her.

Jacob: The War and After (born 1920)

I met Jakob for the first time when he was in his early eighties, almost 60 years after the end of the war. He was a friendly old gentleman, very mobile and alert in body and mind. His wife had baked a cake for us and she showed us around the cozy house and the yard, bordered by a brook. This was very practical for them because one could just dip the watering can into it and water the vegetables and flowers in the garden.

It all looked so normal and safe and content. But as we talked, it came out that Jakob had to take strong medications to get through the days, weeks and years and to appreciate the easy and safe life that was his now. In America one would have called his problem PTSD, post traumatic stress disorder. In post-WWII Germany it was considered normal that many soldiers were not able to shake off their horrifying memories of war and/or their time as PoWs, besides their physical scars. Most importantly: It was considered great and wonderful luck if a soldier came home at all alive, often after many years in Russian or other war captivity.

Jakob had been through five years of war. He had seen horrible sights, had been wounded a few times but one occurrence seemed to be the most horrific for him:

In late June 1944 Jakob and his unit together with a number of others, found themselves encircled by strong Russian forces near the river Beresina (in northwest Russia, east of Minsk). It was almost impossible to get out of this encirclement. Also, most of the German forces were almost out of ammunition; tanks had run out of fuel.

Some German troops, Jakob among them, managed to fight or sneak through the Russian lines. Jakob caught a substantial grenade fragment in his chest but was still able to somehow move. His dispatch rider had stayed with him and the two happened to find a German field hospital, in an area within the woods. The orderlies could not remove the grenade fragment but could somehow bandage him. Most soldiers there were too badly wounded to be transported, let alone to move on their own power. And here Jakob had his most horrifying experience.

The noise of canons had been coming closer and it was clear that the Russians – military and guerrillas – would be there soon. Many of these terribly wounded German soldiers begged Jakob to shoot them because they knew that they would suffer a much more painful death at the hands of the Russians.

But Jakob just could not bring himself to kill his comrades. Would it have prevented their terrible suffering later at the hands of the Russians? Yes, for sure. Would it have kept Jakob from having horrible memories, guilt feelings, anxiety attacks and so on? Probably. Surely not. And – a dreadfully shocking but practical consideration – did he have enough bullets anyway to kill all of the several hundreds of severely wounded soldiers? Probably not. – War is too terrible. And still people are hurting and maiming and torturing and killing other human beings for various reasons or even for no reason at all. Sorry! These are my personal feelings. But let's go on with Jakob's story:

Jakob's loss of blood had made him very weak. As the Russians approached, he and his dispatch rider fled as far as they could into the woods. From there they could hear how the Russians entered the field hospital and they could hear the wounded German soldiers scream as they were clubbed and/or shot to death. The next day it was all quiet and the two of them walked back to the area of the field hospital.

Jakob had written down his whole life's story and I am quoting from this:

What I saw and experienced there, I still experience today often in my dreams. Then I wake up, drenched in sweat and I only see German soldiers how they are being killed by the Russians. Then my nerves are shot and I have to take heavy tranquilizers. On that long ago day I had seen hundreds of dead comrades scattered around lying in the forest.

From this moment on my rage against the Russians was even greater. After this experience I swore to myself, never to be caught alive by the Ivan*. *) the Ivan= Russian military

Jakob and his dispatch rider crept and crawled (seldom walked) westward though woods and fields, having many close encounters with Russians. It was especially tricky when they spotted men in German uniforms but heard them speak Russian at the last moment. Those were guerillas who had to acquire their own clothing, often uniforms taken off dead German soldiers. Jakob's wound had become badly infected and he was in great pain, but he was lucky to happen to come to a German field hospital still alive. He was further lucky to get onto a transport to Germany where he was eventually treated. After he had somehow recovered, he was sent to the western front which by this time had moved to the Rhein into the German heartland.

In the meantime his parents had been informed that he had been killed and was buried at a certain place in Russia. That was because he had lost his wallet during his flight; another soldier had found it and, naturally, deduced that he was dead.

On Easter Sunday 1945 an American tank unit had hopelessly encircled the German troops and they surrendered to the Americans. Now they were prisoners of war. Jakob writes about his blessedly short time as a POW:

First we had to walk several kilometers to the town of Bad Kissingen.*) *)Bad Kissingen in Lower Frankonia, later became an important American military base. *Having arrived there, the Americans took from us everything we had with us: watches, medals, haversacks which still contained some food and cigarettes. We had to throw everything into barrels and were told we would get everything new. Unfortunately, this was not true. We had to spend the night in the yard of the fire station on the blank cement without our coats or any blankets. The next day we were loaded, 100 at a time, unto large trucks to be transported to the city of Worms*) *)* Worms, a city on the western bank of the Rhein, about 200km due west of Bad Kissingen. Later it became part of the French occupation zone. *to some barracks. During the loading onto trucks we were beaten with clubs until we were packed tight like sardines. We were taken to a barrack yard that was surrounded by barbed wire. There we were without coats or blankets. The first two days we got no food and no water. One morning, when we woke up, we were lying in snow that had fallen during the night. We were wet and freezing, but from that day on the weather improved.*

During the drive from Bad Kissingen to Worms a comrade who had managed to smuggle some paper and pencil past the controls, let me have a piece of paper. I guessed we would end up in Worms. I wrote down the address of an aunt who lived in Heppenheim* *) across the Rhein to the eastern bank and then about 20 km east. *I wrote that I was still alive and probably in a POW camp in Worms. When our truck passed along a street where many women were standing and waving to us, I dropped my note and a woman picked it up. Later she could get it to my aunt. Now at least some of my family knew that I was still alive. A friend of my aunt was working with the Red Cross in Worms and she came to the camp and was allowed to speak a few words with me.*

Soon after, we were taken to another large POW Camp further south. There was no shelter there either and very little food. But some soldiers had pieces of a kind of a tent.

We dug a shallow hole into the soil, crawled into it and covered ourselves with the canvas. In between we were called for questioning. When I learned that railroad workers and transportation workers were released first, I reported as transportation worker with my aunt's address in Heppenheim. No prisoners could be released into the southwestern part of the Palatinate where my parents lived at the French occupation zone, because the French were known to catch all former POWs and transport them to France for forced labor. The Americans transported us north to Maxdorf*) *) At this time so shortly after the end of the war, the occupation zones were not established yet. Later, Maxdorf belonged to the French occupation zone. *to release us there so that we would not be caught by the French.**

Jakob walked for several days until he reached his aunt in Heppenheim who was at the time working her family's nursery alone. His older brother had somehow gotten away from his military unit and had also ended up there. After some time even their father showed up there, having come with an old bicycle from his ordered post in the northeast of the country. The aunt's nursery could use all these helping hands and there were enough vegetables for all to eat. Later even Jakob's mother came to the nursery so the whole family was together, even though very crowded. The family apartment in Landau, in the southwestern Palatinate, had been confiscated by the French military and totally ransacked. Jakob writes:

Much later we were allowed to go back to our apartment. It looked like a pigsty. All lamps had been smashed as well as the all the china; the silverware had been stolen and all the bed linen. The bathroom had been turned into a chicken coop. We did not have any money and did not get any unemployment benefits. To get ration cards we had to work one week each month at clearing away rubble from the air raids. When I found that some relatives in a village nearby needed help in their vineyards, I went there each day and made some much needed money for the family.

These were some highlights – or better: some of the very dark points – of Jakob's war years but also of his survival. We all knew at that time – consciously or subconsciously – that one had no choice but to plod on somehow.

I find the years of Jakob's childhood and youth of great interest too, especially in the light of the social and political situations in which they happened.

Jakob's Childhood and Youth in the Palatinate

I very well know the village where Jakob was born because my family had lived there for generation. In fact, as a boy Jakob had tended my grandmother's geese.

In 1920, Jakob's birth year, Germany still lived under the aftermath of WWI that had ended in 1918 and under the unrest that had followed it. The people were poor and they became even poorer during the inflation period that went on through 1923 and ate up any savings that people had accumulated. Factories and businesses had to close and there was massive unemployment.

Jakob's mother had also been his aunt. When his father's brother, Anton, went to war in 1914, he had asked the brother to take care of his wife and two children if he should die in the war. Anton did die and, as it was customary at the time, the brother married his widow and adopted the children. After then Jakob was born into the family.

Jakob's father, Theo, worked at his father's (Jakob's grandfather's) butcher shop where also livestock was bought and sold. In addition, there was work to do at the grandfather's farm and a flock of sheep needed to be tended. At the time no family could live on one job alone. One of the farmers in the village was also a house painter, a professional gardener repaired bicycles (and sold new ones if somebody in the village could afford one). Most families had many children to feed. Jakob's grandfather had 10 siblings who all had families and were more or less out of work. They helped with the farm work as far as they could but they all came to the butcher shop for meat (free meat, of course).

During this time the whole Palatinate (and some more areas west of the river Rhein) was still under French occupation. Jakob tells his experience:

One day around noontime I saw for the first time French soldiers who had stopped for a rest by the side of the road. All the children were very scared and I was too. That's when I saw a black soldier for the first time. The soldiers had put their rifles together on the sidewalk. They were eating sardines out of cans and drinking wine. The next day the empty sardine tins were lying in the ditch by the road and we played soccer with them.

The Human Face of German History

When Jakob was old enough, about 6 or 7, he had to tend geese in the afternoons when there was no school, and also during the summer vacation.

We always had 8 - 10 geese. A neighbor family had geese which I had to tend too. Each week I got 10 pennies for this and I was extremely proud of it. Other boys were tending geese too. My cousin and I tended our two herds together.

Geese, like cows and other livestock, know exactly where they live. When the geese were brought home in the evening, each herd automatically went home.

The summers were especially nice because we would stay out with the geese for several days in a row. We had made us a primitive tent out of a couple of old sacks. We slept on the ground with only a blanket but we loved it. Around 11 o'clock the church bell was rung and one of us would walk home to pick up our food. (The bell was to tell the farm workers it was time for the midday break.) We then made a fire between two rocks to warm it up. It always tasted very good to us. To get water for the geese, we had to go to the nearest brook, scoop water with a tin can into a bucket and take it to the geese to drink.

During these years there was a great trend to bicycle riding. My father Theo had founded a bicycle club. Men from surrounding villages came. There were races and long tours. The bicycle riders' festivals in our village had always been celebrated without respect of social standing and political association. But that ended when the people somehow split into two political convictions.

In 1928 or 1929 my father and some relatives and friends joined the NSDAP.*) *) Nationalsozialistische deutsche Arbeiterpartei = national socialistic German labor party *These men were idealists who believed in the good of the new party. They believed in a better future, as it was promised by many speakers. Nobody foresaw the terrible end.*

A local branch of the NSDAP was founded of which my father was the leader in the beginning. Soon also a branch of the SA*) *)Sturm-Abteilung = storm unit *was founded. All these men were unemployed.*

From now on it was over with the unity in the music club and the sports club. Two large politic groups formed in the village. These were the "brown" ones (Hitler's NSDAP) and the "red" ones (Reichsbanner, extreme left group).

Even the children were told by their parents to which group they should belong. Suddenly friendships were broken. We even fought veritable battles against each other. We even made shields for our protection against the rocks that were thrown. I still have a scar below my lip where a stone hit me.

In the Reichsbanner were united some parts of the former military. Later parts of this group became the "Sozialdemokraten" (social democrats). But for now the two groups fought each other bitterly. The "reds" disturbed the events and speeches of the "browns". The SA tried to fight the troublemaker. There were fierce brawls.

One day during the summer of 1929 my father had been in the next town where there was a festival of music clubs. A friend took him into his car on his way home and dropped him off in our village, then drove off. I had been waiting for my father and we started to walk home together. Suddenly a pick-up-truck drove up, stopped, and two uniformed Reichsbanner men jumped off. They attacked my father from the back, beat him up terribly and then stabbed him with 15 cm (=6") long knives into his lungs. Then they hopped back unto the truck and drove away. My father was terribly wounded. He was taken to the nearest hospital where he had to stay for several weeks. Afterwards he could not work as a butcher anymore because of these injuries.

The perpetrators were later found by the police and were punished. From this event I have recognized for my whole life how cowardly and deceitful people can be.

After this reprehensible deed, the situation between the two parties in our village had calmed down a little but inside the opponents it kept boiling.

Even before this, our family's situation had not been good. More and more people had lost their jobs. Less people had come to the butcher shop because they could not afford meat.

Jakob's father now tried to sell meat and sausages in the surrounding villages. He and two of us children would pull a small wagon loaded with meat products to offer for sale to other villages and to pubs. But not many people could afford to buy this meat.

We lived at the house of my maternal grandfather, a widower. He worked at the local paper mill (for 10 pennies per hour) But there were he, my parents we 5 children, and also two boarders.

For the main meal the local teacher, a bachelor, came too. We always were 11 people at table. I don't know how my mother managed all this work. She even sometimes had to help out at the butcher shop. Most families had goats and/or a pig; anything to help feed the people.

These were extremely hard times and added to all this, the tensions were between members/sympathizers of the two political parties.

But life was not all dark, especially for the young men in the village. There was a tradition – even reaching into my own early childhood – to play pranks on people during the so-called witches-night, the night between April 30 and May 1st, and the young men, probably even unemployed, loved to play pranks.

Fritz, a young man, lived in our village but had work at a brickworks factory in the next village, about 3 miles away. He was very proud of his racing bicycle which he used to get to work. He would never lock up his bicycle overnight, just park it outside. On the morning of May 1st he was searching for his bicycle everywhere and lamenting that it had been stolen. But he should have checked our roof because there it was, bound down. Somehow somebody had stolen his racing tricot, stuffed it and put in on the bike. It seems that my older brother had been one of the pranksters. There were even pictures in the newspaper.

Some other time a farmer in the village had been the butt of the – very big – prank. A group of youngsters – probably in collaboration with the farmer's own sons – had managed to heave a large farm cart onto the roof of one of the barns and cart even filled it with dung.

A gentler part of the "witches-night" was that young men cut birch saplings and place them on their sweethearts' windows. It was advisable to guard the birch saplings until morning to prevent them from being stolen by other youngsters. Even during my own childhood this still happened.

When Jakob was not quite 10 years old he got to meet Hitler, and this is how it came about:

In some town on the east side of the river Rhein a SA-man had been killed (I don't remember how). "Our" SA-troupe went to the funeral, riding on a truck, and I went along. There were several people there who later became prominent during the third Reich. Hitler was there too and after the funeral I had to, or was allowed to present him a flower bouquet.

Today one can say what one may, to me he was fascinating. One felt like hypnotized when standing face to face with him. At that time the people around surely could not recognize that we were facing a very bitter end after a few years of his rule. Who were the actual originators besides Hitler, the warmongers from other countries, the consultants, among them generals? One will never know.

Today Jacob knows more than he could know when all this happened. Now we know that Hitler had made a plan how he wanted to make himself the greatest ruler of his time, no matter what brutally one could and did use. He knew about his almost hypnotic powers over people. He was very smart in picking the most capable people for his ministers and consultants and he recklessly and brutally had people, even friends, murdered, executed if that was to his advantage or if he just felt like it. And he happened to come onto the political stage at the exact right moment in the German history.

Wilhelm and his Friend's Journey to their Double Wedding

in November 1923

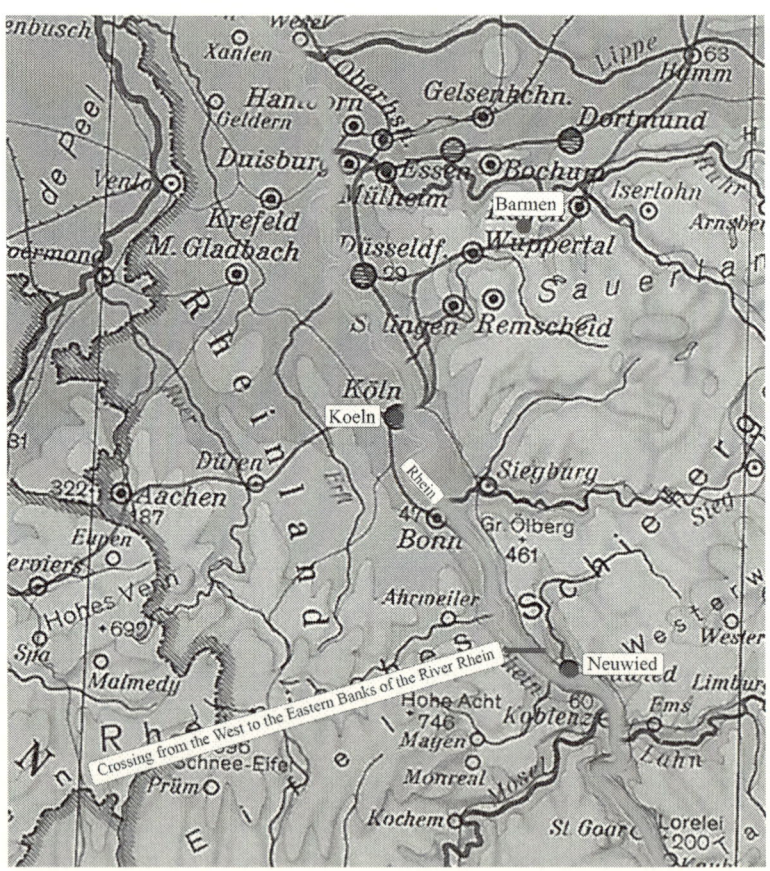

History: After WWI at 1918 How it Helped Hitler to Power

To get a feel for the "mood" in Germany that allowed Hitler come to power, we do have to look at the political and especially the social situation at the time.

Toward the end of WWI, 1918, the German population was starving, even the soldiers did not have enough food and ammunition. The military and national leaders were pulling in different directions. One side wanted to continue the war, the other side wanted to give up the war and accept an unconditioned capitulation. The press – at the time only the government-controlled radio and newspapers – had continuously reported news about victories (there were many at first) but later withheld the actual bad situation on the front. Therefore the people and some groups of soldiers believed that by capitulating, the government had betrayed them and they were very angry.

At the beginning of November 1918 some leaders of the German Navy had the crazy and suicidal idea to turn the outcome of the war around by having a mighty sea battle with the English fleet. The sailors knew that such an attack could only bring the total annihilation of the German fleet and a great number of them rebelled against the order. Following martial law, the mutinous sailors would have been executed. But their comrades did not want to let this happen and they revolted.

The whole fleet retreated to the North Sea harbor of Kiel and there the revolt broke out and spread. First the city was brought under the rule of the revolutionaries and their sympathizers. The revolution soon spread out over northern Germany, then advanced into the other parts of Germany. Especially in the larger cities some kind of Guerilla war was happening. The revolution had somehow been taken over by the so-called Spartakus-Bund,*) *) named after the Roman slave Spartacus who had started a revolt against the Roman lords a group whose goal it was to bring Germany under the influence and rule of the Bolsheviks.*) *)Russia had fallen to the Bolsheviks. In 1917 they had deposed Scar Nicholas II, imprisoned him and his family and executed them in 1918. The Soviet Union was officially formed in 1922.

After the war had practically ended on November 11, 1918, the emperor, as a condition by the Allies, abdicated and fled to the Netherlands. From now on Germany was supposed to be a republic. But the newly formed German government was unsure of how to rule and, as a consequence, the officials changed constantly.

Everywhere laborers and soldiers formed workers' and soldiers' councils who became forces that the government had to negotiate with.

Under the emperor, the German Reich had consisted of several kingdoms, archdukedoms and dukedoms. With the end of the monarchy these kings, dukes, princes were also forced to abdicate, like the king of Bavaria, Prussia and others. Most of them were relieved to retire into private life. But they were still revered and respected by their people.

When my mother-in-law was a young girl and living in Stuttgart, she used to see the former (now abdicated) king of Württemberg walk in the park with his dogs, two Pomeranians. He was a kind old man and one day she got up her courage, walked up to him, curtsied deeply and asked him for an autographed photo of himself. He smilingly consented. The picture is still kept in the family.

The members of the new "republican" government were wavering between making it pseudo-monarchic and a democratic. The government had no real power. So the former military leaders stepped in. To keep the revolutionaries from turning Germany into a bolshevik/communist country and to keep the population safe from excesses, they called on loyal former soldiers and officers to volunteer and fight against these destructive forces. They were called the Freikorp (= free corps).

Wilhelm zur Linden, a lieutenant in the former army and now in the Freikorp, tells*) *) in his book "Blick durchs Prisma" about his experiences in Berlin. One of his tasks there was to find information about the weapons, the positions and manpower of the Spartakists. One foggy and rainy night in March 1919 he went into the area of the revolutionaries, together with two young soldiers. But soon they were caught by some Spartakists, manhandled rather roughly and then, proudly, shown the spot where, the night before, two Freikorp officers had been brutally murdered. Wilhelm's young companions were let go because they spoke the Berlin dialect and could give their home addresses. But Wilhelm, wearing his old uniform, seemed suspicious. He was searched for his Freikorp identification which by lucky coincidence was not found on him. But the Spartakists usually did not bother much with formalities; they just shot suspects. However, for some reason, Wilhelm was taken to their headquarters for interrogation. It so happened that the leader, certain that his prisoner would be killed in the morning anyway, started to brag about the strength of the Spartakist positions, by giving Wilhelm all the information he had set out to gather.

But by morning the two men had also exchanged so many war memories that something like a bond had been formed between them, and the Spartakist whispered to Wilhelm that he should sneak out. He did and the dense fog helped him to escape. But getting back into the Freikorp area was also dangerous. Called to by the posts, he had to give the password and drop down on the ground as not to be shot. Wilhelm was taken to the Freikorp headquarters where he could report all he had learned.

Slowly the country became relatively safe again. The new government had not set up again in the former German capital, Berlin, but had chosen Weimar, a smallish city in the state of Thuringia. Weimar would have been relatively easy to defend against revolutionaries, contrary to Berlin. And Weimar had a special significance to Germans as the city of the famous poets and writers Goethe and Schiller.

But still this new government was anything but stable. There happened a lot of infighting and constant changes. The conditions of the Versailles peace treaty made for specific stress. Two of the conditions were especially burdensome: the paying of huge (and actually unbearable) reparations to the allies and the prohibition of any remilitarization. To undercut the second, a German military force was very secretly built up on Russian territory in exchange for Germans training the Russian military in "modern" warfare.

The way the German government chose to reduce or even do away the reparations, seems, in hindsight, insane and it turned out to cause a financial and social catastrophe in Germany: inflation, at first a slow but then a racing inflation. It was supposed to make the German Mark utterly worthless to the Allies, especially to France. But the inflation also made it worthless to the German people. All savings were lost, all financial properties were lost. Only land properties were safe, especially agriculturally used land. Suddenly the farmers were kings.

At the end of WWI, the Mark in relationship to the dollar had stood at approximately 1:10. In 1922 one had already to pay more than 20,000 Marks for 1 US Dollar, during the year 1923 it was 1 million, then 1 billion. By the end of 1923 it was 4.2 trillion. The official mint's capacity was not enough to print the enormous amounts of money. Other printing companies had to be employed and the money had to be transported across country by freight trains.

At first it had not been too bad for the labor force because during the relatively slow inflation at first, their wages could be raised along with the devaluation of the money. But by 1923 the inflation ran so fast that some factories paid their workers hourly and they (or rather their wives who were waiting at the factory gates) had to buy food and necessities immediately. People suffered terribly. It is believed that this inflation was the biggest reason for Hitler's coming to power.

As the German "financial system" was being destroyed, Germany was not able any more to pay the (enormous) reparations. But France was determined to get something out of it anyway. In the Treaty of Versailles the part of Germany west of the river Rhein had been ordered to be a demilitarized zone and French troops had occupied it (with the half-secret goal to eventually annex the area to France.) But at the worthlessness of the German mark, France had sought other options of income from Germany and therefore occupied areas on the eastern side of the Rhein, especially highly industrialized areas.

My father, a young journalist at the time, had found a job at a newspaper inside the French occupation zone. I found his "Arbeitsbuch" (record of employment) from this time and it was written all in French.

At the time my Aunt Lisa was a young schoolteacher just out of seminary. Like all young schoolteachers at the time, she was sent to teach in a small village for two (or more) years before getting a permanent position. Aunt was extremely lucky to have rented a room at a farm in the village. State employees, like teachers, were paid their salaries at the end of the month. Soon, by the time she received her pay, it was not enough to pay rent and board but the farmers were very kind and housed and fed her anyway. She once told me that at one month her pay was only enough to buy one cake of soap and a small strand of embroidery yarn.

At the time the only way to survive was, to plant vegetables in any space one had, keep chickens if at all possible and/or take valuables, heirlooms, etc. to exchange them at farms for food. Many people were starving.

The situation was desperate. One did not know how long this terrible time would continue. But people can be resilient and they can be inventive.

Like Aunt Lisa, the male young teachers also had to serve in small villages first before they could get a permanent position. And they had learned – like everybody else – that food was the only real necessity to survive. Therefore many of these young men saw the solution in marrying farmers' daughters. This usually worked out well, even in the long run, but only sometimes it did not. Several decades later I knew a teacher in the town where I grew up, whose wife was sweet but very, very shy and easily scared. Later I learned her story. Her husband had been one of the young teachers who, during the inflation, had been looking for a farm girl as his bride. He befriended a family who had two daughters, one outgoing and pretty, the other quieter and a little less handsome. Naturally, his plan was to get the prettier sister. One late evening he met the girl in the – dark – cow barn and started to make up to her. She was not adverse to his advances and later they walked hand in hand up to the house to tell the father that they wanted to get married. When they entered the lighted house, the teacher, to his great horror, saw that he had made love to the wrong sister. But he had to marry her, and it seems that he never forgot or let her forget that he had not wanted her but her sister.

Another wedding that took place during this time had a perfectly happy ending. During the first beginning of November 1923, at the height of the inflation, Wilhelm, the former young lieutenant who had helped in some way to make Berlin safer and later several other cities, was on his way to get married. At the same day his friend was to get married to Wilhelm's fiancée's sister. The two friends and soon to be brothers-in-law met in Barmen where Wilhelm was working as a young physician at the hospital. Under normal circumstances it would have taken a 3 or 4 hour trip by train for them to get to their brides' town. But not only took their trip them in and out of different occupation zones, there was a German government advisory (willingly followed by the population) not to use the trains operated by the French occupation forces except when absolutely necessary. This was an occasion that was necessary.

Barmen, Wilhelm's place of employment was just outside the French zone. But to get to their next point, Köln, the men had to take a train (at 4 o'clock in the morning) that took them into the French zone and then into the British. Wilhelm's friend did not have a visa for the French zone but by some lucky coincidence the French officers who checked the people on the train, overlooked the friends, and then they also made it safely into the British zone. From Köln they took a steamship up the river Rhein planning to get off about 200km further south, near the hometown of their brides.

But the ship started hours late and when a dense November fog came up, the captain anchored in the middle of the river. The fire under the steam kettles was let die down to save coal and it got really cold. A last meal was given out. It cost several billions. Later the ship ran out of drinking water, with about 500 passengers on board.

Nevertheless Wilhelm's friend was confident that they would still make it to their brides' home near the city of Neuwied on the east side of the Rhein. He still had about 200 billions. Little did he know how fast the money's value would decrease.

Around midnight the fog lifted a little and a moon came up. The kettles were fired up and the ship started moving again. The ship landed some way from its next planned stop, but it landed on the west side, the French zone, instead of the river's east bank. For Wilhelm's friend who did not have a proper visa for the French zone, this was another dangerous situation, but the friends managed to circumvent the French guards when gotten off the ship. Now they needed to get across the river. It was one o'clock at night but they found a skipper who was willing to row them across – for 15 billions a piece. They were now on the right side of the river, and after walking for more than five hours through the night, they could finally fall into the arms of their worried brides.

The double wedding was celebrated and everybody was happy. But the wedding guests, by that time, had no possibility to travel home again because in the meantime the price for a ticket on the boat from Neuwied to Köln had risen to 10 trillions. Luckily the family had enough food to feed the guests for a few days and then found a way to sell some valuables to pay for their tickets home.

This was during the beginning part of November 1923. On November 15 a currency reform was enacted and the whole "spook" was over. People did not have to pick up their meager earnings with a laundry basket anymore and take them to the grocery store right away. But whoever had had savings and financial assets, had lost everything.

After the currency reform, a new ruling was passed that included German reparation payments that were somehow bearable. In the Versailles treaty the "new" western borders had been treated somehow vaguely. Now it was determined that France had to withdraw from the areas on the east side of the Rhein and respect the western border (that made the Pfalz a regular part of Germany again). On the other hand Germany had to keep all areas west of the Rhein demilitarized after the French and British occupation would have ended (which it did in 1930) and officially give up any rights to Alsace and Lorraine.

In hindsight it looks like a crazy financial situation: The United States were the wealthy banker while England, France and especially Germany were the "poor cousins". England and France had only been able to support the war because the US had given them credits. These credits had to be paid back now to the US. The US apparently realized that Germany had to be built up after not only the war but the catastrophic inflation. So the US gave Germany credits. Germany paid reparations to England and France. England and France used these reparations to pay back their credits to the US. A somehow crazy circle!

But for Germany it brought something good: The American credits to Germany amounted to about 25 billion while Germany's reparation payments to England and France were only about 10 billion each (per year). This left money to rebuild the German economy and to export well. Germany recuperated. Times became more normal even though the enormous financial losses caused by the inflation, could never be recovered.

In the meantime people in the Weimar government thought that the German people who lived outside Germany proper, the "Reich", should work toward having the areas where they lived (because their forefathers had immigrated there) united with the "homeland". And they especially wanted Austria to become part of the German Reich. Many Austrians wanted this too, among them Adolf Hitler who, already in his youth, had seen himself as an Austrian-German.

The "circle-financing" had helped Germany to get on her feet again. But then came the "world-economic-crisis" of 1929. It started in America. The US could not pay out the credits to Germany anymore, quite the reverse: the Americans now demanded them back. This hit the German economy hard. Businesses went bankrupt, more and more people lost their jobs. And now the Weimar government (it kept changing often) got the idea – and acted upon it – to make Germany (again!) so poor that reparation payments as well as repayment of American credits were not possible. This time they did not instigate another inflation but they deflated the money.

My friend Mariann lived in Dortmund with her parents. She told about the situation there:

> *The time before Hitler came to power, was very turbulent. And everywhere there were beggars. We had our apartment at the 3rd floor of a large house. My mother was always fearful when the doorbell went off. There was a piece of frosted glass at the top of the door through which one could see if a man or a woman was outside. Very often it was a beggar. When my mother had a few coins in the apron pocket, she would open the door and give it to the man. But when she didn't have any money on her, she would not even open. If this would happen that the man would have put his foot in the door to be sure she would come back with some money. She would feel in great danger, rightly or not.*

But she felt it would be cruel, not to help these poor, unemployed men at all. She herself knew how it felt to be poor.

Mariann's parents' families had lived in Bromberg (North-Prussia) for generations. The area had sometimes been Polish, sometimes German – as many areas in the east had been. After the end of WWI the area was declared to belong to Poland. All Germans there were asked to either opt for Poland and became Poles or leave. Mariann's parents had just gotten married and the bride's sister had moved to Dortmund (in western Germany) some time back. So the young couple decided to join her there at. He was a musician and had been concertmaster*) of the Bromberg symphony orchestra. *) The concertmaster/first violinist of an orchestra has almost the importance of the conductor. He/she works with the orchestra, practices the pieces, etc. before the conductor comes in and maybe, maybe not, makes slight changes after his own taste. In Dortmund he was lucky after some time to be able to work as violin teacher. Later he got a job at the orchestra of the municipal theater.

Mariann experienced the change:

> *And then Hitler came to power. I was 11 years old. My parents had not voted for Hitler and I sensed that they were not happy about the political situation. But there seemed nothing to do. My father was glad that the theater had not been closed and he had not lost his job. There were no beggars around anymore, most men had jobs now. Everything seemed safe and orderly now. Only much later I learned what the price the country would have to pay for this order.*

History: The Coming of Hitler

Adolf Hitler was born on April 20, 1889 in the Austrian village of Braunau. We know almost nothing about his childhood and youth, except that he dropped out of school when he was about 16 or 17 years old. He probably had some small talent in drawing and painting, but not enough to be accepted into the Art College (Kunstakademie) in Vienna. This was a big disappointment to him. Imagine what might have happened to the world if Hitler would have had real talent, would have attended the Art College and would have become a famous painter!

Hitler had always been especially interested in politics. At the time many people were too. It was customary to read the newspapers, to discuss the events with others, to try to form a personal political opinion. Hitler felt that Germany was superior to Austria and a better country to succeed in with whatever he dreamed about. When he was about to be drafted into the Austrian Army, he "emigrated" to Germany. Many Austrians felt like he did. Moving between the two countries was easy. He stayed in Munich. He got a small orphan's allowance from home because his father had died. It is said that he sometimes painted postcards and sold them. But he did not try to find a real job or try to start a career in a specific field. His interest in politics, political events and connections was all he lived for.

In 1914 when Hitler was 25 years old, WWI started and he immediately volunteered. He had avoided entering the Austrian military because he did not believe in Austria but he was willing and eager to fight for Germany. He apparently was a good soldier, was even decorated, but never made it above private first class. It seems that he showed no leadership qualities.

Fun has been made about Hitler's little mustache. During that time, especially before the war, most men wore handlebar mustaches. My grandfather did too. There is a picture of Hitler wearing one. But the story goes that he was forced to cut off most of it so that it would fit into his gasmask and after the war he did not grow it back.

The end of the war (1918) found Hitler in a field hospital because of gas poisoning. He stayed there for a whole year but even after that he had no plans for a specific profession. In the fall of 1919, he became a member of a small, unimportant, right-wing party and soon became its leader. He went on speaking trips and discovered that he had a real talent to impress people through his speeches.

It was not so much what he said and how he spoke but he seemed to be able to hold hisaudiences spellbound, like hypnotized. People would hang on his every word and they believed what he said.

In the meantime his party had grown and he had changed its name to "Nationalsozialistische deutsche Arbeiterpartei" (= national socialistic German laborer party) or NSDAP. "Nationalistic" stood for everything German, excluding everything that was not German. With this he tuned into the general nationalistic feeling in the land. "Socialistic" should draw the laborers who had leaned towards communism or at least towards the social democrats*). *)The "social democrats" party were organized as an international party, not only German.

Hitler also felt that it had to be emphasized that his party, the NSDAP, was not just directed towards the middle class but especially to the masses of the laborers who were suffering special hardships after WW1 and who had not been really respected and their needs recognized.

As Hitler and his party gained ground, special fighting groups were formed who protected NSDAP meetings and speeches, the SA (=Sturm-Abteilung = storm section). Most of their members were laborers, mostly unemployed. They were not just rednecks and thugs*) but people like Jakob's father who were seeing in Hitler finally the hope for a future of order and employment and security (financial and social) and for pride in their country. *)remember that Jakob's father was beaten and stabbed by social democrats, that the two "fronts", even in a small village, made even children fight against each other, according to their parents' political convictions.

Hitler, despite his lack of higher education and his, so far, rather aimless life, was intelligent, he was clever, he had great talent for organizing, he could surround himself with exceptionally capable people, and he could and did use the moods and dreams and needs of the people to build on them and fill them with his own ideas.

The people wanted to have pride in their country or rather their "Germanhood" that had been beaten down and humiliated after WW1. Hitler built on the patriotic ideas that had been there long, even before the war.

In this context I just have to tell you the story about Arminius the Cherusci (Hermann der Cherusker). Living from about 17BC until about 20AD, he had been the first one who tried (and failed) to build a strong and united German Reich.

He stayed the symbol for German unity and greatness through the centuries.

In 1875, almost two thousand years later, when nationalistic feelings and dreams were again high, in Germany a monument was finished and erected, that showed his figure, 87 feet high, on a base of about the same height. It was 185 feet high in total which made it about half the size of the statue of liberty. Even in Minnesota a 103 feet high monument was put up to honor "Hermann the German".

At the time of Hermann's birth, southern and western Europe was part of the Roman Empire. But the middle and north-eastern part of today's Germany had not been totally subjugated yet. The Romans wanted Germanic*) governors *)" Germanic" is very different from "German". The first are one of the races of people living in the country, as Germanics, Celts, Swabians, Alemans, Dinarics and more. The English saw mostly of the race of Germanics, they named the whole country "Germany", the French met Alemannic races and named it Allemagne, the Dutch named it Duitsland. For example, I have been told I am Dinaric. Hitler was not Germanic. for these parts and therefore forced tribal leaders to give their sons into Roman custody so that they could be educated in Rome in Roman administration and war techniques – at the same time to hold them as hostages to keep their fathers from revolting against Roman rule at home. Roman education and training was much superior to what was available at home, so some Germanic tribal leaders, among them the Cherusken tribal leader, voluntarily sent their sons to Rome.

Hermann, or Arminius as he was called in Rome, distinguished himself as a commander and was sent home when he was about 25 years old to become the Roman governor of his Cheruskian tribe. But he found that his people suffered terribly under Roman rule. They were treated with cruel brutality and heavily taxed. Several Germanic rulers were already plotting to fight the Romans and chase them away and Hermann became their leader. He pulled the more than three dozen Germanic tribes together against the Roman enemy.

His Germanic army consisted of 11 ethnic groups. Hermann organized them trained them Roman style and taught them to act collectively. Their time to act, came when in 9 AD a large Roman army marched from their summer quarters in the north to their winter quarters in the south. Hermann's Germanic army beat them terribly. There were apparently several battles in which about 50,000 Roman soldiers lost their lives. (It is better, not to imagine how soldiers were killed during that time when the weapons were swords, spears, and plain brute force.)

The Roman commander (Publius Quinctilius Varus), seeing his army destroyed, is said to have killed himself by throwing himself into his own sword.

The Germanic army had won. Hermann, wanting to include Bohemia into a new united German(ic) Reich, asked Marbod, the Bohemian ruler, Rome-educated like Hermann, to join forces with him. He sent a messenger to Budweis (the city where later the Budweiser beer was made) carrying as proof of evidence Varus' bloody head on a spear. (Thus were apparently the customs of communication at the time.) Marbod refused and Hermann himself was murdered a few years later. Thus died the very first attempt to form a united German Reich/country. But the dream of a strong and proud Germany always stayed alive and was, of course, taken up by Hitler.

Now back to Hitler and how he got from the leader of one of the many parties to the office of chancellor.

To the outside the Weimar Republic looked to be on a legally firm base. Even though the Reichspräsident*)   *) In the German system, contrary to the US, the president has no ruling function, only the chancellor does. had little influence into the details of governing. However, he had an important voice about the direction of the government and the appointment of the chancellor.

In reality there was constant infighting among the powerful members of the government, most of them still wanting to recreate a monarchy-like ruling system. More than once the parliament was dissolved, the goal being to strive for a government where only one man would rule. Political murders happened frequently. Coups were planned, even by the government, to bring this about. Wide sections of the population were longing for one powerful leader who could make the country safe and ordered and prosperous again, like an emperor.

In 1923 in the middle of the horrifying inflation, many people felt that a new and strong government was needed. In 9th November Hitler and friends got together a great number of people and marched to the Feldherrnhalle (Field Marshal's Hall), a monumental building, built after a loggia in Florence. The police tried to disperse the masses; it became a shooting fight and several demonstrators and a police officer died. Hitler was arrested and sentenced for five years for treason. But it turned out that he had only served for 9 months. During this time Hitler wrote his book "Mein Kampf" where he pronounced his political ideas and plans.

In the meantime, the social situation in Germany kept worsening and the NSDAP became bigger and stronger because the desperately poor all streamed to it. In the last election of 1932, there were about 10 parties all vying for a majority. The NSDAP came out as the strongest party, it got about one third of the votes. among them and, after long discussions, the Reichspräsident appointed Hitler chancellor. It was thought that he might be easily guided by the "gray eminences" (wire-pullers). There also was the condition that Hitler should chose his government members not from outside his own party.

And this is what Hitler mostly did. But he was extremely skilled and smart in finding people who were the most able and competent for the jobs concerned and who were somehow loyal to him.

In the US there have been basically two parties for a long time: the Democrats and the Republicans. Not so in Germany and also most of Europe. There are many different parties, (about 10 at Hitler's time, more than 14 today). Usually there is no one party who gets the absolute majority (except the "Christian Democratic Union", CDU, right after WWII and Adenauer was voted chancellor.) Then a coalition government is formed. The leaders of the strongest party negotiate with the leaders of several other parties to find some common ground to form a workable government. The strongest party provides the chancellor. Today it is this way. In 1933, the year of Hitler's becoming chancellor, it was similar. He had gotten 1/3 voters and he had to take several small right-wing parties to get the absolutely majority.

When Hitler became chancellor on January 30th, 1933, there were 6 million unemployed in Germany. To get a feel for what this really meant, I did some raw calculations:

In 1933 Germany had a population of 66 million. At that time most women did not work outside the home. Of course there were teachers, nurses, secretaries, seamstresses, servants, washerwomen, and others. Many might have lost their jobs because their employers could not afford to pay them anymore but it is dubious if more than a few reported themselves as unemployed. If they were single, they would have returned home or found shelter and maybe food with relatives and friends.

I therefore will look only at the approximately 33 million of German males. If I presume that only the males between 18 and 70 years of age were "in the job market", this makes 24 million. 6 million unemployed out of 24 makes one forth, meaning that every 4th able man was unemployed. Since almost each, now unemployed, male was responsible for feeding his family (with, usually, a large number of children), one may perceive the poverty of the population. There existed some kind of unemployed welfare at the time, but the weekly payment was not enough by far to support a family.

There was misery everywhere. The government was somehow in disarray and even wanted to dissolve itself and return to a pseudo-monarchic leadership. People were yearning not only for financial and social security but also for order, discipline, a clear leadership and pride in their country. Under the emperor (even though he had been a rather weak man) the country had been enjoying a mild contentment and order in the peaceful time between the wars of 1870/71 with France and WW1. Now, after WW1 and during the Weimar Republic, it seemed that a charismatic and powerful man was needed to lead the masses out of the misery. Election posters were seen everywhere showing a group of poor and depressed people with the words: "Our last hope: Hitler". And Hitler did fulfill this hope – at least in the beginning and at least partially.

As mentioned before, Hitler had a rare talent to pick people for his staff who were eminently suited and skilled for their posts. They created jobs for the millions, they built up the economy, he re-awakened the sense for pride in the German history and culture. The time before Hitler, the Weimar Republic, had been rather chaotic, people were murdered, others just vanished, brutal fights among opposing parties were common. Therefore, now the great masses were not too surprised that many of Hitler's opponents would be found murdered or locked up in Jails. (Many were even released after some time.)

Jews had always been living in Germany and most had become an integral part of the population, many having converted to the Christian faith. Jewish physicians, visual and performing artists, financial experts were highly respected. Then in the eastern part of Europe the Russian and Polish governments started to drive out their Jewish populations. (remember "Fiddler on the Roof") Now these groups*) that had kept their Jewry with beards and clothing and strong religious rules, streamed into Germany and were rejected, even by the integrated German Jews. *) Often these were not even Jews by race but only by ethnicity, having been converted by Jewish "missionaries" a long time ago.

Hitler had been an anti-Semite for a long time, and so were people in many countries around the world. At first in Germany the actions against Jews were rather moderate. Later when Jewish neighbors and friends just disappeared and were thought to have moved away or fled the government.

Nicole, a French friend of mine spent some time in Germany around 1935 when she was about 15 years old. One day she had been on an excursion with a group of young German people. It was getting later than they had planned and one young man asked her to please use a nearby telephone booth to call his mother and tell her that he was alright. Her natural response was: "You go and call her yourself!" But the young man told my friend that he as a Jew was not allowed to use a public telephone. She was shocked.

Unfortunately and incomprehensibly, anti-Semitism exists, to some extend, almost everywhere.

Marie, Jewish from her mother's side, had managed to flee from Germany to Brazil in 1942. She did not have an easy time there and hoped to immigrate to the US because this was – as she thought – the land of the free, the land of tolerance and goodness. In 1949 she had received her entrance visa and was traveling to the US. During her trip she befriended an American woman, a refugee from an east European country. The airline had reserved rooms for them both at a hotel in Miami. When they registered there, her new friend was given her room key right away but when the clerk saw Marie's last name, he told her, that her friend had gotten the last room available. There was none left for her. Now, Marie's father was not Jewish. His name even pointed to old noble German ancestors but the clerk must have thought it looked Jewish. Her friend recognized the situation immediately, put her room key back on the counter and took Maria away with her. Outside she pointed to a small sign with the word "restricted".

This was the first disillusionment Maria suffered in the US. The next one came on the day after when she boarded a city bus, sat down in the middle of the bus and was rudely ordered by the driver to move forward. A black woman sitting next to her begged her to follow orders as not to cause trouble.

So far I have only told about the German masses and how Hitler made them trust and follow him. But many German people mistrusted him and would have loved to get out of his sphere of influence but could not. There was, for example, the family of Gertrud (whose story has been told already). Her father had a good insight into what was happening around him. He was a jurist and knew that he would not be able to support his family in any other country. The law in other countries was different from the German law that he had studied and practiced, and he did not know any other languages sufficiently well.

As I recall from my childhood years, the word „Nazi" was never used in normal speech. It was a swearword only used, in secret, to describe a bad, immoral, etc. national-socialist. Only after WWII was it used openly and then it became the term for all persons who had in any way been involved with National Socialism. However, I cringe when I hear people speak about "Nazi soldiers", "Nazi aircraft" and so on. The military itself was apolitical. There were, of course, soldiers and officers who were firm believers in Hitler. However, the majority were just fulfilling the oath of loyalty and obedience they had had to swear. I am rather certain that it would not occur to people around the world to talk about "US Republican soldiers", "Republican war planes" or "US Democratic soldiers or war ships".

Many people celebrated Hitler's coming to power in January 1933 with jubilant demonstrations on the streets. This was for them the fulfillment of their hopes for a new time, for work and possible prosperity, for order and discipline and a new "emperor" who would be a strong and charismatic leader.

From looking at the life stories of my friends and the people I interviewed, I got the impression that Hitler's chancellorship had been viewed by most as just another change of government as there had been so many during the Weimar Republic. Some were rather pessimistic about it but for most life just went on. Personal small and large problems had to be solved, jobs had to be worked on, people fell in love, married, had children, died.

Did a farmer or shoemaker or even a teacher in a village really care what happened in the capital Berlin? And how did people know anyway? My grandfather, Opa, was a tailor. He was very progressive and he interested in anything new. He was the very first one in his village to own a radio. That must have been in the 1920s but I doubt that there were many more radios in the village by the time Hitler came to power. People had become poorer as the years went on and a radio would have been an unaffordable luxury.

What did happen in Berlin? As mentioned already, Hitler was named chancellor by the Reichspräsident*) Hindenburg. *) In Germany the president does not have a real political power than, like for example, the British king or queen, but not have very much more. When Hitler was made Chancellor, somebody asked the Vice Chancellor (Papen): "You have made Hitler Chancellor?" but he, a member of the "old guard", replied: "Oh no, we have employed him." – How wrong he was!

Because Hitler had his very definite plans on how he would develop his power and he carried them out.

One month after Hitler had been nominated as chancellor, in the night from January 27 to 28, 1933 the "Reichstag" building, the parliament in Berlin, went up in flames. It clearly had been arson because fires started simultaneously at different parts of the enormous building. It has never been determined which group laid the fire. But the official version was "The Communists have done it." and: "This is the beginning of the communist revolution. They will launch the attack. Not one minute must be lost!"

Hitler was prepared for action. He and his Vice Chancellor had the 86 year-old President, Paul von Hindenburg*), sign an emergency decree that practically annulled the constitution and all fundamental rights of the people. Anybody could be arrested without a reason given. *) In 1930 Hindenburg had already signed a similar degree during the very painful economical depression. This degree had made the newly installed chancellor (Brüning at the time) and his government exclusively answerable to him and had also dissolved the parliament. The day after the fire already saw all communist leaders (who could be caught) either arrested or shot. Anybody else who had any connection to the Communist party, was arrested. The prisons could not take in all and temporary concentration camps were established. (However, later many prisoners would be set free again.)

New elections for parliament had been scheduled already for a week after the fire. The NSDAP distributed handbills with the text:

"The Reichstag in Flames!

Set on fire by communists!

This is how the whole country would look like if Communism and the affiliated Social-Democrats would have the power for only a few months!

Good citizens would be stood against the wall as hostages!

The red rooster will be put on top of the farmers' roofs!

Like a cry it has to go through Germany:

Stamp out Communism! Crush Social-Democracy!

Elect Hitler, List 1"

But the election was disappointing for the NSDAP. The party only reached 43.9%. Nevertheless, they managed, together with several other smaller parties, to get a 2/3 majority because not one (of the 81) communist representatives was there. The Reichstag (parliament) could therefore confirm the decrees and dissolve itself. Hitler was now the only one in power. When President Hindenburg died about a year later, Hitler declared that it would not be necessary to nominate a new president. He himself would take over the office together with his chancellorship.

One has to keep in mind that Hitler was smart; and he was egotistical to the extreme. In his view the welfare and lives of people had absolutely no value. Only his own success counted for him. Many people followed his devilish ideas and plans. However, many others did very good things for many people, most often under the name of NSDAP but in reality apolitically and help humanity.

I believe that nobody really took seriously his proclamations that during the war Germany should rather die than give in. But he meant it. The air raids were horrific and inhumane. It is said that the allies wanted to erode the fighting morale of the German military by killing their loved ones and destroying the land. This did not work. The people who had survived the terrible air raids stood together more try to find food and shelter and hate the "enemy". If people would have been written to their soldiers to end the war, they could not have done anything.

When the atomic bombs were dropped to Nagasaki and Hiroshima, the Japanese emperor immediately gave up the war because he wanted to save his people from more horrors.

When Germany was bombed so terribly, Hitler did not give up. He did not care one bit about "his" people. He felt that they should be proud and happy to be allowed to die "for him". I think there was probably nothing human in him.

History: Hitler's Years

Two things about Hitler marked his time above all others:

First, he had an enormous ego. He was absolutely certain that he would make Germany great again after the hopeless devastating times after WWI, even greater (and larger) than it had ever been before. However, his emphasis was not on Germany and the Germans but only on himself as the greatest leader that ever was. And he possessed the, somehow hypnotic, ability to lure some masses to him.

Second, he was a very good organizer. He had plans and ideas. Mostly, he had the ability (or the instinct?) to pick the very best people to make his plans a reality. And most of these people he had picked, did not realize that the good they were doing to Germany and the Germans. All this was for him only a step on the way to his own glory, his own power that he wanted to extend over the whole of Europe. People were dispensable; even his friends and loyal collaborators could be and were murdered whenever he felt like it.

We have to understand the German situation at the time. The country had been deeply humiliated after WWI. The reparations that the treaty of Versailles had imposed, could not be fulfilled in reality. The German post-war government had tried to circumvent the payments by triggering an inflation that should make Germany too poor to pay the reparations but that also made most of the German people extremely poor, took all their savings away, caused unrest and misery. The French had occupied the area west of the river Rhein right after the war and were trying to make it part of France. But later they also occupied several highly industrial areas on the east of the Rhein. The German government gave out a "passive resistance order" to the population (meaning Germans should not work for the French in the occupied factories) but people needed to eat. So this meant more unrest. Finally in 1930 the other Allies ordered France to withdraw from German soil.

During all that time the NSDAP had been growing, mostly by unemployed workers. The SA troops fought against the Communists and the Socialists and other groups. The difference between these groups showed in the fact how they were well organized*): the SA were as brutal as the others but they marched in sync, they were proud and had faith in a better future. *) As mentioned before, Hitler was a very good organizer. He had loved the order in the military and there he had also learned a lot about tactics.

Let me insert here the impressions of Nicole, my French friend that she had in Germany in 1935 when she spent time in Köln as a 15or 16 -year old. She told me:

The young people, the people I knew, they were really happy. They marched in the streets and they sang. For me it was: Oh they have so much discipline and order! which, of course, we did not have in France. Not that I envied it. But I enjoyed it.

A few years later, much had changed. Nicole's family had the daughter of German friends visit her in the summer and she kept saying to Nicole:

"You have it so good in France, you have so much freedom. You are so lucky. You can read whatever you want, do whatever you want."

Nicole recollected: *We often walked in the woods together and once I sang a Hitler Youth song I had learned in Germany. She looked at me and said: "My gosh, we are in France and you can sing that?" And I said: "Well, nobody is going to hear it in the woods. I would not do it in front of a church or anything." She said: "Oh, but in Germany we would not do anything like that, even if it was hidden. We wouldn't dare to sing a French song in public." I still remember her. She could not believe the freedom we had in France of expressing ourselves.*

In January 1933, when Hitler came to power, there were many people who distrusted Hitler and were afraid for the country's future; but more people saw him as the leader who could make their lives better, who could restore order to the torn country. However, the country started to become a dictatorship.

Hitler met and befriended Heinrich Himmler who led of a group of young men. (Himmler was 25 at the time). This group had the motto of resurrecting Germanic "culture". They learned the old Germanic runes, ancient behavior and also the importance of their own tribes keep "clean". Himmler took this as his goal to make and keep German people "clean", even though most Germans are not Germanic but Celt, Dinarian and others. He even tried to chase off the Polish laborers had worked at estates in eastern areas German for generations. (Foreigners should not even touch holy German soil.) Hitler made Himmler first chief of the police, then Gestapo and finally the SS. In secrecy the SS-men were taught and brainwashed. Some of his quotations were:

"The best political weapon is the weapon of terror. Cruelty commands respect. Men may hate us. But we don't ask for their love: only their fear."

"Some SS-men have disobeyed this order. There are not very many – and they will be dead men – without mercy!"

"I hope to see the concept of Jewry completely obliterated."

"We know the clashes with Asia and Jewry are necessary for evolution."

"Atheism is the only world-view. Religious view is not tolerated within the SS."

"We shall not rest until we have rooted out Christianity."

"Anyone who thinks of homosexual 'love' is our enemy...." (all from Wikipedia)

Not only were the target Jews, but in the Concentration Camps were also:

Men who had shown that they opposed the government, Roma (Gipsy), foreigners, criminals (were treated the easiest), priests and ministers, asocial, homosexuals.

When the Concentration Camps were opened after the war and later gruesome pictures were published, we used to the false Hitler propaganda, at first did not believe what really happened. Then it turned that it was true. Some returned soldiers, among my uncle told the truth and they cried.

Hitler was extremely clever in choosing his ministers and the circle of consultants around him from the pool of the most capable and intelligent. Not that he felt any personal relationship or even responsibility toward them. He would order them killed for no reason if he felt like it. At the Nürnberg trials some psychologists tested the accused for intelligence and found them in the range between 130 and over 140 QT. (It can be assumed that they were not judged especially favorably.)

On the other hand, during Hitler's time did indeed bring good things, some big and some little ones to the German masses. Many people did good positive helpful especially socially and cultural. These things were not associated to politic. I remember that my Aunt Lisa, the teacher, was often ordered to give lectures for women, especially young mothers. Before Hitler came on, Aunt Lisa had been interested and even trained in an educational philosophy that taught free thinking and creativity to children. At 1933 all these schools were closed. In her lectures she told the women about this free education philosophy. They liked aunt's lectures but they had no idea where this philosophy came from.

My Aunt Lisa had, in the meantime, received her permanent teacher's position in a small town. All teachers were ordered into social service in addition to their teaching job. The town was poor. The men were employed now but the women still worked as day laborers on the fields of the few wealthy farmers whenever there was need. The babies were left at home. To make them sleep or at least be quiet and content for long hours, the mothers would put poppy seeds into little fabric sacks and give them to the babies to suck. Families slept on straw pallets. The straw would get old and possibly moldy, insects would grow in it. The children would get rashes. The teachers were ordered to go into people's houses and teach them the value of hygiene, how to exchange the straw in the mattresses, how to clean their houses, get the children healthy and not dull their minds with poppy. It happened regularly that Aunt Lisa came home in the late afternoon from such a task, but she did not enter the house right away. She went through the garden gate directly into the washhouse where Grandma had prepared hot water so that she could take a bath, wash her hair and put on fresh clothes before she came into the house and to me.

Also, now physicians visited the schools to examine the boys and girls, without being paid for it, of course. Once a little boy in Aunt Lisa's class was asked if he didn't itch, which he denied even though his whole body was covered with bites from bedbugs. The physician's explanation to Aunt Lisa: "This poor boy is so used to being bitten all the time he doesn't feel it anymore."

Hitler himself surely had not given these and other specific orders but idealistic people who were in important positions, had seen the need for social improvements for a long time. Now there was a way to act upon them until. Before this, teachers would have been willingly into people's houses to show them how to take better care of their children. But now it was an order from this government and the families allowed the teachers in their houses.

It had given the men work and dignity, and therefore it was alright.

By 1936 there was full employment, the economy was booming. Hitler himself did not understand much about economy. But he had chosen the very capable banker and economist Hjalmar Schacht who had already had had an important position during the Weimar Republic. Now under Hitler he could put his, very good and practical, ideas into reality.

Wikipedia tells: "Schacht, the minister of economy, disagreed with Hitler's unlawful activities against Jews and with his military spending. Upon realizing Hitler's plan to do away with all Jews in Germany, Schacht developed a plan under which Jews would be allowed to leave Germany, even be given traveling money. Their property would be held in trust back in Germany. But it should be used as collateral in case they applied for loans in the new country of their choice. Surprisingly, Hitler agreed to the suggestion and authorized Schacht to negotiate with England. The governor of the Bank of England and a prominent British Jew considered Schacht's plan favorably, but Chaim Weizmann, the spiritual leader of the London Jews opposed it. (It is, however, dubious if Hitler would have allowed this plan to be actually implemented.) Hjalmar Schacht, never a believing National Socialist. He later supported the German resistance. He was arrested after the failed coup of July 20, 1944 and put in a concentration camp. At the Nürnberg Trials he was found not guilty and set free."

Financial stability was also reached by freezing prices and salaries, by prohibiting strikes, punishing demands for raising prices or asking for higher salaries. Subordination of the population was guaranteed by the fear of revenge, often brutal and inevitable. After all, from practically the beginning of Hitler's rule the country was living in a state of emergency where the rights of people were suspended. But so many people felt about Hitler: "The man might have his faults but he gave us back work and bread."

Another large "gift of pride" to the people was the re-arming of the military. Some people it would have needed a military to feel dignify. The Versailles treaty had allowed Germany only a small number of soldiers. Now Hitler started the compulsive military service and built up weaponry and tactics. Hitler had been an enthusiastic soldier and he had learned a lot during WWI. Actually, military tactics was the only field on which he had some true knowledge.

The general mood in the country was mostly: feeling safe, content, even cozy. One had to be very careful of what one said and did, one had to admire the "Führer" and say "Heil Hitler" when greeting people but otherwise life was alright. This was mostly due to the clever machinations of Hitler's Minister of Propaganda, Josef Göbbels, who gave the people the illusion that now the time was normal and safe and people were free to learn any news they wanted.

But this was far from the truth. Göbbels had a firm hand on anything that was made public. At the time there were, of course, only newspapers, radio and newsreels. All journalists had to be party members. Anyone who broadcast international news, could face the death penalty.

Every day the main representatives of the newspapers had to meet with him. They were given the news – as Göbbels wanted them told to the people, but each newspaper had to present the news in its own style, in different spots in the paper. This way people could have their favorite paper because one felt they would get the news there in the best way, not knowing that all the other papers brought the exact same news only just worded a little different. The movies produced during the time, were either lighthearted or nature oriented, not political at all.

Propaganda, for the war, against Jews, against foreign leaders, cultures and anything that was not German, was widely distributed. But it was done in clever ways as to make people take it for true. Most people were busy with their own lives, families and careers. As long as they had jobs, a home and food, who really cared about politics!

In the meantime the Concentration Camps were built up and out. There is always the question if the German people knew some about them. Yes, almost everybody probably knew the name and took them to be similar to ordinary prisons. But did people have any idea what happened there? No and infinite times more: No!!

The Concentration Camps had started soon after Hitler came to power in order to take out the communist officials and any communist or socialist supporters. They were accused to have been the arsonists who burned down the Reichstag. Ordinary prisons were not big enough to take in the enormous number, therefore at first makeshift camps were put up that later were turned into permanent buildings. These were kept secretive and strictly guarded. Nobody could have an idea what was happened. As the years went by, more and more concentration camps were built, also specific death camps. Most of them were outside Germany and mostly in the – by then – German-occupied Poland.

68

Now we know that even in these first Concentration Camps some people were murdered, but some also were set free again. Nobody could dare to talk about all. They were also used to "re-educate" called work-shy, criminal individuals.

After the war, reports of the incredible horrors in the concentration camps were shown. There were pictures. These were mostly about the death camps. But nobody could have taken pictures about the horrendous, hellish situations in the other camps. Some prisoners survived. But these did not and could not talk about the camps. Also, during the time after the war, people were starving. The country was in chaos. There was no news except some local ones. Newspapers contained one single page. At most occupation zones all personal radios had been taken by the military as well as also cameras, typewriters, etc. Only recently did it become public. On the other hand, the bomb raids created imaginable horrors. All large and most small cities were strafed. For example, Dresden had been bombed in early February 1945. Almost 4,000 tons of high explosive and incendiary bombs were dropped. Tens of thousands of people were burned alive. It was reported that Hitler was jubilant when he learned about the Dresden bombing.

Unbeknownst to most people, war had been an important part of Hitler's plan on his way to rule at least over all of Europe but also over Russia. He started with some areas in the east that had rather large German population parts. It is said that he was somehow surprised that he could do this without meeting real resistance. His reputation inside but also outside Germany grew. British and French government officials visited and kowtowed to him. They realized too late what was happening. War.

Hitler did not really want to "save" his country but only dominate the population. He said he would never surrender. He seemed to have realized already in November 1941 that the war was lost. But he still had the ruinous power. Hitler seemed to even have to jubilation at destruction. He said: "We can perish. But we will take along us a world." (Wir werden untergehen. Aber wir werden eine Welt mitnehmen.)

For months Hitler lived in his extensive bunker, 33 feet below the ground from, where he gave his orders. Moreover, on 19th March 1945 he emitted the so called "Nero-Order" meaning that everything should be destroyed, such as the industry, the public utilities, the streets, the bridges, the canal system, so that the enemies would find nothing but a desert without civilization.

Luckily most people did not follow this order beyond what was destroyed already. Hitler made the generals come to his bunker each day to receive orders. The generals did not dare to contradict him for fear of death

Several assassinations of Hitler were attempted. Before the planned assassination at July 20th 1944 a new government had been prepared physically whose goal was to end the war right away. None one of the assassinations were successful, mostly just by coincidences. It was said that the devil always protected Hitler as being his best helper.

So much of Germany was destroyed and so many people killed with inconceivable brutal pain. Hitler had said that when he would die he would take his world with him.

But this "world" has been built up again with incredibly hard work and diligence and a lot of time. Germany does live.

Meinrad's Story (born 1933)

Before I even met Meinrad, I had walked in his shoes for quite a while – literally. As the war*) (WWII, 1939-1945) went on and everything became more scarce, children's feet kept growing, but there were no new shoes for them, except sometimes wooden sandals. When Meinrad had grown out of his shoes, they were given to his cousins whose parents were close friends of our family. I, however, was in between these two stations, age-wise and foot-size-wise, and therefore I was the temporary beneficiary between Meinrad and our friends' children.

Eventually I got to meet my "temporary shoe sponsor" at our friends' house. Through the years and decades we happened to see each other sometimes,. and when I had started thinking about putting together this book, Meinrad was one of the first people I asked for his story. Little was I prepared for his "family chronicle" as he called it, that he had written for his children and grandchildren. On about 300 single-space typed pages he had described not only the family's ancestors but also, in precise detail, the time of the war and his – sometimes horrifying – experiences. I got a totally new view of a man who I thought I had known since childhood.

I will let his story begin around the beginning of the war:

In 1938 Austria had been annexed, "returned into the German Reich" as it was euphemized. Shortly after, the crisis over the "Sudetenland") rose up.* *) The Sudetenland is a region in the east, having been settled mostly by Germans centuries ago. Since the end of WWI it had been included in the newly formed state of Czechoslovakia. *People started to be afraid of a developing war, including my parents. But their trust in Hitler did not seem diminished too much. Later a historian*) *)Sebastian Haffner in "Anmerkungen zu Hitler explained it this way: "The economy bloomed, the man had so many foreign successes and he could talk to German citizens, male and female, out of their mind." One more factor was the peoples' memories of the time before Hitler's coming to power, when there was so much unrest and poverty and the fear of communism. When my mother had been very pregnant with me (in late 1932), she had been overtaken on the street by a communist demonstration. A woman had grabbed her with the words: "Are you hungry? Come along!" and made her march along. Communism was all around.*

I think it was even before the actual beginning of the war, when we all had to report to a certain city office, where we had to try on and then take home, our gas masks.

It was a thing out of green rubber, which had to be pulled over the head with great effort. It covered the head, airtight, down to the neck. It had a space for the nose and there was glass in front of the eyes. A filter was screwed into the round, metal-bordered opening at the bottom. One had to breathe through the mouth.

Hitler's first years had brought a great economic upswing. Now, since the war had started, this was followed by breathtaking military successes. The radio brought one victory report after the other. Of course, we were only allowed to hear the German, controlled, broadcast stations. People were ordered to attach a piece of cardboard to their radios' station control knobs, which carried the warning that listening to enemy stations would be punished with at least two years hard prison time, up to the death penalty. The British Broadcasting Company sent out news in German but one had to keep the volume extremely low because their broadcast signal was the first two measures of Beethoven's fifth symphony, a sound that was recognized by everybody.

Black-out blinds were attached to the windows and one had to be extra careful not to let the smallest ray of light show outside. One time my older sister was sick in bed with a high fever. My mother had apparently not been careful enough with the black-out blinds. Suddenly a policeman stood in my sister's bedroom, scolding and threatening in a loud voice because there was little light coming out. But my mother scolded right back at him quite angrily, asking how he had dared not only to enter our apartment without asking but also the bedroom of a young lady. He left, grumping.

The streetlights had all been turned off, the, extremely rare, cars drove with dimmed headlights, and only when there was no air raid alarm. When the sky was overcast, one was totally blind. To prevent pedestrians from running into each other in the darkness, little brooches were given out that were covered with fluorescent paint. But they only helped when there was at least some light.

We had our apartment on the second floor of a four-story house. The cellar underneath seemed quite sturdy and my father put some simple bunk beds there, covered with straw sacks so that at least we children could sleep or rest during the frequent air raids at night. At first we only heard the noise from the Flak canons*). It was not too bad to get up during the night because if the alarm lasted past midnight, school would start later, *)(Flak is an acronym for **Fl**ieger-**A**bwehr-**K**anonen = airplane-defense-canons).

In the morning we children would go hunting for grenade fragments to take to school for recyle, the bigger and the more jagged, the better. But soon there were so many around that our interest waned.

The rationing of food and other necessities did not hurt at first. Later the rations got smaller and smaller. After the war, when ration cards were given out by the occupation forces, it was hardly possible to survive on them.

On advertisement pillars in the cities, on streetcars and everywhere else one saw posters that ordered people not to waste anything but to save whatever they could to further the war effort. I remember a picture of a black-clad man, wearing a burglar's mask over his face and a large bulging sack on his back. He was named "Kohlenklau" (coal thief) and the wording on the poster was "He steals the electricity, robs the light, steals gas and coal; don't tolerate this!" (In German it rhymes.) Another poster showing a sinister looking man carried the slogan "Pst! The enemy is listening". What any foreign spies could have found out, I don't know.

During first and second grade I had a horrible teacher. He was a fanatic national socialist and he was a sadist. Since he also was catholic, he made us pray each morning "for the Führer and the Nation". I was always scared that I would catch his attention and would have to suffer his painful punishment.

Our next teacher, in third grade, was also a national socialist but he was a nice man and a good teacher who controlled our class with keeping our interest awake instead of with anger and brutality. He never gave us political speeches. After several months he suddenly did not come to school and we were told that he had taken ill and would not come for quite some time. My parents learned the truth, probably through some secret channels: Our teacher had dared to criticize the behavior of several higher party officials' behavior that had conflicted with his feel for justice. Finally he went to the party office, threw his party book*) at the officer there with the comment that he, a convinced national socialist and party member from the very beginning, would not go along with this disgrace. He was arrested by the Gestapo. I don't know what happened to him. *) Each member of the NSDAP had a party book, the size of a passport. Written in it were personal data and the date of his/her entrance into the party. Nevertheless, I never got the idea that this whole apparatus, Hitler's German Reich, could be something wicked. Our soldiers were good people, the enemy soldiers were bad.

My mother, naively, kept saying: "One can not deceive a nation of 80 million." She was wrong. Naturally, the enemy military was perceived to be bad. But there was no real hate towards the more and more appearing POWs. Officially it was prohibited to feed them or even let them sit at table with the family. But most POWs were put to work at farms and craftsmen's workshops where their work was needed and appreciated, and soon the POW became almost a member of the family. Were some POWs treated badly? Most probably. There are always people who treat their subordinates unfairly, no matter what nationality they are.

Late during the war we had two Russian POWs, Peter and Paul about whose intelligence and education we were surprised. Our "minister of propaganda and enlightenment" had declared all Russians to be sub-humans. These two had only attended basic schooling but had taken German language courses there. Peter remembered only a few words but with Paul one could have real conversations. He explained to my mother: "Germans good. Russians good. Hitler good-for-nothing. Stalin good-for-nothing" Of course, the two Russians got food from us. The German official at the POW camp had even advised my mother to feed them. He had added that this would make them work better, but basically it was a humanitarian advice, against the official rules.

At the time food was already rather scarce. Our basic food was potatoes. To stretch even those to go further, my mother used to mix carrots from our little garden under the potatoes. But the two Russians refused to eat carrots in any form. They said that in Russia only the "queek-queek" (the pigs) would be fed carrots. Therefore my mother divided the mashed potatoes into two bunches, one pure for the Russians and the other, mixed with carrots, for us.

Whoever has not lived under a dictatorship, can not imagine the characteristic of this system, namely that everything becomes so self-evident. This danger and evil can not be underestimated. People have their lives to live – and these lives are not easy – and they, of necessity, become complaisant toward the rules and these rules soon become natural. It had always been self-evident that one entered school at age 6. Now one became a member of the HJ (Hitler Youth) at 10 and a soldier at 18, and one greeted people on the street with "Heil Hitler!". For people who do not know any other way of life, everything is "normal" that happens after any norms, be they the most abnormal ones.

So far we had always heard the noise of the Flak*) shooting. *) Flak is an acronym for Flieger-Abwehr- Kanonen. But one night in the cellar the noise outside seemed different.

"Bombs" said the adults. My father became more and more nervous. Finally he said, allowing no contradiction: "I have to go to the store*)." *) the family business, a several story high building that sold mostly textiles. I admired him. I was not afraid for him. But when we came out of the cellar after the all-clear, we came into a totally changed world. The sky was blood red, many houses in our immediate surroundings were burning. We could also see those that were damaged or destroyed by high-explosive bombs. As we learned later, the special tactic was to drop at first carpets of explosive bombs and then, also to prevent firefighting operation, to drop carpets of incendiary e bombs. The house across from ours was also burning, all floors of it. The woman who lived there and her daughter were standing on the street, shocked and desperate. My mother went over and said to them: "Come over. For the beginning you will live with us."

Late Sunday morning my father came back, black from soot, with red, inflamed eyes, three quarters blind. Our family physician who lived not far away, called it smoke poison and said father should stay put for three days and put moist compresses over his eyes.

Our store had burned to the ground, the rest destroyed by explosive bombs. As had been ordered on Saturday, most of the merchandize had been put into the cellar. Like each night, three or four sales ladies had been in the cellar as "air raid guards". During the air raid my father had had the scary vision that the burning elevator might drop down into the cellar and burn everybody and everything there. Indeed, he managed to get there in time to keep the cellar free from fire even though the water soon dried up. And he could comfort the scared women.

While my father was standing in front of the smoking ruins of his business, the man who had been his business competitor across the street walked over and they talked. Both men confessed to each other that it was somehow a relief that now the worst had happened. Little did they know what was still to come!

In radio news the air raids were called "terror attacks". That's how Göbbels, the minister for propaganda, had ordered the journalists to call them. As we learned much later, this description was quite correct. The strategic goal of the allies, especially of one "Bomber-Harris"*) whose monument stands in London, was, to bomb the people ripe for capitulation. *) Sir Arthur Harris, 1892-1984, also called "Butcher Harris" in England, was marshal of the royal air force, air officer commander-in-chief and led the whole air raids to Germany. After the war he emigrated to South Africa. When he was asked 30 years after the war if he would do everything the same again, he said yes. (Wikipedia)

On September 7, 1943 I learned that the dream of schoolchildren worldwide had been fulfilled for me: our school had been burned down and destroyed. But it turned out that it was not after all a good thing for me and my schoolmates. It was degreed that grades one to four should be taken away from the bomb war and sent to a relatively safe place in Lorraine (Lothringen) where they could sleep and learn undisturbed – and also be taught to behave in a disciplined manner.

On the day of the departure we had to line up at the train station wearing our HJ uniforms. It turned out that we would have to wear them during all the following weeks and months at camp. I do not recall that there was any opportunity to have them washed.

We first took a train to Metz, then another one further into the country and then we had to walk for about ten km on the hard road, carrying our backpacks. Our destination was an old, somehow dilapidated little castle. On the front steps stood a brown-clad young man, our HJ camp leader, yelling at us: "What a bunch of lay-about pigs comes marching here!" And this was the tone and lifestyle that we would be exposed to day and night. There was little school teaching; the teachers did not have any control. We spent most of the time being drilled and doing punitive drills. Usually the whole group had to do these punitive drills. I was lucky, not to come to the leaders' attention. It was reported that some boys did have to do push-ups and sit-ups in their bath trunks in spots of stinging nettle. Some of us boys were sent to work at nearby farms. The Lorrainers hated us but we preferred to work on the fields, even with our backs hurting, than being drilled.

We got much less food than the common supply at the time. Since we could not even get enough potatoes to satisfy our hunger, we ate the potatoes with the skin. We could not have peeled them anyway because there was only one knife for every three "men" at the table. Once there was half a boiled egg for each boy. At our table of twelve I was the only lucky one whose egg was alright. Two or three of the other eggs were somehow edible. The others stank so much that even the worst hunger had to refuse them. The leaders were fed much better.

Many farmers had left their farms and gone west with the retreating French army. After a few weeks our group of boys was moved to such an empty farmhouse nearby. We slept on bunk beds on sacks of straw. Since we were all malnourished, we were always cold. We kept our underwear on underneath our pajamas; some even wore the pajamas over their uniforms. From time to time one of the leaders would come by and he would order a boy to open his pajama and then some punishment was to follow.

Luckily I was never caught but I was fearful each night.

But I learned something at this place, that was a lesson for life: to "organize" which meant to search for and find things that one did not have but needed. We were cold; therefore we went to other abandoned farm houses to find a woodstove. We had no fuel: therefore we found furniture at these houses that we could demolish and burn. We were hungry; therefore we went to the fields at night to find potatoes and corncobs that we could roast on the stove.

We could not tell our parents about the bad situation at the camp because all letters had to be given to the leaders, open. If a boy complained he would be punished. Some of the older boys had run away but I did not dare to do this. My parents and I had suspected that the mail would be censored. Therefore we had agreed on a code sentence for me to write if the situation was real bad. It was "how is my Hansi?" (the canary). Finally I became really desperate and I wrote this sentence in my letter but no reaction came. My letters were more and more filled with questions about Hansi but nothing happened. Later my mother told me that, in all the turmoil of air raids and the struggle for food, she had forgotten our agreement.

Finally one day I saw the mother of one of the boys sitting with him in our bedroom. I asked her if she would take a letter to my parents and she agreed. I started my letter with: "Now I will finally tell you the truth." I put no great hope on my cry for help. But two days later suddenly my mother stood before me, saying: "Come and pack your things, we will go home." The camp leader had wanted to intimidate her but she had stayed firm. We walked the 10km back to the train station, managed to catch the last train to Metz and found friends of my mother's there who had a hotel where we could spend the night. The next morning, wonder over wonder, there were rolls for breakfast and as much rye bread as one wanted to eat. I ate half a loaf and then I was full for the first time in a long time.

By the way, not all children camps were as bad. Some "children's country evacuation camps" were really nice. I had just had bad luck again.

There had been enough boys left in my hometown Ludwigshafen or, like me, had been picked up again from camps, that schooling had to be arranged for us. There was no school available for us in the city but the high school in Speyer, an hour away by train, was willing to take us for afternoon lessons.

Our classes lasted from 1 to 5pm which meant that I had to leave home around 11am and returned at 7pm   In the school in Speyer we got almost no nationalist-socialist indoctrination.

The allied fighter planes came around often. Once I had to walk home several hours because the train tracks had been damaged.

We still had to report to HJ meetings but our leaders were nice and they were not eager to indoctrinate us. We just did fun things and often the meetings were canceled.

When my sister needed special medical attention, my mother and I went with her to a specialist in another city. We were shocked and scared to see posters in the physician's waiting room, made by himself, on which the government was denounced as the root of all evil and the people were called to resistance. We feared that so much bold daring would bring the man into trouble. But nothing happened to him.

More and more people were drafted by the state, this Moloch, to work in places where men, having become soldiers, had worked before. Whoever had four intact limbs, was drafted. Older and older men and younger boys were drafted, first as "garrison capable" but later to the front. Women who had not at least three small children had to work in the factories. It was said in our family that certain relatives got their third child only to circumvent this draft. Young girls had to work with the military, first to do telephone and wireless services, later to be with the Flak.

The assassination attempt on Hitler on July 20, 1944 did not register much with me. For me he was some far-away entity, almost abstract, not quite real. Later I have often thought about and discussed with others, how things might have developed if the devil would not have protected his most eager scholar and Hitler would have died. Surely hundreds of thousands of peoples' lives would have been spared; Dresden, Würzburg and many other beautiful cities and houses would have come through the war. Maybe the would-be assassins would have been able to negotiate a more lenient peace. But in reality, the allies had already determined how Germany would be treated.

One afternoon in October 1944 I had been out collecting greenery from the side of the road for my rabbits. When I stood at the door to our apartment, the air raid siren wailed. I had heard this sound countless times.

But this time I felt a horrible fear as I had never felt it before. I begged and pressed my parents not to go to our cellar this time but to run the few hundred meters to an uncle's cellar that he had had reinforced with steel and concrete. I don't know if I transferred my fear to them or if they just gave in. We ran to uncle's bunker-like cellar. When we came back out again, we stood before our ruined house. A bomb had fallen through all four floors into the cellar where it had exploded. The seven people, who had been there, had all been killed.

This was the only supernatural experience I have ever had, and I hope it stays the only one.

I don't know if I suppressed my feelings, but I don't remember either relief that my family had survived or sadness about the loss of my home. Members of the emergency service came to dig out the buried. They were all dead. My father had ordered me to stand close by in case any items that belonged to us, would be unearthed. I saw body parts carried out and I could not look.

One corner of the house was still somehow standing and we could spend the night there. The next morning my mother went a few houses across the street to the bakery that was still standing. She hoped to get some food but she came back right away, crying uncontrollably. In the dark hallway of the bakery she had stumbled over the corpses that had been deposited there.

We were lucky to find an unused office where we could live. When this was destroyed, we got a room in a small house that had not been bombed yet. We even managed to celebrate Christmas somehow. On New Year's Eve we trusted that the allied airplanes were busy celebrating too. But suddenly there was a tremendous bang and then the siren wailed. A single airplane had dropped an "air mine" over a neighboring district.

Air mines were very large explosive devises that exploded already in the air and affected large areas. The whole district was in ruins.

Soon it became the rule that the sirens sounded only after the first bombs had already fallen. I lived more and more in fear. I slept in my clothes and my parents had to make me take at least my shoes off. People did not rely on the air raid sirens any more but rather on the radio. One sat there in front of a special map that had Mannheim-Ludwigshafen in the center. Around it were concentric circles in distances of 25, 50 and 100 km and numbered squares.

The voice of the speaker came, interrupted by banging noises: "enemy bomber units in square X, flying towards square Y." This way, at least I learned the geography of my home state.

Because Mannheim-Ludwigshafen had been bombed from early on, above-ground bunkers had been built. They were reported to withstand even the worst bombings. Now we did not trust uncle's reinforced cellar anymore but went to the nearest bunker. The bunkers became more and more overcrowded.

So far I had always found comfort with my little dog, Struppi. But no dogs were allowed into bunkers and so his little life had ended when we stood before the ruins of our third make-shift living quarters. It seemed to me that he had looked at me especially sad when I left him at home. So much more horrible things are done to children but I still remember my pain and sorrow when Struppi was no more.

Our family physician gave us a room in his house where the four of us could sleep. During the day we stayed in a cellar that was still intact.

*After a while a new danger came up: "Jabos" (**Jagd-Bomber**, hunting bombers). Warning posters went up in all train stations on how to protect oneself. These planes had two bombs on board but, low flying, they attacked anything that moved with their machine guns. They also attacked trains. A few of the pilots still had some sense of fairness. They would first fly a few rounds over a train. This gave the engineer time to stop the train and sound the steam whistle. All people would rush out of the wagons and hide at some distance as well as they could. Only then did the fair pilots destroy the train. But there were also many others who attacked the trains without warning and also seemed to have fun to kill civilians on the fields or on country roads with machine guns and board canons.*

Our small business truck had withstood having debris and parts of walls fall on it. With its two-cylinder two-tact motor it still ran, even though slow, noisily and stinking. When we had to drive overland, my father made either me or my sister sit on the hood to watch out for Jabos. We were lucky. We were never attacked.

During these last weeks of the war, Göbbel's propaganda had become more and more all-embracing. In our world of ruins there was hardly a piece of a wall that had not been inscribed with some rallying calls: "Wheels have to roll for victory" (Räder müssen rollen für den Sieg,) "Our walls may break but not our hearts"

80

(Unsere Mauern mögen brechen aber unsere Herzen nicht.), "Men between 16 and 60 don't belong in the bunker but at the front" *(Männer zwischen 16 und 60 gehören nicht in den Bunker sondern an die Front.)* In between these slogans former inhabitants of their ruined houses had written, with chalk, messages for relatives and friends, like : "We are still alive and now live at ..."

My father had turned 57 in November 1944. He and uncle Edi were drafted for the Volkssturm in January 1945. Being in the Volkssturm meant to wear an armband for uniform, when ordered to, stand in a tank trap and throw all their ammunition, 2 or 3 bazookas, at oncoming tanks – and subsequently be flattened as the tanks would roll over them.

Father had been able to get a "ration coupon for a make-shift home for air raid victims". It had been easy to get the coupon but getting the building materials was almost impossible. That's why most people did not even apply for a coupon. Many years before Father had bought a large stock of oak wood to be stored at his friend's, a carpenter's, yard until he would be 60 years old and the wood well seasoned. With it he then wanted to build a cabin, maybe in the Black Forest, near a stream where he could fish for trout.

This wood had been commandeered by the government at the beginning of the war and the carpenter had been forced to use it to build military barracks. Now, however, the carpenter, my father's old comrade, managed to get some wood for us. On March 17, 1945, early in the morning, we were all standing on a meadow in a valley near a small village in the vicinity of the town of Dürkheim, about 30 km from Ludwigshafen. Each of us was helping as much as possible to put up our make-shift home. First, posts were driven into the ground with a heavy sledgehammer; beams were fastened on top and then came prefabricated plywood sheets. By evening our provisional home was ready to move in. I don't remember how and when some make-shift furniture arrived: two bunk beds with straw-filled sacks, a cook stove, a folding table attached to the wall. There was, of course, no water or electricity at the house; but a well, about 100 m away, gave us and the nearby village enough water.

The next day was confirmation Sunday for the protestant children of the village, a very special day in these dark times for the children and their families. We had walked to the small village restaurant of friends where we got some food.

On our way back along the main road we had to squeeze along endless lines of soldiers marching east towards the river Rhein. From time to time there was a horse-drawn wagon or a truck that pulled two others.

As soon as we were home, it might have been 1:30pm, the air raids started, lasting, with a few breaks, until Tuesday night. They hit the town of Dürkheim just as they had hit the big cities, with the difference that there were no bunkers in Dürkheim. Together with their houses, the inhabitants were destroyed. Decades later I learned that the just confirmed children, as they came out of the church, had been shot by Jabos. Maybe the weapons had been blessed by a man who stood as a successor of Jesus Christ and Martin Luther, just as the man who had shortly before spoken the blessing over the children.

We fled into the woods that started right behind our new home. In my fear and ignorance I ran deeper and deeper into the forest but got closer to the road which was the main target of the attacks. An earsplitting detonation pushed me to the ground. For one moment I believed to be lying in a hollow and fires burning around me. I thought that I had been killed and was now in hell. But luckily the bomb had exploded on the hillside above me so that I had not been grabbed by the air pressure. I got up, went for the others and found them. On my way I met Father who had been searching for me desperately.

During a firing break we dared to go back. Our little house had come apart at the seams but it was still standing. Father took the big ax and hammered the parts together as well as was possible.

The next morning some people from the village came by and took us with them into a narrow side valley. There we built a shelter out of small pine trees and branches and covered it with smaller branches. Inside this we were not visible to low flying planes.

The next night we dared to return to our house. At dawn the next morning Father went out to try to find something edible but he came back after a few minutes, reporting: "the road is full with American tanks." I thought: Today is Wednesday, March 21ˢᵗ, 1945, the beginning of spring. The war is over. No bombs will fall anymore. I don't have to be afraid anymore.

In the evening, we had found something to eat, Mother, teary-eyed, said to us that Father wanted to tell us something. It was only a few sentences.

*He told us that, despite the lost war, we should never forget that
we were Germans.*

*For some time we still heard the firing of canons and a
while later the explosions. One morning, weeks later, my mother
woke me with the words: "We have lost the war." I only answered:
"Oh, let me sleep on", turned around and went back to sleep.*

*White flags (probably bed sheets) were hung from all
houses, except ours. When the inhabitants of the make-shift house
next to ours were gone for some time, I took advantage of the fact,
went over there and ripped their flag down. Was I a patriotic ass? I
did not care that we had lost the war. I was so relieved that no
bombs were falling anymore and no Jabos were shooting at us
anymore. And at the same time I felt like a good German who
would keep his pride and not kowtow to foreign soldiers. I had just
turned 12 a few days before.*

*In the meadow next to our hut we found two horses
grazing. Heaven knows how they had separated themselves from
the back of the military. They awakened in me the same feelings
that I had had for my rabbits: lovable creatures that one wants to
pet but that, nevertheless, can be butchered and eaten with good
appetite. Now I had not only a good appetite, I was starving; we all
were. A man came by who could butcher horses and cut them
apart. To keep meat for some time was not possible. The freezer
had not been invented yet, nobody had an electric refrigerator
(there would not have been power anyway to run it), and the people
who had an ice box could not buy ice. The meat was distributed to
everybody in the village. And what I found so astonishing
afterwards: there was no quarrel over the distribution of the meat
and nobody tried to take the second horse during the night until it
was its turn to feed the neighborhood.*

*I could eat my fill for several days; just meat, meat without
anything else; full, full, full! Father tried and succeeded in salting
some of the meat and smoke it in the chimney.*

*Soon the orders of the occupation forces were made public:
No going out during the night and a large part of the day. The
place of residence may not be left. At the outside of each house a
list had to be attached with the names, ages and genders of the
inhabitants. Everybody was registered and received a primitive
piece of paper on which one's personal data were listed, as well as
a fingerprint.*

A note on the paper proclaimed that it did not convey any rights. Together with this paper one got a ration card with which one could buy bread in "homeopathic doses" at the bakery. Once I watched our neighbor come back from the bakery. She cut and weighed the daily bread ration, gave it to her husband outside, saying "this is your ration for today". It was one slice. Nevertheless, the hunger was suppressed by the feeling "I have made it through alive".

Now the war was over but after some time I started playing war. I did not play killing, I played surviving. From somewhere I had gotten a few lead soldiers. In the woods I built bunkers for them out of sandstones with a layer of sand on top. Then I hit these bunkers with stones. Everyday my bunkers became stronger and safer and my stone "bombs" heavier. For a few months I still feared thunderstorms (because of their similarity to bombs exploding) but then I had "played away" the war fear from my soul."

Edith's Story

Edith's Story (born 1930)

When I asked my friend Edith to share her experiences during WWII, she felt they were not "dramatic and traumatic" enough because her family had been able to stay in one town and their house had not been destroyed by bombs.

However, years later when, at her children's request, Edith did share memories, it was apparent that her family had been deeply hurt and affected by the political and social events of the time.

When the war started Edith was nine years old and her younger brother was four. Her father was a dedicated, much loved and respected teacher. Her mother was an artist and spoke several languages.

Edith remembers:

In 1938 there had already been talk of war, but Chamberlain (the British prime minister), Daladier (the French prime minister) and Mussolini (the Italian dictator) came to München (Munich) Germany to confer with Hitler. Thus so the danger of war was averted for another year.

In the summer of 1939, we were on vacation in the Black Forest. Our whole family was together: my mother, father, younger brother Henning and I. Suddenly there was an atmosphere of panic because war really was going to start. Father said he would have to leave right away because there was mobilization (draft). Later I learned that the year prior, he had received a simply gray postcard informing him that in case of mobilization, he would have to report to a military core of engineers in the Pfalz (Palatinate) region to build up the Westwall.*). *(The Westwall, also called "Siegfried Linie", was a line of fortifications, bunkers and dug-outs, along the German to the border to France to stop a possible French invasion. Along with military core engineers, soldiers and civilians, and even some 16 year old girls were sent to work on these fortifications.)

We took the very next train home. And as we were walking up our street, local officials were already walking along delivering ration card to all the homes. These ration cards had, of course been printed well before the war started. *These first ration cards were simple. Printed segments - each the size of a postage stamp - were allocated for almost everything one would need such as flour, sugar, milk, meat and sausage, shoes and clothing. Vegetables were not rationed. During these beginning war years, one had enough to eat.*

Now our family was no longer together. Father was leading this military core of engineers at the western border of France. He was allowed to return home almost every second Sunday. His visits were turbulent. His uniform had to be washed, by hand, and hung up to dry either by the woodstove, the attic or outside weather permitting. *(Washing machines did not exist yet here.) *Even his cap had to be washed. Everything had to be finished by the time he had to leave again. Also, most probably, a loaf cake was baked for him to take along.*

During this time we did not notice much of the war since there were no air raids yet. The first inkling of what was to come was when the family of my mother's brother was ordered to be evacuated to the east away from Saarbrücken in preparation for the western front.) *)Saarbrücken, close to the border of France, is the capital of the state Saarland which throughout history was sometimes French, sometimes German and was currently a state of the German Federation.

His wife, Aunt Lizzy, was pregnant and they had a little son. She was a saucy, cheeky woman with a sharp tongue. None of the relatives wanted to take her and the little boy in. It was said: "If anyone can get along with Lizzie, its Millie", my mother. So they stayed with us. The baby was born. It was a beautiful baby girl. All three of them stayed at least a year with us. They were the first guests in our apartment as the war went along.

I don't remember when the air raids started. When they started, the air raid sirens wailed, we scrambled into the cellar day or night, and the bombers roared over the houses. At first the bombs fell mostly on outlying fields. Then Mannheim and Ludwigshafen were hit with a small number of bombs. We thought this was very bad and worried about our relatives in those cities. However this was nothing compared to what happened later.

Edith's town was about 10 miles west of Mannheim and Ludwigshafen and the river Rhine. It was about 10 miles south of Heidelberg. Probably the proximity of her town to Heidelberg gave it some protection. Planes kept dropping leaflets printed with the propaganda rhyme: "We will spare Heidelberg. We want to live in Heidelberg."*) *)"Heidelberg wollen wir schonen. In Heidelberg wollen wir wohnen". But nobody could feel safe. Indeed, there was little damage to Heidelberg. Similar leaflets had been dropped over the city of Dresden, citing its important cultural and historical buildings. So the people of Dresden depended on this assurance only then to be betrayed in the most horrible, cruel and torturous way towards the end of the war.

Sometimes there were little funny occurrences while we waited out yet another air raid in the cellar. One night, when all the occupants of the house were once again sitting in the cellar, my little brother let his windup toy mouse run around in the semi-darkness of the cellar. One lady, she was tall and thin, mistook it for a real mouse and screeched "a mouse, a mouse!" and lifted her legs as high into the air as she could. We all had a good laugh despite our situation.

We would wait until the sirens would sound the "pre-all-clear". Then we would sit in the first floor living room of the people who lived in the first floor apartment. When finally the "all-clear" sounded, we could back to bed. For us school children, we hoped this would happen after midnight because then the start of school would be delayed by two hours.

As time progressed, the air raids came more frequently and the attacks more severe. We would find out where the bomber squadron were and in what direction they were headed. The entire area had been drawn up as a system of coordinates and then superimposed over a map of the area. By listening to a specific radio station, one could hear numbers of the special locations.

Later, we went to a better cellar in our street. The lady of this house graciously accepted everybody. But the air raids became even more serious and very, very bad. The explosive and the incendiary bomb attacks on Mannheim and Ludwigshafen were too horrible to describe. The planes flew loops over the wide valley and hills at the river Rhein (Rhine), and flew in for their attacks.

These attacks used explosive bombs and the incendiary bombs. These phosphor bombs where fire accelerants, and ignited fires that spread with explosive speed. These enormous fires instantly consumed all available oxygen, in the process sucked all air and everything in its path, toward it. Everything was pulled to the fire with enormous force. Running, fleeing people were thrust into the fire, like an unimaginable, colossal burning tornado. Those people who might have been able to flee and tried to escape the falling buildings, were powerless, no matter how steadfast they tried to hold on, in the face of these super inferno winds, they were inevitably sucked into the inferno and burned. This was systemically carried out in all other large cities Berlin, Hamburg, Köln, Stuttgart, München, Dresden and all others. Incendiary bombs could not be extinguished with water. If one happened to see a just fallen building, one might have a chance to pore sand on it. All houses had ready a pail with sand. So you could do it. Also smaller towns were hit. One could never know where the bombs fell.

Edith recounted:

Naturally at first we did not fear for our own life. The fear was for the people ten miles away in Mannheim and Ludwigshafen. We bodily felt the shockwaves of the detonations. Our houses shook from the carpet bombing, and sky was lit with the firebrands. There were also the so-called air-mines, special large bombs that detonated in the air right before the ground and could destroy a whole block.*) *)The planning and executing/carry out had been done by Sir Arthur Harris (1892-1984), marshal of the royal air force, air officer commander-in-chief and the whole air raids to Germany during the last two or three years of the war. He was a friend of Churchill. Many British called him "Butcher Harris" (Wikipedia).

I remember one night as most surreal and terrifying, it was in September of 1943. We neighbors were standing in the street that night, but it was lit up from the fires ten miles away. Nobody spoke. It seemed like we could actually hear the blazes. Black scraps were flying through the air. Suddenly we heard a bird sing. Somebody said it was a nightingale.

(It needs to be explained that in Germany and most of Europe the houses are built of stone or concrete blocks or concrete cavity blocks, because many ruins stayed standing.)

Towards the end of the war, we did not go to house cellars anymore, but ran to the hospital's bunker. It was some distance away, up a hill and then down again. A tunnel had been dug into the hill underneath an old fort. This is where we hid. So, in the middle of the night when the air-raid sirens would start to wail, we would start to run. We only had to put on our shoes and grab our little packed case with our personal papers and a few valuables. One night, as we were running, the Christmas lights*) were on already. My little brother, running along hand in hand with my mother, sleepily asked: "Mami, are we going to the shoemaker through town or around the town?" He must have been sleeping and dreaming while running. *) What people called "Christmas lights" were actually signal flares dropped by planes over target areas. These flares were attached to little parachutes to illuminate the area to be bombed.

Then my father's military corps of engineers was deployed to Norway. Many of the men in his company were from our neighborhood, or villages and hamlets in our area. Someone had arranged that soldiers coming back to Germany on furlough, would be given Norwegian fish in brine to take with them. Some came in tiny little wood barrels, with herrings in brine. But most of these German soldiers were from these landlocked farms and did not know how nor want to eat this canned fish.

Knowing this, my father suggested they drop off their canned fish at mother's house, which they happily agreed to do. Food was scarce, and my mother knew how to prepare fish, so we enjoyed them and shared them with friends. We were also very lucky because sometimes the parents of these same soldiers let us buy a few vegetables from their farms, probably as a thank you and to curry favor to my father.

A neighbor friend was sick with such terrible puss filled throat infection that her throat was a septic wound, even possibly diphtheria. My mother advised she gargle with salt water as a disinfectant. But salt was scarce and at times hard to get. In desperation our neighbor croaked: "give me some of your salty fish watery-brine!" She actually gargled with the salty fish brine, and the puss coating in her throat came off and healed.

My little brother Henning also put the canned fish to good use. Across the street lived a family whose father had a position at an important industrial plant. Sometimes these higher employees received special amenities not available to ordinary citizens. Henning was playing with one of their two children at their house, and while using their restroom, discovered to his amazement that they had real toilet paper. For a long time toilet paper was not available any more. At our house, as all houses, we judiciously used newspaper cut into squares. Henning took heart and asked his playmate: "Do you think that your mother would give my mother a roll of toilet paper if my mother would give your mother a can of herring?" I don't remember if the barter actually took place.

But then my father was transferred. The gifts of canned fish and vegetables ceased, and finding food became much more challenging. My little brother Henning, 9 at the time, decided to try and find some food on his own. He took a small hand cart and made his rounds among the farm families he knew, begging for something edible. He returned with an empty cart and an empty stomach. My mother cried, hugged him and said: "My child, you must not go there anymore."

Before we had lived in a different town and there my mother had employed a washerwoman. This woman had a daughter, Gretel. My mother taught Gretel to knit, crochet and especially sew.

This became especially important during the war and afterwards when nearly no fabric was available and one needed to sew things from old clothes. Old sweaters were unraveled and knit some warm things.

Gretel never forgot how Edith's mother had taught her, and in such a sweet and patient way.

Gretel had married into a family who owned a grocery store. It was in a different town where normally more things were available. Gretel had kept the relation with our family. During the hungry times after the war, my brother and I would sometimes bicycle there the approximately 20 miles, up and down hills. Gretel would give us always what she could give us: vegetables, potatoes, once even a small package of margarine and even a piece of cheese. What Gretel had managed to find extra food and she shared it with us. Always these days always were festive days. We were fed and, of course, we took food home to mother. I think that my parents' charisma was the reason of the close families between us.

Food had to be grown but there were no able men to harvest. All they had been deployed. In one large farm had been planted fields and fields of peas and they had to be harvested. So the day to day work fell upon women, the aging, and children. In 1943 or 1944 in a nearby village we children were "drafted". At first we thought it would be great not to attend school. But it became: Bend down – pull entire plants out – straighten up – pick pea pods off of the plants – throw pods into basket – bend down – pull plants out – straighten up – remove pea pods – throw pods into basket, on and on, all morning. Our backs and hands were so sore. During one harvest, our elderly mathematics teacher was sent with us. He must not have been drafted because he was too old. He worked with us pulling the plants out and picking the pea pods off of the stems and throwing them into the baskets. In doing so, he groaned, perspired profusely and his face became red and wet from the sweat. Nevertheless, he persisted. As young as I was, I felt such high respect for the old gentlemen. Whenever we did this backbreaking labor, we were allowed to purchase some peas at a discounted price. From what I brought home, mother cooked pea soup in a large laundry kettle. It made for a truly festive meal for everyone living with us.

It must have been in 1943/44 when my mother was drafted for war service. All women who had children over 14 had to work in factories. I was 14 but my brother was only 9, therefore mother had to work only half days in the factory about one mile away. When there was an air raid alarm during the day, she would run home to be to be with us children in case something should happen.

At the factory mother met a woman who became her friends for life. We called her Aunt Trudy. She was an interesting woman, being witty and clever and very pretty. Her husband was older and therefore had not been drafted. Later she and her husband helped us through some hard times.

Even though they lived in a small town in the country, Edith's hometown was not safe from Allied bombs. Edith's Latin teacher's and parents' house was destroyed, only about 200 yards away. The family could not find another place to live. Our apartment belongs to a small room at the attic. So they came to Edith's home and stayed all through the war and even after the war.

Many houses at the town were crowded because the people's houses in Mannheim/Ludwigshafen had been destroyed and they had to live somewhere.

Every room was our apartment was actually occupied. Aunt Lizzie with her little son and baby had come to us. Now we were 9 people together.

Then a friend, Wilhelm, brought his wife, Juliette, to us when their house in Mannheim was destroyed. Later her son was wounded at the front line. When he was discharged from the hospital, he also came to live with us. Shortly before the end of the war, another aunt came to us too.

Those that had actually survived the destruction of their homes had to crowd into the dwindling number of standing houses. In the cities many people had no choice but to live among the ruins. Unfortunately even ruins were still target by bombs.*) *)When survivors' homes being reduced to ruins, and they had found another place to stay, they would write with chalk to their ruins where they had gone. This way, other people would know they were alive, and where to find them.

Juliette's husband, Wilhelm was a close family friend. Juliette was French and was an interesting woman. The saga goes that Wilhelm met Juliette in Paris and she followed him, on foot, to Germany. I don't know if she really did this, but it seems possible since she was vivacious, peppy, and had her own mind about things. Additionally, she did not keep quiet about her political opinions saying dangerous things like: "this dopey 'itler!".

After their house had been bombed, the couple found an apartment in Mannheim, but only for a short time. There the following happened: One day, Juliette appeared with us, dirty, unkempt and desperate.

"My Lord, you look awful. Where have you been?" my mother asked. "In prison!" she answered, and told all. She had been homesick and so wanted to listen to French music and speaking on the radio. Naturally because of the war, it was forbidden to listen to any foreign radio stations, even though some people did it secretly. Juliette recounted my mother that she would click on the radio, but her husband, Wilhelm, would turn it off. She would click to turn it on, he would turn it off again. And so it went back and forth. It must have been quite a noisy fight. The police arrived and took Juliette to prison. She was not treated well. She and the other prisoners had to remove the long quill of goose feathers to be made into soft goose downs. Apparently a guard would come from time to time, stick his hand into a sack of downs, falsely claiming to find a quill and dump the entire lot onto the floor for them to painstakingly gather up again. This, of course, was pure harassment. Luckily Juliette's husband had a rather high position in a company that produced war related items. Therefore he was one of the more highly regarded and indispensable people and was able to get Juliette out of prison after a few days. But her spirit was broken. She stayed with us, even for quite some time after the war. Her husband had said about my mother: "you are the only one who can handle Juliette," which was probably true. My mother was patient, understanding and loving and Juliette stayed with us after the war.

A couple of years after the war my mother found a very small and cheep apartment and we moved there. All our guests had to leave. My mother begged Wilhelm to take Juliette back. He finally did this, but Juliette never forgave my mother for not keeping her indefinitely. "Millie is dead for me", she would say, "she has thrown me out."

It was not uncommon that some people would fall in love and marry across borders. Now during the war Juliette must feel her heart ache with the realization that her German born son, now a German Lieutenant, would be shot at a French soldier, possibly even relatives of his. Indeed he was shot, but luckily only wounded.

During the war, propaganda was disseminated to warn ordinary citizens of possible real, but more probably imagined enemies. Posters on pillars and other visible places warned of foreign spies. One poster depicted a figure of a man holding his pointer finger in front of his mouth in the typical "shush" gesture, with the caption "Shush, the enemy is listening in." ("Psst, Feind hört mit"). Of course, no enemy could have learned anything from an ordinary citizen. To the contrary, it was the government that was secretly listening in to the private conversations of their own ordinary citizens, not the enemy.

Edith recalls how she got into trouble:

In our small town it was customary that, when school let out, the children who had a similar way home as their teacher, would walk with him or her. The older kids were allowed to carry the teacher's books and other belongings. The younger ones just walked along. We usually conversed amongst each other. One day when our group had just passed one of the aforementioned posters warning of spies, I said something like: "Last night while I was lying in bed, I heard the woman who lives close to us listening to her radio, but I could not understand anything. It was in a foreign language." I was later told it was English.

At the time, I did not know it was highly forbidden to listen to foreign radio stations. German people were only supposed to listen to the government-approved news from German stations. My mother had not told me this. The adults in my family did not talk politics in front of us children. But Dorle, my best friend did know it. And she had nothing better to do but tell other people: "Edith said...." It must have gotten around because my very nice elderly teacher came to my mother, asking her to tell me that it was dangerous to talk about such things. Nothing happened to anybody so I can only surmise that none of the people who heard about my faux pas, were no Nazi informers.

However Dorle's mother came to my mother and said that from now on, her daughter and I were not allowed to have anything to do with each other because I was talking about dangerous things. This was hard on both of us girls. Only about 15 years later, long after the war, Dorle and I met again and rekindled our friendship which lasted until she passed away. For our mothers, the situation must have been much harder. They had worked together as young women, been close friends, lost touch and had much later reconnected. Unfortunately their friendship cooled due to this incident, and never recovered.

This shows how "oppressed" and scared people were. Dorle's mother was a nice and intelligent woman. But she was deathly afraid (and with good reason!) that Edith's naïve mutterings could bring her family into danger. Occurrences like this could and did rip friends and families apart. On the other hand, most Germans at the time would stand with people who made much bigger mistakes than the one Edith had made, often simply by not reporting things to the authorities, contrary to what one was supposed to do.

Despite the constant fear, people made sure to ensure that life went on. Edith remembers:

School space was tight and few teachers, so the day was split. We "little ones", I was in 5ᵗʰ and then 6ᵗʰ grade, had school in the afternoons. The "big kids" had their lessons in the mornings. And so on my free mornings, I helped the milk distributor on his route. Milk was rationed, of course. On his handcart, he had two large cans, one for whole milk, the other for skim milk. The whole milk was only for infants and toddlers and probably pregnant women. Everyone else received only skim milk, or as we called it, blue milk, because it was so watery. For me the milk distributor filled up two smaller cans, handed me a miniscule measuring cup, and instructed me on measuring out the exact allotted ration for each family.* At the end of the tour I was rewarded with a cup of milk. *At the time refrigerators were mostly unknown and milk was not pasteurized. So it was delivered each day. Every morning one placed a jug on the ground floor windowsill of the house one lived in. The milkman or milk woman or child measured the allowed amount of milk into the can. This is how it was in my village.

However, having virtually no access to news that presented the true state of the war, many, if not most people, believed that even after the American invasion, the front could still be halted at the river Rhein, or somewhere east of the river, and Germany might still be able to win the war.

When the front came closer, another aunt came to live with us also. Right away she urged us to evacuate about 100 miles to the southeast. But mother did not want to leave, one reason being that she wanted to be there when father came home. Somehow we all had such naïve ideas about father coming home. Our thoughts were legitimate and no one thought otherwise.

In March the shooting stopped and all was silent. We neighbors had accumulated in a villa to wait on there what would happen. It was told that the American soldiers would rip of women's chains off their necks and their watches off arms. Women would be harassed. Then it was told that a house would be demolished if they found any Nazi-literature. Mother realized that we had Hitler's "Mein Kampf" in our book shelf, mandatory but never read. She took the book and ran again to find a place to hide it. When a shot was heard, she slipped into the next house; it happened friends' house but nobody was in. The cooking stove burned a lively fire. Mother put the book on the fire. The book did not want to burn well but, nevertheless, she ran back. Nothing happened.

A few days later our aunt went out to find some food. When she came back she told that a black American soldier stopped her in the street and asked what time it was.

Aunt showed her arm and her watch, being sure that she would lose her watch. But the soldier only looked at the time and then passed. After this occurrence we felt a little easier.

Many black soldiers liked children and often give them some food. One day my brother and other boys were prowling around the military kitchen. One officer saw the boy and he cursed him and chased them away. The cook, a big black man, came out of his kitchen, furious. He took two loafs of bread and threw them to the boys so that they could pick them up.

When the Americans had come through, they commandeered houses in our neighborhood for their officers and soldiers to live in. This was quite common all over Germany. One of our friends' house was taken away from. Them and their small foster child, Lieselotte, come to live at us also. Mother had no space for herself, no quiet, nor private time.

Then, during the second half of May 1945, I was 15, I was sent on my bike to the next village to pick up salad plants. Arriving, I knocked or rang the doorbell. I don't remember. The door opened but nobody said anything. I led into a semi-dark kitchen. A man sat there, in a chair, with gray-green clothing. I was told it was the woman's husband. Thoughts started to tumble over each other through my head. 'This man, father's batman, is here but my father is not. Maybe he is dead.'

It was explained to me that my father had been killed during a Russian Guerilla attack. I was told he had received a shot between his eyes and was dead immediately.

I don't remember how I got out of the house. When I started perceiving my surroundings, I realized I was on my way home. I only remember that I pushed my bicycle along the road. Then a man spoke to me. I came back to being conscious and recognized the man as my piano teacher.

"Edith, what is wrong with you?" he asked. "My father has been killed." He let me talk and talk. He only listened to me and brought me home. One of the tenants stood by the entrance to my house. She saw our stricken group approach and asked: "Edith, what's wrong?" Little Lieselotte was playing in the road. Childish curiosity might have attracted her to our group. I did not actually see or hear anything anymore. I only answered: "Our father is dead."

The little girl ran up the stairs to our apartment. Before I myself could have brought the message, she yelled: "Aunt Millie, uncle Luddel is dead."

Mother collapsed silently. Somebody brought her to bed. I don't know how the rest of the day progressed. Later it turned out that her wonderful singing voice had been broken by the shock.

The morning before, an American officer, who lived across the street, had spoken to my mother in the yard telling that she should do his laundry. One did not dare say no to such demands. He gave her his clothes, a piece of soap and said he would come back the next day. When he returned the next day to retrieve his laundry, he was told by a woman in the house that it was not done since my mother was sick in bed. The American officer asked to see my mother and would not let be deterred. So finally he was taken to her bedroom. He quietly sat down beside my mother, gently stroked her hand and said: "War is terrible." When he came back days later to pick up his clothes, he brought a small ration of real coffee*), something for us children and allowed us to keep the leftover soap. *) During these times real coffee made from coffee beans was not available anywhere. So substitute coffee was made by roasting barely or other grains.

Mother was sick for a long time. Only our elderly, good family doctor brought her to herself again, mainly by forcing the people who lived with us, to give her some space of her own.

Mother had not been in perfect health even long before this incident. Despite this, she had to work in a factory during this time. Every time an air raid happened during the day she ran home to us each time to take care of us. She handled all of this in addition to having the 11 people living in our apartment.

Now our family was just the three of us. Father would never be with us again. After "the dust had cleared", mother should have received a widow's pension as other widow's fallen soldiers did. And we children should have been given orphan's allowances. But some totally insane ruling did not allow for this. The occupying American government rationalized their rule, incomprehensibly.

In actuality and officially the war ended May 9th 1945 with the signing of the German capitulation. But since the Americans had invaded our area in late March, that date that was used to declare the end of the war for our area. My father had been killed on April 6th, 1945. Therefore soldiers who had been killed after late March and before May 9th, no matter where, after to this American invasion or entry in our area, were declared to have not been killed during the war. Between late March and early May, were classified as being killed after the war. And those families whose husbands fell into this second group, were disqualified from receiving monetary support.

To add to the problem, my father, having been a teacher, of course had had no choice but to become a NSDAP*) member. *) NSDAP= National Socialist German Laborer Party.

A very small number of teachers could avoid being become party members. It was sometimes avoidable if one lived in a hamlet so small that party officials were likely to overlook the tiny hamlets and therefore the inhabitants. However, everyone else was given little choice but to join the party, if they wanted to keep their teaching job or at least suffered inconveniences. Many individuals were signed up automatically. Also those turning 18, were automatically registered into the party. One did not dare question. Additionally, it was impossible to retract this party membership.

Not only not receiving mother's war-widow pension but even the money from father's life insurance policy was frozen. Mother was only allowed to withdraw a very small amount from her savings bank account each month. Just recently I found a letter that mother had written to the occupying American military government. She asked to be allowed to withdraw a little more from her personal saving bank account. The request was denied.

But one needed money, even if there was almost nothing to buy. But one had to pay rent, electricity, water, private tuition because the schools had been closed from summer 1944 through the fall 1945, and transportation. All these had to be paid with money. Additionally, one needed money for those things necessary for survival. Naturally, we could not afford to buy goods on the black market.

Luckily mother found work that brought a little money in. My mother, being a talented artist, had previously decorated costumes for a dancer friend. This friend knew a gentleman who was looking for people who could paint for him. He had fairytale figures cut out of thin plywood. Mother painted these figures beautifully with lots of detail. We all helped painting dwarves and other figures. The man was enthusiastic about mother's designs and even added some of her suggestions to his assortment. This did not bring in much money, but it kept us above water. More than half a century later, one of these designs is still hanging on a wall in my present house.

Juliette and I were helping these figures to paint. We made beautiful fairy figures. After painting the fairy figures we painted little hearts with cut out to put small photos inside. Mother had insomnia and most nights she worked until 2am. Also Juliette sometimes worked through the night.

One morning we found her still working. Asking why she was not in bed, she said: "I have to make miniature spots, spots, spots, for poor Millie to get money she can buy for bread for the children." We all laughed about it. It is absurd that one finds something funny despite the terribly sad situation. It must have been some type of self-protection.

Food was so scarce. Suddenly one day spread the information that a freight car stood at the train track, containing all kinds of necessities. We neighbors, mostly children who were fast, climbed down the hill to the train tracks. The freight cars were stormed. We got a handcart loaded of large boxes, the size of moving boxes, all full with pasta, not in packages, but just loose. We shared with others who had not heard. We brought Aunt Trudy and her husband, who lived at a different section of the town. Trudy said they did not have anything to eat otherwise.

Another time Trudy's husband had heard that there was cut and dried turnips*) for cattle in Heidelberg. *) These are the large turnips that are normally eaten by cattle. *He drove his bicycle to the 15 miles on his wheel rims wrapped with an old garden hose. He did find the dried turnips. We soaked them, cooked one and ate with not much excitement. At that time he also kept rabbits. This was not easy. One had to get a female who had to be covered. Then the young rabbits had to grow large enough to eat. Trudy's husband, was such a kind-hearted person, but he had to butcher the rabbits. The hunger just dictated this.*

After a couple of years after the war we found another apartment just for us three. It was built in an attic and contained two very small rooms and a good-sized kitchen. There seemed to be no place for our piano so we put it in the kitchen.

It was the time when local officials went to all houses to find out if anybody had any spare rooms for evacuated and refugees. The officials at first declared our live-in-kitchen to be a luxury living room because there was a piano in it. My mother said that this was a kitchen and that there was no law not to have one's piano in the kitchen. Nobody came back.

Over the years life normalized slowly and it became easier for people. In 1948 in the three government occupations western Allies did a currency conversation. All monies and all savings were only 10% worth. Even though Edith's mother's savings were, relatively, free now but their former value had now shrunk to one tenth. In 1949 the military governors were replaced to civil leaders (Adenauer).

At these so very hard times Millie, Edith's mother, survived raising her children, helping other people. Now one slowly worked one into better times. They went through danger and hunger and private problems that all people also went through this. This family and most others made it through the times and never gave up.

I met Millie several years ago. The old lady seemed satisfied with her life. She was charming, and had an inner strength. Her wounds were invisible. She was never bitter.

Edith became a teacher. She shared with her father the talent of treating students in ways that they needed. She was a teacher of handicapped teenagers, emotional and physically. Edith has many of her students "healed" so that they could live a full life.

Edith is the most creative person I ever know. Not only is she a tremendous artist and writer, she helped old people to find meaning again. Edith can make the most fantastic festivals and birthdays that have a theme where her children and grandchildren participates made cultural, funny, reflective and memorial experiences. To summarize Edith, I have to say: "Edith is full of life and she is life herself".

Susanna's Wanderings Through Europe

Susanna's Wanderings Through Europe
(born 1919)

Danzig ("Gdansk" in Polish) was Susanna's birthplace and most beloved city. As a settlement at the Baltic Sea it had started more than 1,200 years ago. It grew to the proud trade city with old city wall, beautiful medieval houses and churches, busy industries and about a half million inhabitants. Over the centuries it was alternatively German, Polish, Russian. The city had always been politically special. Napoleon had made him a "Free City-State". Now it is Polish. At the time when Susanna was born there lived 98% Germans and 1% Poles.

The Reichsbank, the German government bank, had a large branch in Danzig, and the father of my friend Susanna was an executive there. Susanna was born in Danzig in 1919. As her father was promoted, he was being transferred from one city to another, and his family moved with him. (see map that shows the family's moves within Germany as well as Susanna's through Europe during the war) From Danzig they moved to Marienburg in East-Prussia, not too far from Danzig. Next, the family moved west to Stettin on the river Oder. Susanna's sister was born there. Later they moved even further west to Schwerin, a pretty residence town. Susanna recalls her childhood and youth as being safe and sheltered:

I was so very sheltered and protected. I didn't know what went on in the world. I was an obedient child. I listened. When my mother said: "go this way!" I did. When she said: "do this!" I did. Well, that's how it was everywhere during this time period.

Susanna was indeed an obedient child, living in a sheltered and protected environment. I feel that in her later life she, subconsciously, transformed this experience of being protected into an awareness of the special moments and events of safety and protection, however miniscule, which occurred in her life and gave it a slightly different, and safer, direction. In her narrative Susanna kept pointing out these occurrences to me. She would say: *"in this instance I was protected"* or *"here I was protected again"*.

While the family lived in Schwerin, Hitler came to power. Susanna recalls that on the evening of this fateful 30th of January 1933*)
*) the day when Hitler took up his office as chancellor, she happened to walk through the town to meet her father at the train station.

On her way she encountered a troupe of SA-men marching along the street, marching very precisely and orderly, to music played in a brisk rhythm. Susanna was 13, and she was very impressed. Here was something new, something very organized and disciplined, and exact and seemingly powerful. (see Françoise's impressions of marching HJ)

Did she have any reactions to Hitler and his take-over of power? No, absolutely not. She did not know what was happening. It is very likely that her parents did not discuss any political issues in front of the children, and Susanna did not care anyway. She was just very impressed by the very disciplined and orderly marching of these uniformed men.

The changed political situation did not infringe in any way on everyday life. The family had moved again, this time to Wittenberg, between Berlin and Leipzig the city where Luther lived and worked. Susanna was very happy there, in part because she had quickly found a nice group of friends at her new school. She was even elected class-speaker, an unexpected honor that brought with it a wonderful privilege. Susanna's last name started with Z, a fact that had always made her the very last in everything. Now, as class speaker, she was always called first and she had to walk as the first one in a line. She loved it.

When Susanna's family had to move again, she stayed behind, at a friend's house, to finish the school year, then joined her family in Sommerfeld, a town southeast of Berlin.

Susanna had become a member of the BDM. (That was mandatory.) She went to the weekly meetings but she does not remember much of what they did there. She liked the sense of community, and she was impressed by the discipline and order. That's what she had been used to from home. One had to obey what the parents wanted. But she was not too fond of the occasional camping excursions with her BDM group. Sleeping in a tent was not her style.

And then one morning as she came out of her room, her father scolded her: *"Here you have been sleeping while we have a war outside."* It was the 1st of September 1939. Susanna was almost 20 but she had not been interested in anything political. She did not know what being at war would mean.

So far Susanna had only taken some courses at an arts and crafts school but the skills she had acquired there, could not be turned into a good career. She decided to learn about business and office work. There were no real opportunities in her town but Susanna's father had a friend in Danzig who agreed to receive her into his family there.

Danzig together with the health resort town Zoppot and the sea port Gdingen had over time agglomerated into a loose economic unit. Susanna lived in Zoppot and took the tram to her business school in Danzig every day.

She reminisces:

Zoppot was wonderful, and its greatest attraction for me was its Forest Opera. There Wagner operas were performed in the forest and I could hear the music from my room. The echo was unbelievable. I still get goose bumps today, just thinking about it. There was also the pier and the seaside promenade where one could walk among beautiful surroundings. Here everything was much more relaxed than in the Reich. I could even buy my favorite chocolate that had not been available anymore at home.

And here I met a wonderful young man who would become my fiancé. He was, of course, a soldier. He flew a Ju 52 and he also taught blind flight, which was a rather new thing at the time. I admired his versatility of talent, and we were very much in love with each other. But then my parents did some investigations into his background – they even put a detective on the case – and they found something about his family that they did not like. I still can not grasp it how they could do something like this. I shake my head and I could still cry about it.

My mother wrote to me that I should break my relationship with this wonderful and talented man. And then she got my friends to write to me daily, telling me things like "he is not for you; think about it; it's just not possible". My fiancé had gone back to the front, so I had no support from his side. After some time I started to have doubts. Could my mother and my friends be right?

I had been brought up very strictly. I was used to be very obedient and to do everything my parents told me to do. I wrote my fiancé a letter telling him that I would break the engagement and I sent it to him by registered letter through the military mail. I can still see the road to the post office and I thought "how may this letter find him?" And then I became very unhappy.

About a year before all this happened, I had graduated from the business school and started working at the army's armament inspection office. But after I had broken off my engagement, I wanted to get away from Danzig. I wanted to get as far away from everything as I could. I had been well liked by the admiral and also by his aide for whom I worked.

When I asked to be transferred to another country, I was asked: "where do you want to go?" Imagine this luck! I said, I did not want to go to Paris, everybody was going there. I wanted to go to Athens. But before, I had to go to Dresden, everybody had to go through headquarters in Dresden for physical and other check-ups. I was allowed to pay a brief visit to my parents and then I was off to Athens – or so I thought. On my way there I had to pass through the Belgrade (Yugoslavia) headquarters. After being there for a while I was told: "Nix Athens, you stay with us."

In Belgrade many apartments had been confiscated by the army for Germans to live in. I got my own apartment with a bath. I worked for the aide of the general and I first had a very hard time because of all the "szlc"s in the names of people and places. I tried to transfer them into shorthand but that didn't work, of course. All the other secretaries found my boss a very difficult man to work for. He was very precise and he was demanding. Nobody wanted to work for him. But I did not perceive him that way, I just accepted it. I liked hard and disciplined work and got along fine with him.

We did not notice much of the war. I worked for the military business headquarters (Wehrwirtschaftsstab) and we had to manage roads and bridges and all traffic issues. We had nothing to do with the specifically military things, with marching and weapons and such. We were responsible not only for Yugoslavia but also for Greece, Bulgaria, Albania and Croatia. Everything came together at the office of the general for whom I worked.

In 1942 my father died and I was allowed to go home for the funeral. It was a great privilege that I was allowed to go. After all this was in the midst of the war.

A year later I got a special decoration for working so hard. I was proud of it and always wore it on my uniform. As a reward for my work I was sent to a Romanian spa, together with 30 or 40 other girls who had worked hard too.

Suddenly there was word: Athens will fall. That was probably 1943. My boss and I (and others) had still believed that everything would turn out well. We thought "when will we march into Cairo?" Rommel was there and he was strong. Suddenly Rommel retreated. Cairo was out of the picture, and Athens was out too. I had been protected. If I had gone to Athens I would have had to leave there and would not have known where to get another job. In Belgrade I was protected, and I was secure in my job. Now all those who had worked in Athens came to us and subsequently had to go to Dresden.

In 1944 the first bombs were dropped on Belgrade but there were no real air raid cellars. I had lived on the outskirts of Belgrade but now all female employees were moved into the city and into hotels. We were assigned rooms, always two to a room. I was very apprehensive because I had never slept in the same room with another person. I was probably a little arrogant. But then it turned out that my roommate Hilde and I became great friends. That was in 1944 and we were still friends 60 years later. At the end of the war it was her name and address in my address book that saved me and helped me to get released from a prison camp into West Germany. How wonderful!

The two of us had a bedroom, a living room, and a large bathroom, and we had a beautiful view onto Belgrade's main street. While we were together, my friend met her future husband. I still have to laugh when I think about it. Hilde was a little lyrically inclined; she loved to read Rilke and other romantic poets. One day as she crossed a street in Belgrade, a military vehicle stopped in front of her and the lieutenant who was riding in it was very shocked. They probably got to talking and, well, they later got married. He had been an actor and had played at the Theater in Hamburg together with Heinrich George who was probably the most famous actor of his time.

The war situation got worse. Athens was gone, Bulgaria started to boil, and in Belgrade we got the bombs. Then the order came: all females have to go to the homeland. This meant the Dresden headquarters. We were transported in a military train and we all were afraid of being bombarded. But then I thought: I have all my precious things on me. I can hide quickly. We arrived safely in Dresden. The city kept getting more and more overcrowded.

I lived with an older couple a little outside of Dresden. And then fate interfered again. For the evening of the 13th of February 1945 I had planned to see a certain movie that played in a cinema close to the main railway station. But then I felt too lazy to go and decided to stay home and read a book. Suddenly we heard loud noises. We were in the cellar and had no clue to what was happening. Dresden was being bombed. First came the explosive bombs that destroyed everything and then came the incendiary bombs that made the asphalt and everything else burn. The people who wanted to get out of the air raid shelters got onto that asphalt and they burned from their feet up. Think on it: all this was planned. They had carefully thought about it: How do we destroy these people? The next day some survivors met at the banks of the river. Allied fighter planes came and shot everybody, just like a hunt.

I learned that later. At the time when it happened I did not know. After two or three days I went into the city. I wanted to see what had happened there. I did not know where I was. The ruins of a church next to the river were still recognizable but everything else was destroyed. I did not know where I was.

At the day of the bombing, the train station had been packed with trains crowded with refugees, and they were all suddenly killed. That's how they had thought it out: How do we best kill them all? Had I gone to that movie near the train station, I would have been killed too.

The Allies had always said that Dresden was the Florence of the north, that the architecture and the wonderful works of art had to be protected, that no bombs would be dropped there. The people felt safe in Dresden. And then they changed their mind. It was so cruel, so cruel.

When I came to Dresden from Belgrade, I was incorporated into a military company. I was unhappy but I told myself that I could cope with this. Then we were all transferred to an area near Gera, about 80 miles west of Dresden. We were housed in military barracks, every small room packed with girls. And now I was really unhappy. Luckily I had managed to get a small job. Most girls did not even have jobs. We were more or less warehoused.

After a while I went to the director and asked if I could not go somewhere else. I was told that Denmark was still possible and Czechoslovakia. Imagine, that was 1945, February 1945 and nobody had a clue about the end of the war.

For a long time I had not heard anything about my mother and my sister. There were no mails anymore. I did not know if they were still alive. I felt that my life did not matter much. I had nothing to lose. Maybe my mother and sister would mourn me. I had no responsibility towards anybody, only towards myself.

Denmark was overcrowded with refugees. I chose Czechoslovakia. I was supposed to report to Kudnafore, a place southeast of Prague. But I had to see how I got there. I first tried to hitchhike with military vehicles (private ones were already prohibited at the time) but none stopped for me. With my heavy suitcase I walked from the autobahn back to town. I happened to know a woman there, and I could leave my suitcase with her. I packed only the barest necessities and tried again, this time at the train station. It was very crowded but with my military pass I got onto a train.

I made it to Kudnafore which was a beautiful place and the people were friendly. Work started very early every day but I still managed to take a little walk through some green space before work. One morning, it was after April 30, I realized that the native people I met on my walk acted strange. At the office I was told: "Watch out! Hitler has committed suicide, the townspeople know that we have now lost the war."

When I woke up the next day, I was told: "The war has ended. Take what you can carry. We leave this place." I packed only what I really valued and could carry easily. We were loaded onto a truck that went west. We were moving in a trek, that is, one truck behind the other. Suddenly one truck had disappeared and somebody said, they had probably lost their way and gotten into the hands of the Russians. We heard the bombs falling behind us. We were in real danger. Around us on the road were the refugees. They were all on foot. And I was in a military vehicle. Only because of my job I was in a military vehicle.

And then we came to the borderline between where the Russians were and where the Americans were. The Russians were right behind us. And somebody said: across this border is America.

Somehow the night passed, with us thinking: tomorrow we will be with the Russians. We knew that this meant being raped and possibly losing our life. But the next morning there was a rumor that all women might go to the Americans. Imagine that! I was again protected. It was good that the Americans thought to take us women. It was, of course, very hard for the soldiers but the women were more helplessly exposed.

We did come to the Americans and were put in a prison camp that was a barn. We were all laying there and then it started raining. Everybody tried to find a spot where it would not drip too badly, where the rain was not coming through strongly.

Over time I had collected some cigarettes that I could use as payment when somebody helped me. But then I realized that they had been stolen from me. I was so disappointed because that had never happened to me. But I was there and I was protected.

After a few days one could go just outside of the barn, stand on a cart and look where the soldiers, the other German prisoners, were. Further down was a river and across the river I could see the prisoners standing, shoulder to shoulder, they were standing shoulder to shoulder. And then came the rain. Oh God, these poor men. They were far away, one could only see the circles of their heads. My future husband could have been one of them.

He went through something like this too.

I had brought a tiny sewing kit with me. One day I helped an American soldier with some sewing thread and then he gave me something to eat. That was really nice, that showed some kindness.

Then there was a rumor that the Americans might slowly be starting to release us. But they would not release anybody to the eastern part of Germany, only to the west. I still had my address book with me, God be thanks, and in there was the address of my friend Hilde with whom I had been in Belgrade. I did not know where her hometown was but she had once told me that she had visited the Drachenfels. I knew that the Drachenfels was a rock formation on the river Rhein, and the Rhein was in the west. I gave that address as my home address and I was released. If I had not had this, all would have been lost.

In this barn I had made another friend, Gisela. She is still my friend today, and her son is my godson. Later she wrote to me that after I had left, the situation became really bad, very, very bad. There was nothing to eat, etc.

Now I was in the train going west. It was the very first train and we were all prisoners of war. It was the first train that had been released. The wagons were all cattle cars. We were standing in there, packed densely, standing shoulder to shoulder. And we thought: Oh God, how will the night be? and the next night? Where will I get something to eat? – How I survived, I don't know.

Once in a while the train stopped so that we could go. For that it stopped. After all, a person does have to go. It was really bad when one had one's period. That was terrible.

When the train stopped, people, civilians, came running. They probably thought: "Oh, the first released. That means our soldiers will come home soon too." And they threw us potatoes and sometimes they gave us to drink. From the people that accompanied the train we did not get anything. Nothing. I do not know how I survived. I don't even know if I was hungry or what; survival was the only important thing. I only know: lucky the one who got such a potato. That these people thought of bringing some potatoes was so great. They didn't have anything themselves, just their meager food rations.

Susanna, like so many others, must have blocked out much of her bad experiences. When we talked about her train ride from the American prison camp towards the west, her story had many blank spaces.

I asked Susanna if she did have her period during that train ride. She did not remember. I asked her if the potatoes were raw or cooked. She did not know. Did she catch a potato? She did not remember. I asked her, how long, how many days, the train ride had lasted. She did not remember. I asked her, where she got off the train. She did not remember. – Her story goes on:

Then I landed somewhere and I knocked at some door. I asked where I was and how I could get to the town that was Hilde's hometown. The people said there might be a possibility of transportation. They told me about a place from where sometimes trucks were allowed to run. There was no traffic at all, no trains, no cars, nothing went. But when I came to the place that the people had indicated, there was indeed a truck, loaded high with cabbages. The driver took me on because I had my release document. Without it he would not have taken me. He read the address to which I was being released and he nodded. I had to climb onto the cabbages and beside me was a soldier who had been released too and then, I believe, there was somebody else. I believe we were three. I don't know. And then the truck started. Imagine how one survives! These hard years!

I made it to the village where Hilde's parents lived. I found the house, knocked on the door and said: "I am a friend of Hilde." And the woman asked right away: "And where is our daughter?" That was hard, very hard. I said: "I don't know." But they took me in anyway. A few weeks later Hilde did indeed come home too, and she had already married her lieutenant-actor. Wonderful, isn't it!

I am certain that Susanna had needed some time to recuperate. She was lucky to have landed in a village where people had a little more to eat, especially potatoes, than in the cities. But when she had regained her strength, she was ready to move on.

After a while I said to my hosts: "You have taken me in and cared for me in such a sweet way. I have to stop living with you. I will go to the next town and see if I can find a job there." I did go there and located an office that found jobs for people.*) Such offices were leftovers from the 3rd Reich where everybody was assigned work. I was told that there was absolutely no office work to be had. Nothing was alive yet, companies had not reopened yet. I was very disappointed and I said: "What am I to do with myself? I can not be a burden to these people anymore." The man looked again and he found a request for help at a corn distillery. I only heard the word "corn" *) (Korn = rye in German) and thought of bread.

111

I was so naïve at 26 that I did not know that Korn *) its full name is Kornbranntwein, is also a term for a certain type of schnapps.

I went to the place, it was a long trip for me. The people were very nice and they did indeed hire me and I found out that my job was to do the housework. (The family members probably worked in the distillery.) The daughter of the house became a close friend of mine. She told me later how they had been in stitches, watching me to try to shine her father's shoes. They had laughed so hard. Well, I learned to do housework and I had enough to eat. They could exchange their corn schnapps for food.

While Susanna worked at the distillery, she met the man who would become her husband. When they had already known each other for some time, Susanna became very ill with appendicitis. Her problem was diagnosed too late. The appendix had already broken through. This was the time before antibiotics – at least in Germany. There was not much that could be done for her and she had almost given up. Then one day her male friend visited her in the hospital and brought her a golden ring. He had collected little bits and pieces of gold and had found somebody who could make the ring for her.*) *) In Germany engagement- and wedding rings are simple golden bands without any stones. He talked to her about a future together and put the ring on her finger. This gave Susanna back her will to live and she had an almost miraculous recovery. Later the two got married and had a happy life together.

But how did Susanna find her mother and sister? When Susanna had been transferred from the military barracks near Gera to Kudnafore near Prague, she had left her suitcase with a woman who was also an acquaintance of her mother and sister. After mail service was reinstated, Susanne wrote to this woman and her mother did the same.

During and after the war many families and friends got separated and, if they survived, they often found each other by extraordinary means. After bomb raids, the surviving inhabitants of destroyed houses would often write messages on the ruins like "Peter and Lotte are still alive and on their way to uncle Martin in X-town." Letters to mutual friends or relatives were another way but this only worked if the mail did not get destroyed or lost.

Well, Susanna had found her mother and sister. They had not had an easy time either. Towards the end of the war it was the American army who came first to where they were living in East Germany. Susanna's sister Claudia, had always been good in English and soon found a job with the Americans.

But then it was determined how Germany should be divided up into the four occupation zones, and this area was made part of the Russian occupation zone.*) *)see map   Before the Americans were to leave, Claudia's boss told her that she, as an army employee, could come with the American army to the west, but only she herself. She could not bring her mother. Claudia contemplated this offer for one whole night. The next morning she told her boss that she would either go with her mother or not at all. Her boss must have been touched very much by her loyalty. He said to her: "Your mother may come." This was very much against the rules but he managed to slip both women onto the military truck.

Susanna's mother and sister were taken into the newly formed American occupation zone but from there they had to fend for themselves. They walked and walked, just like the many, many other refugees. They had several relatives in the west but whenever they called on them, they found that their houses were already overfilled with other refugees. But the two women were never turned away. They always could sleep indoors for a night (if on the floor) and they probably were also given some of the very little food their hosts had.

Finally they came to Hamburg where Susanna's and Claudia's mother had a brother. He took the women in and could even get them a room. By that time it was the dead of winter, and an especially cold winter at that. There was, naturally, no heat. People had no fuel, especially not in the cities. Susanna remembers:

My mother and sister had one of these washing bowls in their room but when they wanted to wash in the morning the water was frozen. But they were always living inside a house, never outside. It was a start.

Then my sister got a job with the Royal Air force), *)* Hamburg was in the British occupation zone *and later she got a job with a Greek shipping company. Yes, they were protected, just like I was protected. We all made it.*

Susanna did not know much about her mother's and sister's experiences and wanderings. She said:

I do not know where they had been living when my sister worked for the American who took them to the west. I do not know where they were set down, and for how long they walked before they got to Hamburg. I do not know any details All this was told so very quickly.

This is typical for that time. The only important issue was to survive. One talked about where to find food. The past was over (or rather buried deep inside). Now, one had to look into the future, to move on with one's life.

The soldiers, who had come home from war and from prison camps, normally did not talk about their experiences either. I remember an uncle who came home a few years after the end of the war. He had been in a Russian POW camp. For years after, he spent all of his free time doing crossword puzzles. He never talked about any of his experiences and his family soon learned not to ask. Many decades later his daughter, my cousin, found her husband doing a crossword puzzle, and she panicked. She remembered her father sitting at his desk doing puzzles, totally secluded and isolated from his family and the world around him and, probably, trying to distract himself from the memories of his experiences. My cousin's husband had done his crossword puzzle only on a temporary whim. Seeing his wife's distress and learning her reason for it, he, good-naturedly, gave up this pastime completely.

I met Susanna a long time past the war. She was content with her life. When I asked her what was most important to her in her life, she said:

"I am so grateful. I was always protected."

Klaus' War Story

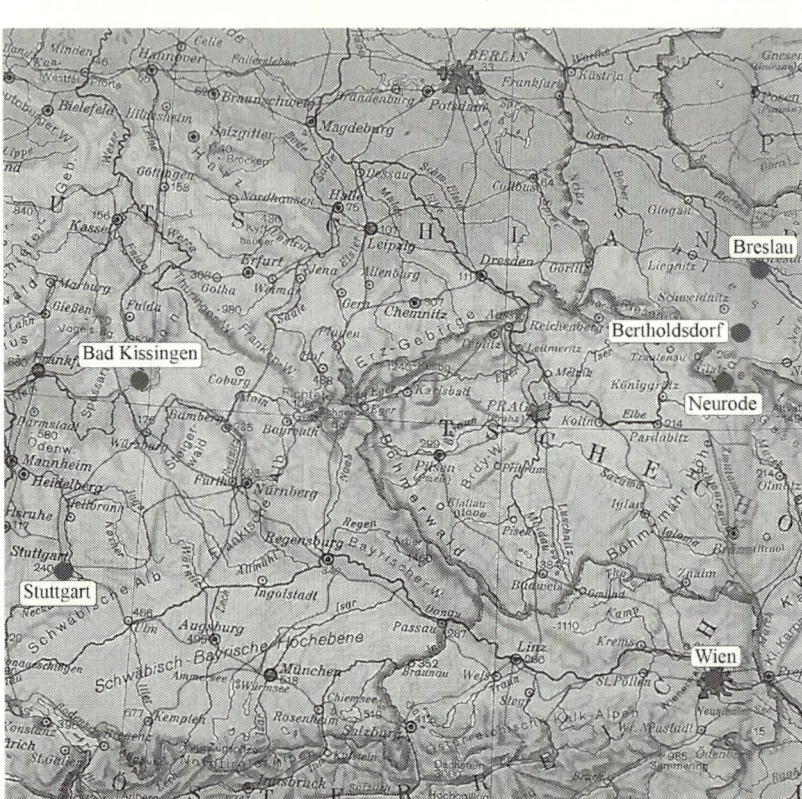

Klaus' War Story (born 1934)

In 1925 my mother, Maria, got a letter from a friend who lived in the city of Breslau, suggesting that she also move there. Breslau was a long way from Maria's home in the Palatinate, but it was not much further away than Berlin or Hamburg and it was as much part of Germany as these two other cities were. Maria was young and adventurous. She went to Breslau, accepted a teaching position at a college there and spent a happy time in this, more than a thousand years-old, and very cultured city.

The University of Breslau had always been a center of sciences, arts and humanities and had attracted the best of researchers and teachers. In 1912 the Bavarian-born Alois Alzheimer*) *) 1864-1915 went there, assigned by the emperor Wilhelm II as a professor of psychology. Alzheimer had already done important research at various universities about the disease that was later given his name.

At the same time, namely from 1897 to 1916 Ludwig Wilhelm Stern was also a professor at the Breslau University*) *)1871-1938. Stern was Jewish and had to flee Germany after 1933. He first went to the Netherlands then to the United States where he taught at Duke University and changed his first name to William. Stern was working on discovering what made up the personality of a human being and found that intelligence played a large part. He coined the term "I.Q.", Intelligence-Quotient, to describe the level of intelligence of a person. Now-a-days people who determine a person's intelligence by using IQ-tests, don't think of professor Stern at Breslau University.

Today, that is after 1945, Breslau is called Wroclaw and it is part of Poland. The city and its inhabitants suffered horribly at the end of the war when the Soviet army captured it after heavy fighting and they suffered afterwards under the Soviet occupation.

My friend Klaus' family lived in Breslau, or rather in one of the suburbs. Klaus told me how they managed to survive the horror and how they finally came to the west.

Klaus (born 1934) and his two brothers had had an almost idyllic early childhood. They enjoyed the surrounding fields and meadows, even a brook, shallow enough for children to splash around in. Politics were not important and did not enter into the family's life. But everything changed in 1939.

Here is Klaus' story:

> *One day in August 1939*) this peaceful existence was shattered when my father was called-up to the military. I was 5 ½ years old. I was told that father had to go away because he had to become a soldier. I had no idea what this meant. My younger brother, Manfred. was 4 years old, he understood even less, and my older brother, 12 years old, did not explain anything to me. We accompanied father to the military barracks inside the city. It was sad to have him leave, but that was just it.* *) WWII started on September 1ˢᵗ 1939.

> *A few weeks later the terrible thing happened. Our house had been built to house three families: one on the third floor, then we on the second and a young couple on the first. Suddenly we heard a shrill scream from the woman above us: "War has broken out!" The women rushed together, talked and lamented, but my mother said: "God be praised! Our children are too young to get involved in it." Unfortunately she was wrong. Five years later my older brother was drafted and he died shortly before his 18ᵗʰ birthday.*

> *The actual beginning of the war has been re-enacted, filmed and shown on television after the war. It seems that several, somehow harmless looking, German military jeeps came to the Polish border. They stopped and some soldiers got out. One of them lifted the barrier and the German vehicles drove through. The Polish border guards didn't know what had hit them. Maybe they were taken into custody. I don't know. By the time Poland realized that she had been attacked and could mount some resistance, the German units were already 20 to 30 km inland.*

Klaus' story picks up again towards the end of the war. He was 10 years old at the time, his younger brother was 9, his older brother had been drafted into the military. The Soviet troops were advancing.

He remembers:

> *It must have been around January 18, 1945, in the middle of the very cold and snowy winter, that we saw the first people who had been evacuated from Upper Silesia, passing by our house on the street. They moved in long treks with their sleds, on which they had loaded all kinds of luggage. If they were farmers, they had horse-drawn sleighs.*

My older brother, now 17 was stationed at some military barracks in Breslau, and he had asked my mother to come and pick up his private possessions because he would be moved to the front in a few days. When she came back, she was very upset and reported that the Breslau railway station was overcrowded with people who were trying to get out of there and to the west, Görlitz, Dresden or so.

When Klaus' father and a close friend of his, Walter Bauer, had, years ago, been in the position to build houses for their families, they had built them next to each other in this pleasant suburb. Walter had been a sports teacher but, because of some health problem had not been drafted like his friend, Klaus' father.

After my mother had told the Bauers about the situation at the railway station, Walter took the initiative, and told my mother: "Elsie, we will leave this evening. If you want to come along, pack your things, take the children and come. I don't want to wait until Breslau will be officially evacuated and the civilians will be ordered out. By that time the roads will be blocked and the help stations on the way will be even more overcrowded. We will go this evening at any rate."

And this is what we did. Manfred and I were at the time 9 and 10 years old, as old as the Bauers' children Christl and Dorle. As far as I remember, we left around 8 o'clock in the darkness at about -20° C (-4F). We had an ordinary sled onto which my mother had strapped two suitcases and a backpack on the top. At the end, when she had packed the most important things that we could take, she said to us two children – and this was so sweet – "Now each one of you may take his favorite toy". I took my Waldi, a stuffed animal, a dachshund. He was a pretty Waldi who I loved very much. And then I also took a spinning top. It was very small, so I was allowed to take that too.

We were wrapped up warmly, one piece on top of the other. Long johns over pants, some shirts and jackets and on top of all that a thick, warm winter coat. Grandma Bauer, who was a seamstress, had made us these coats from wool blankets. They even had leather covered edgings. They were wonderfully warm but they were also rather heavy, and since we were wearing jackets and all the other things underneath, we were somehow stuffed and this was cumbersome while walking. We soon became tired.

We started: the Bauers with their two children, my mother with us two boys and also a young woman with her baby who had been born only around Christmas 1944.

But she only walked with us until we came to a military airport from where she was promised to be flown out.

On this evening we walked probably 20 km (12 ½ miles), a good distance, and it was hard for us at the end, especially because of our heavy clothing. We didn't feel the cold too badly because we were in motion all the time, and we were used to walk.

Funny, that this leaving was not hard for me. Mother had even said: "We will lock the door so that nobody will get in." just as if we were to be gone for a weekend.

And now it became adventurous and exciting for us children. In a village whose name I have forgotten, Walter had knocked at the door of a house where there was still light and said, we were so and so many people and we needed a place to spend the night. This was no problem at the time. We had come to a farm and we four children were allowed to sleep in the hay barn. This was special for us and it was warm. The parents slept in the house. I am sure that we even got some breakfast the next morning.

The next day we went on to a village with the name of Tambadel. The Bauers did have acquaintances there who kept them over night and we were taken in at the forester's lodge that was a few hundred meters further on.

Later we separated from the Bauers because we wanted to get about 25 to 30 km (15 – 18 ½ miles) further to Bertholdsdorf (which is close to the county-town of Reichenbach in der Eule). My uncle, my father's brother, had a nursery in Bertholdsdorf and he took us in. We stayed there probably until the end of March, maybe even to the beginning of April.

Around most of the city of Breslau the railroad ran on a dam. The political head of the district (Gauleiter) had ordered, in total disregard of the actual war situation that this dam should be fortified and the whole city defended as a fort. There had been some destruction already in the city and women and even children were commanded to move the rubble from ruined houses into barricades. Government officers had full control over the population and only later in January, almost too late, were women and children allowed to evacuate out of the city. (Klaus' family and their neighbors had been living outside the "ring" and could therefore get away on their own.) It is said*) *) Wikipedia states that during that evacuation 18,000 people froze to death in the icy snowstorms.

Many people, especially the older ones, had stayed in the city, among them the parents of Walter Bauer.

Life became harder as the bombardment of the city increased. The people lived mostly in their cellars. But one needed to get food from time to time. One day grandma Bauer (the one who had sewn the winter coats for Klaus and his brother) went out to find something to eat. She was hit by a grenade fragment and died. Grandpa Bauer learned this by coincidence.

The front had been halted east of Breslau and my mother had decided to go back to our house to get some more of our possessions. Surprisingly trains were running in the area. We left my brother at the nursery and took a slow train to a station close to our suburb. The next morning, we walked back to this station but were told: "No trains are going anymore. The Russians have broken through the front. Breslau is probably even encircled now." My mother was shocked; my younger brother Manfred was outside, we were probably inside. We left our two suitcases standing at the station. Theoretically they must be there still. We started walking and some lucky circumstance helped us there. Near the station a man approached my mother, asking her if she knew the area well. She didn't know it real well but she knew a little and she answered: "Yes, I know my way around here." The man was happy about that and started telling that he only now had been allowed to leave the city and gotten a permit out. He cursed the Nazis who had held him back in the city so that he should help defend it. For my mother it was probably a bit of protection that he came with us.

We started walking in the direction of Schweidnitz but we were not sure exactly where the front was. We kept meeting German troops but they were not sure either where exactly the Russians were. We saw no fighting, just heard canons but those were not too close. Then we met soldiers who told us: "Yes, you are lucky, the Russians are 3km (1.9miles) away on this side and 5 km (3miles) away on that side. If you keep going straight, you will probably make it to get through." We walked like he had suggested and some time later soldiers gave us the important news: "You are through, you are outside." A little incident happened as a grenade came flying and hit about 50m (54yards) from us. This was a little scary. We kept walking and spent the first night in Jordansmühl, a little town at some people's house on the floor, probably in their living room. The next morning the man went his own way and we went ours. Now we knew exactly how to proceed. We walked through Langenbielau which is famous from Gerhard Hauptmann's play "Die Weber". This village is really very, very long. I was very tired but mother kept saying "It is not far anymore, Bertholdsdorf is right after Langenbielau. Finally we did arrive at uncle's. We were happy to be together again. The undertaking had been for nothing, we had not been able to bring back anything; that was left standing at the station in Klettendorf.

But we were healthy and together again.

The German army tried to keep up the discipline of the troops. Any action that looked like desertion was punished by death right away. I remember that a young tank soldier had hidden himself in an empty house while his unit moved on. When he came out, he was recognized by another unit as not belonging to them – he was wearing the black tank unit uniform – and hanged for desertion.

In the meantime life had been somehow quiet, that is, there was no direct danger. We were well housed at the nursery. Uncle had a horse and a dog and there was also our dog, the German shepherd Hella. We had brought her to uncle earlier during the war when it was known that dogs were being drafted for military service. We wanted to save her from that. When we came to Bertholdsdorf, she was very, very happy to be with us again.

I want to talk about "guest-laborers", the POWs or displaced persons who were put to work at German businesses and farms. There has been talk that they were treated badly and there might have been single occurrences by people who were mean to start with and who treated everybody badly. Uncle had a Russian worker at the nursery. He lived at the nursery, had his own small room, he ate with the family, worked when everybody else worked but had his free Sunday like everybody else. After the war he took leave of us in a friendly manner and went home to Russia.

Then the front came closer and we had to flee again. We fled to Neurode in the mountains, that is a little outside the Glazer Kessel, very close to the Czech border. This was the farthest we could go within the borders of the German Reich. There we were assigned a room. That was still organized by the local government. We even received ration cards.

It was there that an accident happened to a friend, a boy my age, also a refugee. We had played at a dump looking for things to play with and he had found an unexploded bomb or grenade. It was, of course, dumb of him to play with it but he was a child and for us everything to do with weapons and shooting and airplanes, was interesting. The bomb or grenade exploded and he was dead.

Shortly before the capitulation the food depots were opened for the population. Mother sewed little sacks out of flag fabric and they were filled with dried peas.

The capitulation happened on May 8, 1945. That is how long my father was a soldier. He probably got into American captivity at that date near Weimar. He managed to escape rather soon and reached Breslau in September.

On May 8th the Russian troops entered the town of Neurode without any fighting. This was, of course, lucky for us. The German population was called to the market place by funnel microphones. It was in the afternoon. A Russian officer gave a speech: "You may be happy, the war has ended. We, the Red Army, we have liberated you from this wicked Hitler regime, from this Nazi regime. You may all go home again now and now everything will be well again." That's what the man said but as he had just finished, the first Russian soldiers started to take the people's wrist watches who had any. (These soldiers had been posted on the market place, not to guard us but to prevent riots that could have happened.)

I have to insert what happened during this time to an acquaintance in Berlin. He was approached on the street by a Russian soldier who showed him his arm with a large number of wrist watches on it. He looked at the man's wrist watch, apparently to check if it was working, then demanded the working watch. Then the soldier gave him the whole assortment of watches. They had all stopped working and he did not know that they had to be wound up. (This was, of course, long before watches had batteries.)

I do remember other, funny happenings. The Russians had these Panje-Wagons that were box carts pulled by Panje horses, these small, tough steppe horses. Onto these wagons the Russians had placed the most beautiful easy chairs and now drove them, sitting in these upholstered chairs. Some even had put toilets on their wagons and were sitting on top of those. These were some funny occurrences.

My mother had taken literally the Russian officer's words that we could all go home now. After a few days we went back to Bertholdsdorf to uncle's nursery. The walk, over mostly flat terrain, was not hard. In Bertholdsdorf we learned that uncle had been thrown out of his nursery. It had probably been given to a Pole. We stayed there for two or three weeks, collecting food, which would be easier there than in the city. And then came the Bauers. They knew, of course, of my uncle and wanted to know if we were still there.

Walter Bauer, he was a competent and prudent man, had somehow managed to acquire a wagon and two horses.

Maybe he had gotten them when the military was dispersed or he had gotten them from a farmer. Anyway, he came with this horse-drawn wagon, which later would play a very important role in the Bauers' life. Walter said to my mother: "Elsie, of course we will now go back to Breslau." And then we all went to Breslau. In the meantime I was well used to walking on the road and at the time it was not dangerous yet. That only came later.

When we arrived in Breslau, or rather in our suburb of Breslau, we found our house as well as the Bauers' in ruins. But a few houses further my aunt's house was still standing. She and my grandfather had fled when there was still time, so our two families moved into this house. We nailed the ground floor windows shut to prevent any Pole or Russian to climb in and we barricaded the door. Of course, somebody could have rammed it in with great force or shot through, but this never happened. We just tried to protect us a little. The problem lay in getting food. There was no provision of food anymore, no office that would have given out ration cards, and if there would have been those, there was nobody who would have had any food for sale. One had to care for oneself. The cellar of our, now destroyed, house was still standing. It had been reinforced with concrete. Strangely enough, part of the terrazzo floor of our bathroom on the second floor also was still there. Even the bathtub still stood upon it. Some of the outside walls were still there too. But from the street level we could look up all the way through to the sky.

We first looked in our own cellar for food and found potatoes. One also checked the cellars of other abandoned houses and often found some preserves. Some things grew in gardens, either by themselves or they had been planted. And there were berries. In our garden we had gooseberries and currants and strawberries. That way we could survive for some time.

The Russians, like all occupation troops, wanted to live as comfortably as possible in the occupied territories. A house, a short distance from ours had taken some Russians' fancy. An old couple lived there. When Russians came and commanded them to leave, they refused. The Russians simply shot and killed them and moved into the house.

Now comes the story of the Bauers' horse-drawn wagon which Walter defended against everybody and everything. One night something real dangerous happened. The horses and wagon had caught the Russian soldiers' attention and they would have liked to have them. One night there was an attempt to break into aunt's garage, which Walter had changed into a horse barn.

It had an ordinary door out of sheet metal. Walter had apparently suspected that the Russians would come sooner or later. He had drawn a cord from the garage door through their bedroom window and had tied it around his arm so that he would feel immediately when somebody would open the garage door. He had been a sports teacher and was also skilled in fighting sports but against a group of Russian soldiers he would have had only a limited chance.

When one night he felt the pull on his arm, he leaned out of the window, it was of course, very dark, and he shouted and roared and yelled incredibly loud. He could also whistle so piercingly. The Russians must have had their guns with them but it was dark night and somebody roared and whistled like hell and they became scared and ran away. Walter went downstairs and kept roaring because he wanted to chase them far away, not only around the next corner.

Walter had chased the Russians away but they, and their superiors, now knew about the horses. And somehow they wanted and trusted a German carter and so they hired him, together with his wagon and the horses to transport things for them. Each morning he went to work and when he came back in the evening, he brought a container of food that would not only feed his own family but also our family. It was not enough to fill us up but it helped a lot. This food was Walter's salary. Were the Russians humane or was it just utilitarian thinking, like: This man shall live as long as we need him?

To get water was almost as difficult as getting food. The whole infrastructure had been destroyed. There was no water, no sewage, no electricity. We were lucky that not far from our subdivision there was an old abandoned farm with a well from where one could pump up water. Without this water we would not have been able to live. It was, of course, contaminated and had to be boiled. There were a lot of dead soldiers buried in shallow graves and other contaminants.

In August 1945 I became very ill with scarlet fever and paratyphoid fever. My mother was afraid I would die. She learned that there was still a German physician, a lady, living about ½ hour away from us. Mother went to her and this lady really did come to see me. She had to walk the whole distance, of course, which was somehow dangerous for a woman at the time. She examined me but had no medicine for my illnesses. She had, however, some medicine to strengthen my heart and this, probably, helped me to make it through and survive.

*After about four weeks I could get up but was still extremely weak
and could hardly walk. But soon I could help the others to glean
left-over grain shafts on the harvested fields.*

*I have to tell about my older brother. He was seven years
older than I, eight years older than my brother Manfred. We two
little ones admired our older brother and appreciated and enjoyed
it very much when he played with us once in while.*

*Now he had become a soldier and he had been wounded at
the beginning of February, soon after he had been put at the front.
We were in Bertholdsdorf when we received a postcard from a
hospital for wounded soldiers in Breslau. How this card had found
us and how the postal service was still working during these last
weeks of the war, I can not imagine. My brother had dictated to a
pastor or priest or monk that he had been shot in the head, which
was not necessarily fatal, but also that his lower body had been
torn to pieces. He sent us his love. He must have been very weak
but had managed to somehow sign his name. The pastor had
written underneath: "His life is in God's hands." This told my
mother that there was no hope anymore. The card was dated
February 11, the day my brother died. It was a miracle that this
card reached us at all and in Bertholdsdorf.*

Years later Klaus shared with me that he kept thinking that his
brother might have had to suffer horrible pain before his death. I asked
several German physicians who had served in the war and they all
assured me that morphine was freely given to wounded soldiers. This
made Klaus feel easier. It seems that at the time morphine was widely
used in the allied armies too. British soldiers apparently carried with them
syringes with morphine ready to inject.*) *) The book "Der rote Faden" by
Wolfgang Heintzeler

*A second miracle happened when we came back to Breslau
about the end of July 1945 and my mother immediately went to
this hospital where the postcard had come from. It was not
destroyed even though downtown was destroyed at 75%. And the
hospital was not empty, there was a gate-keeper sitting in the
porter's lodge. Mother talked to him and said that her son had died
in this hospital. He asked for the name and date of death, then
opened his large book. And he found my brother's name and the
date of death and could tell her that his body had been buried in a
row grave. He told my mother which grave it was and as what
number he was buried and he said to her: "My lady, just calculate
50cm (20 inches) for each soldier, then you will know exactly where
he is lying."*

This was like a miracle. Of course we went there and put flowers on his grave. I remember that well. In the meantime everything has surely been leveled and nobody knows anything anymore.

But these are points that give one a little hope for humanity. I am sometimes a little cynical and biting and I keep saying: The worst creatures that God has created are humans, the sum of people. What terrible things develop today at many places, this is monstrous, it is a wrong evolution. Animals don't do this. But because of these small miracles one must say, there are also light-points, points that give us hope. Such points were also on our flight route where there were people who could have fled but who told themselves: "No, I have been put on this post, I am needed here and I will just stay here." And this is why we could survive in this chaos of flight. There were support bases that helped us and surely saved many lives. Many people died who had not managed to reach such support bases but many others got helped.

We had not heard from my father but in September he suddenly appeared in Breslau. Right after the capitulation he had become a POW with the Americans in Weimar. In the turmoil of these first days he had managed to escape. I do not know where he was hiding and how he came to us, but if he had not escaped, he would have been transferred from the Americans to the Russians and would probably have ended up in Siberia. I do not know why it took him so long to get from Weimar to Breslau but he could, of course, only walk during the night and even then had to be very careful not to be caught by the Russians. They transported every man who looked able to work, to Russia. That happened to two playmates of ours. They were 5 or 6 years older than we (probably 15) and had often been the leaders of our group. One day they were loaded onto a Russian truck and never seen again. From a book I know how that was usually done. The Russians already had so-and-so many men working somewhere. Let's say, there were 100 in a certain group. If in the evening there were only 98, the Russian officer who was responsible for the group just grabbed two off the street to have the full number again. This probably had happened to our playmates.

Many Poles had come already with the Russians. It had been decided from the beginning that Breslau and everything around it would become part of Poland. Not that the Russians treated the Poles well. In rare instances they even favored Germans over Poles. Since Walter Bauer was now somehow an employee of the Russians, no Pole could touch his horses without fear of being killed by Russians.

The Russians also needed Germans in other ways. The city was destroyed to 75%, there were no utilities. The areas that were still fit to be lived in, needed to be supplied with water, electricity, gas. Only a few Germans who knew how the utilities worked and who were still there, could build up the infrastructure again, and the Russians needed and protected them.

My father had realized right away that we would not be able to survive the coming winter in town. We needed to be in the country where we could have food, if only the bare minimum. So we went back to Bertholdsdorf. Before father had returned, we had made the trip there a few times, walking the approximately 50 km (31 miles), to pick up some food. This was always dangerous because in the meantime, the area had become more and more Polish. We also met Russian soldiers on our way. Luckily, nothing really bad happened to us. Our greatest fear, that on the way back the food would be taken from us, was not realized.

Now we were back in Bertholdsdorf. Uncle's nursery had been taken over by Poles, therefore we had to find some rooms elsewhere. Luckily we found a small apartment in a private home. Upstairs lived several women refugees, and there something terrible happened. Some Russian soldiers had found out that women were living there and one night they brought a ladder and entered their rooms upstairs without coming through the front door and passing by our apartment. The women screamed and we opened our windows so that my father could crawl out to get help in the village. The German men of the village had actually some kind of emergency service. Everybody had a bell or something to sound and then German men came with cudgels. Sometimes this helped to chase away the Russians, sometimes it did not. But my father could not even get out because in front of each window there stood a Russian soldier with his Kalashnikov. Then he went up the stairs but another Russian soldier guarded the door and did not let him pass. And the women were, of course, being raped. First we heard their screams, then everything was quiet. We children did not really know what was happening. After the Russians had left, the women reproached my father terribly. How could a German officer allow that women were raped by Russian soldiers! But if he would have attacked the Russians, they would have simply killed him and the women would have been raped anyway. This was so horrible and I, as a child, experienced for the first time that women were treated badly.

Later we all were ordered by the Poles to work on the fields to bring in the harvest. Many of the farms were given into Polish hands, and we had to help to harvest potatoes and sugar beets. This made it possible to put aside some potatoes for ourselves and also some sugar beets. The Poles tolerated this. We positioned sacks at the side of the fields and put some potatoes and sugar beets in them. In the evening we took these sacks home. The Poles did not prevent it. This way we had enough potatoes to eat through the winter. The sugar beets were cooked, then mashed and the liquid cooked some more until a kind of syrup was produced. This process was interesting for us children. The potatoes and sugar beets were our only food. Maybe we got some grains too. It had been too late in the year to collect grains on the harvested fields; we must have gotten some from somewhere else. They were coarsely ground in a coffee mill and then we got some kind of grain soup. We children did not like it at all but we got used to it and sometimes we could add a little syrup to it. For Christmas my father went into the next town, taking with him a suit or some other piece of clothing, probably from Uncle. He himself had only the clothes on his back. There he bartered the suit for some salt, which we had not had before, and a piece of meat. This was our Christmas meal and the only occasion during all the time when we had meat.

Within the village lay a government estate that had now been taken over by the Russians. It should have been given to the Poles but the Russians had more power and they wanted it. Because we still had our German shepherd, Hella, she and my father were commanded to guard the livestock barn at this estate through the night. He might have received some little compensation. I don't know. Two or three times he took me along for the night which was for me as a city kid something new and interesting. There were pigs and cows and, of course, cats. One time Hella started barking up at a fuse box or something like it and did not stop. My father finally opened the small door to the box and tumbling out came a number of tiny naked mice, little pink mice. As they fell to the floor, Hella just gobbled them up. This shocked me, but that just was the way. In a moment they were all gone. The barn was for me also a zone of security. My father was so-to-speak an employee of the Russian occupation forces and as such he was protected.

This is how we spent the winter. We had enough wood and we had potatoes. We could take a handcart into the woods and some tools and then we felled firs and birches, cut them into pieces and carted them home in our wagon. At home they had to be sawed into logs and split for firewood. We children did not like the sawing very much but enjoyed the splitting. This way we had enough fuel to keep us warm.

One day during early spring my father and we two boys were walking outside the village. It was still rather cold and my father was wearing a thick winter coat. Suddenly two Poles attacked my father and wanted to take his coat away. He did not want to part with his coat and some scuffle resulted. A Russian officer had observed this and walked over. He did not even bother about the Poles but asked my father (I don't remember in which language): "What were you during the war?" My father answered: "First lieutenant". The Russian said: "Well, me also first lieutenant." Then they talked for a while. The Russian clapped my father on the shoulder, chased the Poles to the devil, and my father could keep his winter coat.

Sometime in March 1946 came the expulsion order. The whole German population was expelled. There would have been the possibility to stay and become Polish, but we had nothing to do with Poles and we did not know the Polish language. It was self-evident for us to leave. Then my father thought of some kind of trick that would make it possible for us, not to be expelled as Germans but as Romanians. That was a little more advantageous.

A note about Breslau becoming Polish. When Germany was divided up after the war, the new border to Poland was supposed to run along the two rivers Oder and Neiße. But there were two rivers named Neiße: the Lausitzer Neiße and the Glatzer Neiße. One flows into the Oder way north of Breslau, the other to the south. The Soviets chose the more northern Neiße over the objections of the western allies.*) *) At the Yalta Conference in February 1945 (even before the German capitulation) Great Britain and the United States wanted to make the Oder and the Lausitzer Neisse the border. This would have been kept Breslau in Germany. But the Soviets wanted the more northern Lausitzer Neiße that gave Poland a much larger area of Germany, including Breslau. At the Potsdam Conference in July/August 1945 it was the same. But by this time the Soviets had already installed a pro-Russian Polish government in the area. The western allies then permitted the Poles to deport all German inhabitants to Germany. The border was being debated until in December 1970 the German government acknowledged it. (Wikipedia)

So, now we were Romanians. How had this been possible? During the 13ᵗʰ century the king of Romania had called German settlers into his country. Our forefather, a count, had moved to Romania with all his subjects of his village. They had always kept their German culture and language. My grandfather had come to Germany to study at the universities of Leipzig and Jena. He must have been a very intelligent man. It is said that he knew ten languages. He spoke, of course German and Romanian, plus English and French. Together with Latin and Greek these are already six. He must also have spoken Russian because for a time he was headmaster of the German school in Moscow. Later he settled down in Breslau.

I never knew him because he died at age 70, seven years before I was born. My father was the thirteenth of thirteen children. Therefore my grandfather must have been already rather advanced in years when my father was born.

Now my father just claimed that we were Romanians. He also had some papers that had been saved through all the turmoil of the war. We pinned on small Romanian flags; this gave us some protection. Because of all this we were not expelled as Germans but as "undesirable foreigners". This meant that we could take one more suitcase with us and in the train our cattle car was only occupied by twenty to thirty people while the other wagons were overcrowded. But when the train started moving, everybody became very upset and scared because it did not move in a northwesterly direction but towards southeast. People wailed: "For God's sake, they are taking us to Siberia!" But our fear was groundless. The train stopped at Kattowitz at the border between Germany and Poland where we were taken to a large refugee camp to be de-loused. We had to take all our clothes off and they were put into a hot oven to kill the lice. Then our hair was shorn off. We all had lice *) *) It seems that the bodies of malnourished people are not well able to defend against parasites. *Then we traveled west in another freight train. The Germans were taken directly to Germany, we as foreigners were taken to Vienna. In the refugee camp there we reverted to being Germans. For about three weeks we all lived in a sports hall. It had been divided up by folding screens into family units. Each of us had a cot. Standing up one could see the neighbors' heads but there was still a minimum of privacy. We had food rations. It was not much but the people of Vienna didn't have much for themselves.*

These three weeks were not too bad for us children. We could walk around in the city and there was the Danube. And Vienna was not as destroyed as Breslau.

A refugee in the camp, a lady who was a teacher, offered to give the children some lessons.

It was not much; all different ages were together. But for us it was the first time in over a year that there was at least some kind of schooling. And the lady was nice.

After three weeks we were taken from Vienna to Germany, to Homburg vor der Rhön (near Frankfurt). There was a very large but simple refugee camp. I remember some wooden barracks. From there we were distributed to our final destinations. We had a choice between two cities.

My father chose the larger one, Bad Kissingen at the Franconian River Saale. There we were again put into a refugee camp but this was a large hotel that had been turned into a refugee camp. We were given a tiny room to ourselves. For the first time we had our own space. Everything else we could handle. Most important, we were together even though without the oldest brother.

About four months later we were transferred to another hotel that had also been converted to house refugees. It was a stately old hotel with a beautiful baroque façade. There we had two rooms next to each other just for our family. They were on the attic floor and had been servants' quarters, but for us they were great. Now we had one room where all four of us could sleep and one living room. Some time later we received a small iron stove. We guided the stove pipe through the skylight. Now my mother could cook for us. We also received beds, probably from the hotel stocks. They were only mattresses, framed with wood. But we put wooden blocks underneath to lift them above the floor. From somewhere we got a table and a chair and a few kitchen things. These were given to the refugees. That's how slowly our lives became civilized again. It was very modest, but for us it was wonderful. My father even found a small collapsible piano somewhere. I am certain that it did not have many octaves but we used it, especially around Christmas. Our life was on the way to normalcy.

To my great sorrow my father had insisted that I attend school in June (1946) immediate after we had arrived in Bad Kissingen. I felt it was not worth it because the school year ended in the middle of July anyway. I was not interested in school but my father said: "You will go to school. This is good for you and it has to be done anyway." So I entered 5th grade the grade I had attended last in Breslau. Since all the other children in Bad Kissingen had missed school also, even though they had not gone through the turmoil of evacuation, it was decreed that everybody had to stay in the same grade when the new school year would start in the fall. For good students there was the possibility to take a test and, if one passed it, to advance into the next grade. My father said to me: "Klaus, you are good. You will take the test. You can do this even though you have not been in school all this time." Mathematics was no problem for me, writing essays was easy for me too. Only in geography I encountered the question "What do you know about the forest of Thüringen?" I did not know anything. But I was so self confident and bold that I wrote: "At the time the Forest of Thüringen would have been taught, there was, unfortunately, no school for me and therefore I can not write anything about it." This did not hurt me, maybe even helped me that I was honest. I was advanced and could enter 6th grade in the fall of 1946.

This way I could finish high school and take the college entrance exam in 1953*) *) In Germany schooling lasts 13 years. I have to thank my father for this. Later this let me finish my studies at the University one year earlier. At 24 ½ years old I graduated with a masters degree and became an accredited engineer.

In Kissingen my father had no work at first. It just was not possible. We lived off welfare as all the other refugees did. It was not much. We were, of course, in a worse position than the locals, first because in many cases there was a father who could work, and second because they had resources that we did not have. But that was just the way it was. If one needed something special, for example shoes, one could apply for a coupon. We boys were still growing and we needed new, larger shoes once a year. My mother would buy lace-up boots for us. They had to last for one year and they did.*) *)At the time shoes had leather soles that could be "walked through" rather quickly. Longer lasting plastic soles came much later. I had two shirts. One I wore while the other was in the wash. Life was very simple but it was possible. Since most of the others had to live like we did, it was not too bad. I feel that poverty is only bad if one is the only poor one or belongs to the few poor people while all the others around are wealthy.

Once I was a little sad when my class went on a trip into the Bavarian mountains. I could not go with them because it cost a few marks which we did not have. It was not expensive but we did not have this money at all. Unfortunately, at that time people did not say "we will all chip in". I had to stay home and this hurt a little. Otherwise all went well. When one is young and has a bit of courage, one can carry a lot. We had learned that and I have also realized it later in life. I was more mature than my classmates because I had experienced so much, gone through bad and difficult situations where one just has to collect all one's strength and had to get through and not give up, otherwise one would have fallen by the wayside.

We children did not feel that we were not accepted because we were refugees. Of course there were difficulties from time to time but this is understandable. During the transport from Vienna to Homburg our train had stopped in Schweinfurt. We were all in freight cars. I don't remember if we had to change trains or if only the doors of the wagons were opened. But there was a station conductor standing on the platform yelling at us: "You dirty Prussians!*) Go back where you came from!" *) Bavarians have always detested Prussians for no specific reason. He must have been a low clerk but he was an official railway employee wearing a railway uniform.

This was our welcome to Schweinfurt. But this occurrence was one of the very rare bad things. Maybe there was a train like ours each day and he said what many of us think when now-a-days too many asylum seekers are coming to us. We might think: Is this really necessary? And: how can we manage this?

There were difficulties when a local wanted to marry a refugee. Then the parents asked: "what do you want with this have-not?" Naturally, the locals also had had losses because of the war but they had not lost everything. In Breslau we had been rather well off and now we had nothing. One felt that sometimes. Among classmates there were no barriers. One made friends with the ones who had common interests.

At first we lived on welfare, then my father was employed for some time to manage Jewish properties. Since he had worked in business administration, he was well qualified. And he had not been a member of the NSDAP. He was given several projects to work on. It had been determined that a hotel, houses, other possessions had been taken from Jews and he had to talk to people, had to make sure that these possessions were taken care of. For this work he even was given a jeep because some of the objects were outside the area of Bad Kissingen. I even rode with him a few times. He received a small salary but this job lasted only about a year. After this we were again dependent on welfare. In 1951 my father could start working in Düsseldorf at the same insurance company for which he had worked in Breslau. Now we were a little better off. He could send us money. Of course it was not very much because he had to rent a room in Düsseldorf.

My father had in his youth been boxing with his friend Walter Bauer, the sports teacher. Now he told us boys: "You have to do this too." He founded a boxing club, probably already 1947 or 48. Something like this was being supported by the American occupation forces. He negotiated with the Americans and they gave us material to build a boxing ring. My brother and I learned to box there and we even performed publicly. There were boxing competitions with other boxing clubs. People in the audience kept saying that the nicest fights were when the "little ones" performed, that were my brother and I. We were called "paperweights"*). We were 14, 15 years old. When we were boxing, it looked rather elegant, in contrast to the heavy weight boxers who tramped around and hit hard. I could never have boxed another one k.o. I never could do that. *) paperweight in a sense that the boys were so light weight; "feather weight in English.

*When I went away to Stuttgart to study at the university, I
had about 20 marks in my pocket and I had no idea how I would go
on. But I received a scholarship; I did not have to pay tuition and
probably even got a small allowance. From the beginning I worked
at the postal center office in the evenings sorting mail and earned
there a little money. Of course, everything was a little difficult but I
made it.*

Yes, Klaus made it wonderfully well. He became an engineer
and got a good job. He found and married an especially nice and capable
lady and they raised four beautiful children.

Not only happened so much to him during these terrible times,
but Klaus also had to actively find ways and overcome problems to stay
alive. These experiences and memories have stayed with him of course.
Scars are built into one's person but it can and will one's strength only
larger.

We had met Klaus and his wife a long time ago through music,
especially singing. Later we became fast friends with all his family.
When I remember Klaus, I see him charming and cheerful. He was
always ready to help whoever needed it. Klaus always took a positive
attitude and was grateful for his life given him.

Rolf's Recollections (born 1934)

I like to round out the stories to the recollections of WWII. The time before and after the war was horrible, but since I was only five years old when the war started, and our parents were careful not to discuss politics in front of us, I have no recollection of this event. So here are a few highlights (or better said, "low-lights",) of what came later.

The house across the street

When I was a young child, my mother forced me to take a nap after Lunch (probably because she wanted to take one too). For this, the shutters in my bedroom were lowered and I had to go to bed, which was very boring. However, these shutters must have had small holes so that a little light came into my bedroom. Mainly on sunny days, I could see on the opposite wall of the shutter-clad windows, an image of the house which stood across the street. This house had interesting ornamentations on the roof that were typical for the 19th century. I could clearly recognize them. Interestingly enough for a four or five year old child, I noticed that the house stood upside-down on my bedroom wall. Since the image was particularly strong on sunny days, I concluded that this effect had something to do with light. However, I could not explain the upside-down image. Moreover, our house stood on a sloping road and I could hear from the pattern of slow or fast footsteps that the pedestrians, passing our house, were walking up the hill or down the hill. I observed that the images of the pedestrians were moving in the opposite direction than they were walking. Finally, I saw that the images of the pedestrians were not points, but lines, that started all from a "focal point". All was a mystery to me.

These observations were the beginning of my interest in optics. Unfortunately, one day, after the first bombs had fallen onto Stuttgart, this house across the street was directly hit and destroyed. This was the end of my optical studies (at least for the next 5 years).

The bombing war reached us

When the air raid sirens sounded, we had to rush as quickly as possible into our cellar where bunk beds with straw mattresses were installed. At first, we heard the roaring of the planes. Then came a whistle, followed by a bang. (Where did that whistle come from?) This bomb did not hit us. We all trembled. We prayed. Were we angry with the allied bombers? Did we hate them?

No. Definitely not. Not even today. I considered the bombing as a fortitude of life, something that one has to endure, similar, as it is the case when one vomits. It passes. After seemingly all bombs had been dropped, we went out of the (very demolished house) and saw the devastation and the fires around us. My father saw after one of the bombing raids an American soldier on his parachute drifting down between the houses. He was apparently in deep shock. My father grabbed him and pushed him into an air raid bunker, telling him in his very bad English that there would be no danger for him. Then the neighbors started to dig out the surviving people who were buried in their cellars. Many lives were saved this way.

After one of the air attacks, my mother and I walked to the railroad station in Stuttgart through the burning city. No public transportation was of course operating. After half an hour, we reached the station, where we were told that the train had already left prematurely, before the air raid would have destroyed the station. We had to walk back home through the firestorm. I still see today in my mind this chaos and burning inferno. Nowadays, people go to a doctor for treatment of post- traumatic stress disorder. We did not have this opportunity. We children had to endure this trauma. What influence did this have on our later life? I venture to say: It made us stronger and kinder in contrast to later generations of children who did not have to suffer through this trauma as we did.

Opa Gaildorf

The bombing of Stuttgart became more intense. The attacks occurred day and night. Thus, all children were "evacuated" to the countryside. My grandfather (Opa) who was a retired pastor lived in Gaildorf, a little town about 50 miles from Stuttgart. My father asked him if he would allow me to come to him (and his housekeeper who never had children by her own). He welcomed me warmly despite his 81 years of age. During the day, he worked on a book entitled "Religion and Science". Sometimes, in the late afternoon he played a round of backgammon with me, whereas he stressed that I had to play fair and not to play to win. Each night before sleep, he came to my bed, told me a story from his long life, and prayed with me. His life was for me a role model to be a good human being and Christian. These were the formative years in my life.

Since it was boring for me to live with an old man, (I have little recollection to school or scouting), I befriended a farmer's family who had a boy of my age. There I became familiar with farm life and was sent with other children to keep watch over the cows.

138

Over the years, both my brothers and my mother also came for a short while to Gaildorf. Eventually, however, my father took us all back to Stuttgart because he wanted the family to be together during the end phase of the war.

Optics an Acoustics

Let us look at the following event from a learning point of view that had a positive outcome (at least for me but not for our property). On our drive back from Gaildorf to Stuttgart in a small pick-up truck, we were suddenly attacked by two or three fighter aircrafts. My father commanded to the family: "Out of the car, lay down on the meadow, face down"!! And here they came. I wanted to observe what was going on. I could see the pilots. I noticed that they aimed at the truck. Moreover, what I also noticed was that the flash from the guns came always somewhat ahead of the bang of the shot. Aha, I said to myself: Apparently, the speed of light is larger than the speed of sound. I learned this phenomenon much later at school but I observed it myself a lot earlier. I did not confess my observation to my father, at least not at that time. Are you surprised that I became a physicist?

The Handyman

After the war was over, most of the houses were destroyed and others were heavily damaged, but still partially inhabitable. Everybody tried to recover items that could be fixed. However, handymen were rare to come by for repairs. Whenever possible, I watched them during their work. They were my best teachers. There were, of course, no spare parts available. Thus, one had to improvise by "repurposing" parts from other devices or make new ones from scrap. Soon, I became quite good in this trade. In particular, our washing machine needed constant attention. Or, the strings of the window shutters tended to rip off from their rollers. Radios did not work anymore. Windows and doors needed adjustments and the inserting of new pieces. Plumbing and electrical failures were my specialties. I learned from a plumber how to solder. Before repairing them I firstly found out how they were supposed to work. Since most house devices utilized gas stoves for cooking and matches were hard to come by, I invented a primitive electric "spark generator" which I sold to relatives and friends. Eventually, I became so good (being only 14 years of age) that I was asked by neighbors to perform repair work for them too. It was a common phrase by my mother: "I send you Rolf". This habit of repairing broken items rather than replacing them still follows me today. No wonder that my first car (a VW bus camper) is already 56 years old and still running.

The UF country club

The next story is very short. When I was already a professor at UF, I was invited to the "University of Florida Golf and Country Club". Since I do not play Golf nor do I have much interest in club life (which is a mistake as I recognized later). I virtually did not know anybody at that party. What do you do in such a case? You ask the next best person in which department he or she is a member of. And then, an interesting conversation may begin during which one can learn something from your vis-a-vis. After a few conversations with interesting professors, I approached the next person with my usual question. Well, he said, "I am not a professor but I flew 26 successful bombing raids over Germany." This prompted me to a swift response: "and I was on the receiving end of your bombing missions". Naturally, this response ended our chat relatively quickly (not necessarily from my side). But I must truthfully confess that during my 57 years at UF as a professor, I never experienced any verbal attacks because of my nationality (just the opposite!). There was no discrimination. The same is also true for professors or students of color. We are all human beings.

Food

During and until the end of the war, we virtually did not experience serious shortages of foodstuffs. Naturally, we had ration cards, but everything seemed to be well organized, at least, at the place where we were living. This changed after the allied occupation. I do not know how my parents served a meal each day to a family of five plus a house helper. It must have been difficult. We grew vegetables in our backyard (basically my job), we raised rabbits (my job) and my mother occasionally went to Daniel Mandelbaum who ran a thriving black-market business, where everything was ten times more expensive (if one had the money and he had the merchandise). My father went out to farmers and traded silver items and other valuables for food (a process which was called bartering), and we youngsters went into the forest to collect beech tree seeds (for cooking oil) and acorns for stretching the little flour which one could buy with the ration cards we had. Occasionally we received gift parcels from a former nurse of my mother who lived in America and whom my father had helped out before the war with money in her difficult times. My mother's sister who lived in Sweden also sent us food parcels. Each time such a parcel arrived, the content was displayed on a small table, similar as on birthdays, and admired for days before consumption. Moreover, most children received at school a warm meal prepared from American field rations, (called "Hoover Feeding," named after a former American president).

If one looks at photographs of that time one immediately notices that nobody was suffering from obesity. Quite the contrary. Nevertheless, we survived.

Everything changed in 1948, after the "Währungsreform" (currency reform), when suddenly the value of the money was worth only one-tenth of that the day before. Everybody could exchange only 400 old Marks for 40 new DM (Deutsch-Marks). From then on Germany's economy prospered rapidly in the western zones ("economic miracle") but not in the Russian occupied zone where socialism was supposed to be practiced.

Schooling

There was not much schooling during and right after the war. At the beginning of the war, the young teachers were drafted to serve as soldiers and many perished. Towards the end of the war, we spent more time in bomb shelters than in classrooms. Then, of course, after the war, there were only a few school buildings spared from destruction or they were repurposed as hospitals. Thus, my mother conducted in our slightly damaged living room a small private school for the children of our neighbors and her own kids. This was fun. After the regular schools finally opened again, my mother was immediately asked to teach in a high school. There were not enough teachers available who were allowed to teach until their political "cleanliness" was established (de-nazification).

These old teachers were now teaching the pupils. Most of these teachers had been marked by personal Nazi government's injustices, and also the war horrors. Therefore the children were now on the receiving end of mean, sadistic and yelling (also with expletives) teachers.

I was suffering severely from them and their ugly behavior. Their marks on me were more severe than those I suffered by the bombing war. In particular, the math teacher in my 11th grade insulted me constantly and one day exploded when I answered him that I intended to become a teacher in adult life. If this is so, he responded, then continue the lecture for me, which I dared to do. His face became red in anger and he hurled insults on me. This was the end of my public school career. I declared to my parents that I never wanted to go to school again and instead wanted to become a carpenter. My mother was alarmed. She pulled some strings, together with my aunt from Sweden. As a consequence I was allowed to join a week later a wonderful private school (Waldorf School) which was a blessing in disguise.

Nothing better could have happen to me. It was a turning point in my life because the teachers were encouraging and fostered my talents particularly in physics and natural sciences. My physics teacher even sent me his own child for private tutoring.

I admired my teachers at the Waldorf School greatly, and to mention as a side remark, I found there my soul mate who I married after finishing University studies. This shows that some good can come out of bad. Later on, I paid my positive experiences back to my students at the University of Florida who overwhelmed me with enthusiastic teacher evaluations and initiated that I eventually received 14 local and regional "Best Teacher Awards" during my career.

Gudrun's and Manfred's Separate Journeys

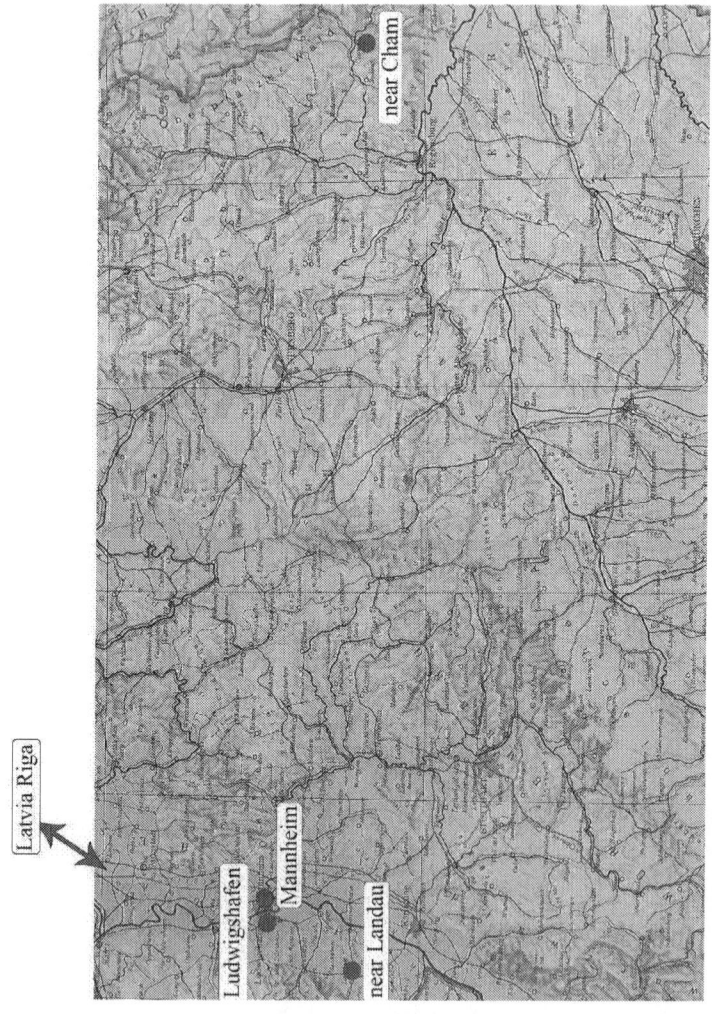

Gudrun's and Manfred's Separate Journeys
(born 1916 and 1911)

I had known Manfred and Gudrun, and even their parents, all my life. Manfred had a motorcycle. When I was still little, he took me in his sidecar on small trips. Later I sat behind him and learned to lean in the right direction when going through curves. I felt very proud of myself and of being taken seriously by him.

Manfred was tall and slim and easygoing and disciplined. I adored him as most children did, including years later my own children, and, interestingly all dogs liked him and minded him.

Manfred was born in 1911, two years before WWI started and his father had to become a soldier. He had wanted to become a teacher but when the time to start his education there was no money. Instead of this he entered a bakery and worked as his apprentice. Manfred became not only a baker but also a great pastry cook. I remember the family's magnificent und delicious cakes. But after his three years of apprentice there was no employment. This was when the German economy was down, unemployment was rampant. He took what small jobs he could and went home to his parents when nothing else was available.

In the summer of 1931 the German government started the program of the "Freier Arbreitsdienst" (Free Labor Service). Young, unemployed men where housed in barracks or camps, were fed and worked on civic and land improvement projects. They drained swamps and built or improved roads. Many years later I was still shown the stream that flowed through my grandparents' village. Manfred's service group had straightened the winding and swampy stream at places. They had also been reinforced the embankments, even built steps into it so that the people having their gardens right there could walk down these steps and fill their watering cans.

For Manfred the Arbeitsdienst was a great opportunity. Even though he was a skilled baker (his cakes were the best I have ever tasted!), he had always dreamed of becoming a teacher, especially a teacher of practical skills which he had in abundance. In the Arbeitsdienst his talents and abilities were soon recognized. After a short training in building barracks, he was given the task to oversee the work in different areas.

In the meantime (1933) Hitler had come to power. The new government had taken over the Arbeitsdienst and in 1934 made it into the "Reichs-Arbeitsdienst". The young men were given uniforms, a spade and a bicycle*) *) which was necessary to get from their barracks to the, changing, projects. When they marched, they carried their spades over the shoulder like soldiers carried their rifles. When Manfred was about 80 years old he still showed my children how to "present arms" – with a spade.

Soon the Reichsarbeitsdienst was made mandatory, all young men had to serve for one year. Manfred had been promoted several times. He was liked and respected by his "students". He once told me: "*These farmer boys, they are as strong as oxen*) but they are stiff and awkward. At first I do exercises with them to loosen their muscles and they love this.*"   *) at the time most farm work was heavy manual work; even holding a plow steady while plowing a field required great strength.

When the war started, the Arbeitsdienst was appointed as to follow the troops to supply them with food and ammunition, to repair roads and bridges, then as auxiliaries to anti-aircraft units. Manfred was deployed to Riga in Latvia which was at first, far away from the front. He could even have Gudrun, his wife, and their new young daughter, Jutta, with him.

Here I want to leave Manfred and Gudrun in Latvia for a while and tell about Gudrun's interesting background. She was born in 1916 on a good-size farm near the French border. I knew her parents well. Her mother would always feed me with good and tasty food, and lots of it. While during and especially after the war food was so very scarce. Much later I learned Gudrun's parents' story and I think that this story is an interesting portrayal of those times:

Amalia, Gudrun's mother had been born around 1885. Amalia had fallen in love with Eduard, a young man with no fortune because he was a second son and his older brother had inherited their parents' estate. To make the situation even worse, Eduard was protestant while Amelia was catholic. Both sets of parents were against the marriage; but the young couple married secretly. At the time Algeria, then a French colony, seemed to present opportunities for people, adventurous and brave enough to make a life, and maybe a fortune, in that country. Eduard and a friend went to Algeria. Amalia was supposed to join her young husband later, after Eduard has established himself there, during she stayed with her parents.

But the parents pressed her more and more to put the marriage aside, which had not been acknowledged by the Catholic Church anyway because the groom was protestant. Amalia finally gave in and the marriage was dissolved. But suddenly Eduard was back. He had decided that Algeria was not where he wanted to live with his wife but he had acquired enough money to start his own farm. He was shocked to find his beloved was not married to him anymore. The two asked her parents if they could go for a walk through the fields one last time and got permission. And there they hatched a perfect plan. When they returned, Amalia "confessed" that Eduard had threatened to kill her with his rifle if she did not marry him again. The parents believed the trick and the couple happily married again.

In time four daughters were born. It had been agreed that any daughters should be brought up catholic, any sons should be protestant. But when Amalia approached the village priest to arrange the first daughter's baptism, she was told that the Catholic Church did not recognize her marriage and therefore the baby could not be baptized catholic, so she was baptized protestant. The same happened with the second and third daughter. But when the fourth daughter was born, the priest apparently thought that more and more future Catholics were being lost to his church. He went to Amalia and offered to now baptize all four girls in his church. But Amalia did not forgive the priest's former attitude and sent him away.

Gudrun grew up to be a very pretty and attractive and courageous young woman. Manfred and Gudrun met, fell in love and married. Gudrun and their very young daughter Jutta followed her husband to Latvia when he was stationed there.

As the Soviet front came closer and the German troops had to retreat, the military and the Arbeitsdienst families were evacuated. Gudrun remembers:

We made it out of there with the very last civilian train. I had two suitcases and I had 4-years old Jutta. To keep her safe and near me, I tied a string from her wrist to mine. From time to time the train would stop because enemy planes were flying overhead. Each time we had to get out quickly and hide as not to be shot. But we made it to Berlin and then to Ludwigshafen/Rhein. As I was standing there with Jutta and my two suitcases, a man approached me and said I should go with him just around the corner. I said no, and what did he want. He showed me a piece of a ham and told me he would give it to me if I would go with him. And he wanted something as payment.

I said no, and that I did not need his ham; and he said: "you are pretty, you go with me." But I chased him away. This happened to me twice and they were Germans.

Home was only a small distance to the border with France. Now Gudrun and Jutta were home again from Latvia. But the western front came closer and closer, and there were many air raids and shootings by low flying planes. Manfred and his unit had in the meantime been moved to near Cham in Bavaria, and he thought, that his wife and daughter would be safer there. Gudrun remembered:

My mother went with us to the railway station and she cried so hard. She kept saying: "Oh please, stay here!" and then "No, go where you are safe!"

When we arrived in the town near the Arbeitsdienst camp, Manfred first went with us to the office of the mayor to ask for lodgings there. But the mayor looked at us and said: "They will stay at our house." He and his wife did not have children and they liked Jutta right away – and later he and his wife spoiled her as much as they could.

As more and more German soldiers died at the fronts, the Arbeitsdienst was added to the military, especially the infantry. Manfred was taken to the eastern front. Gudrun and Jutta stayed in Bavaria. At this point it seemed not to matter where one would experience the end of the war, as long as it was not with the Russians. Gudrun recalls:

The mayor was, naturally, a member of the NSDAP. He had to be. But he was a very nice and kind man and had never hurt anybody. But when the Americans came, they wanted to shoot him. His wife said: "I will go with him. If you shoot him, you have to shoot me too." Somehow then they and we and the neighbors were ordered to stay in the hay barn and lay down on the floor. We had to lie there for about five days. It was dark in the barn and we had to lie very still. Jutta lied between me and the mayor's wife. When one had to go to the toilet, one had to go to a corner. They did not let us out. The Americans came from time to time and they walked over us, just across us. There were also guards outside.

But many Polish POWs or displaced workers had been held in the town during the war and had had to work there. They went to the Americans and said that the mayor had always treated them well and they should not shoot him. And the Poles also sneaked into the barn from time to time and brought us milk and some food.

Nobody knew where Manfred was and if he was even still alive. In early summer Gudrun decided to go home to her mother. Their hosts wanted to keep her and Jutta there longer but Gudrun wanted to go home. She still had one of Manfred's suits and she exchanged it for a bicycle and even managed to get a child seat for Jutta that could be affixed to the handlebars. On the back carrier she had tied their clothes and the food that their hosts had given them: ham and bread-crackers and other foodstuff. It took Gudrun and Jutta 13 days to cover the distance of at least 500 miles. Gudrun remembers:

We could only move on paths across the fields. Germans were not allowed on main roads at the time. I kept asking my way but it was mostly straight west. At 6pm no Germans were allowed to be outside anymore.

Each day around noon I started looking for a farmhouse where I could stop. I would knock and ask if I could get a bit of soup for my child. And then they gave me some food too. I always helped on the fields or where they just needed help. And then they let us sleep in the barn. Some farmers even gave us a few slices of bread to take along when we left the next morning. Jutta always said: "Mama, you have to eat that you have enough strength to pedal."

In the Bavarian town where we had come from, Jutta had often played with some neighbor girls. They had lice and Jutta had gotten lice from them. When I needed a short break during the morning, we would sit in a ditch and I would comb Jutta's hair and kill as many lice as I could. In Mannheim we had to cross the river Rhein to get from the American occupation zone to Ludwigshafen into the French zone. I had been told that the Americans would put all people into quarantine who had lice or fleas. If the other people were alright, everybody had to strip and be sprayed with DDT. I put an undershirt on Jutta that was actually too tight and very hard to get on and off. When we got to the bridge, I made to try to pull the undershirt over Jutta's head. This made her cry and the soldier said to leave it. I pulled the shirt up a bit but folded it over her head to hide the lice, and we made it through. From there it was only two days' ride home.

Amalia, Gudrun's mother was, naturally, overjoyed to have them home again. But she had always known that her daughter and granddaughter would come home safely. In the next village lived an old gipsy woman who was visited by many people for her gift to know the future. She had foretold that Gudrun and Jutta would be alright.

However, several years before she had also foretold that out of the five men of the family, one would die during the war.

Since the husbands of the four sisters were now soldiers, it was believed that one of them would be killed. But it happened the old man, Gudrun's father, Eduard, was the one.

It was the custom to store some of the feed for the winter, turnips, all kinds of roots and beets, on the fields. A shallow pit was dug and lined with straw, the produce put in and covered with more straw. On top of this earth was poured. For extra insulation in an extra cold winter one spread over this a layer of manure, or rather straw from the barn that had some manure in it. On Christmas day – it must have been 1943 or 1944 – the weather suddenly turned bitter cold and Gudrun's father knew that a certain stack had not gotten its final cover, the feed inside would freeze and could then not be used for the people and animals. The wagon was loaded and the oxen harnessed ready to take it to the field.

At the house lived a French POW and worked on the farm. Eduard, Gudrun's father, asked the Frenchman to drive to the field but he refused. So Eduard himself drove the wagon to the field. Sometime later some shots were heard but this was nothing unusual. The American and British low flying fighter planes shot at everything. But then the oxen came home alone, still pulling the wagon. Eduard was found lying on the field, shot to death.

At the end of the war, Manfred was captured by the Russians and – almost – put on a transport to, probably, Siberia. When he later told his story, he used to say: *"I did not quite favor this marching direction, so I chose my own."* Meaning: he escaped. But later he was caught by the Russians again. Only now these Russians had just taken over a laboratory where serum was produced for tetanus vaccinations from horses. The Russians did not know how to proceed but some of the captured Germans did know (or found out from the – German – instructions). Manfred was one of the caretakers of the horses. He loved horses but the men were given almost no food and as they got close to starving, they decided to eat one of the horses. Some of them went to their Russian boss to report that one of the horses had taken ill and should be put down. The Russian, having no knowledge of horses, gave the order to kill the "sick" horse and the men were saved from starvation. But they started thinking of escape anyway. Manfred and one of his comrades were the first to go.

The serum institute was located right at the river Elbe. The pastures for the horses went right down to the water. Manfred tells the story of his flight:

We were at the serum institute in Roßlau. This is on the east side of the river Elbe which was occupied by the Russians. The area across the river was at the time under American rule. And that's where we wanted to go. There was a bridge not too far away. If we would have had some schnapp s (hard liquor) to bribe the Russian guards, we could have used the bridge; but we had none. Therefore we had decided to try to swim across.

The Elbe is a very large and very wide river but they were hoping to make it despite being malnourished and rather unfit as they were.

We had found watertight containers for carrying our clothes across and one dark night we were ready. Along the bank there were jetties to break the speed of the river on one side and keep the other side open for ships. We had taken off our clothes and put them into our containers but as we walked around to find the best spot to start, we noticed a small rowboat, tied loosely to a bush. We put our things and ourselves in it and rowed across. We were lucky that there was mist over the water. However, as we were almost across we heard: "stoio, stoio!" The Russian guards had seen us. We let the boat hit the bank, threw ourselves out and crawled up the embankment. The American guards had heard this too and they came to look what was going on. But they did not come on foot, they drove along the river road in their jeep and let their searchlights play around. They did not see us.

When we had decided to flee, we had told some trusting Germans who worked close by. They had given us addresses from friends at the nearest village of the American occupation zone, away from the river. Now we started to walk toward the village. These people took us in and fed us. Then we walked to the nearest railway station. But no regular trains were running yet, only freight trains. My comrade and I separated there because his home was in the very north while I needed to go southwest. An engineer at a freight train allowed me to lie on the coals on the tender of his locomotive. When I got off, I was black all over. At another station I asked where the freight trains were going. I found one that was going to Cham and it was my direction. I got into one wagon that had loaded lime. After I got off, I was white from the lime powder. From Cham in Bavaria I walked to where I thought Gudrun and Jutta were still living. (about 50 miles)

When I got to the place the people looked at me strangely. Of course, I was black and white in my face and all over. My clothes were rags.

I first thought that they did not want to recognize me because before I had been an officer and now I was a poor former POW. But as I started speaking they called out: "Oh, you are Manfred!" They fed me and prepared a bath for me so that I felt halfway decent again. The next morning I wanted to leave again because Gudrun and Jutta were not there anymore. But they would not let me go because I looked so thin and starved.

When I went to visit an old friend the next morning, the village baker, I learned that he had been arrested the day before because of an insignificant social job at the NSDAP he had held. His wife was desperate, not just for his safety but also because now there was no baker in the village. But I could help out and I told her that now I would be the village baker for a time. Everything was very primitive. There was only rye flour for bread and very little salt. But at least the people got some bread.

At a farm in the village three German soldiers had found shelter. They were high officers and they worked hard at the farm and on the fields but the farmer treated them with utter contempt, saying: "You were officers. You have not done any work all your life. Now I'll make you work." And he gave them not enough food.

In the village a French transport unit was stationed, even though the whole area was in the American occupation zone. I had met some of the French soldiers because they baked their own bread at the bakery, using, of course, their own wheat flour and other ingredients. Somehow I also got to meet the commander of the French transport unit. And then he invited the three German officers and me. As we were talking he started telling stories from the time he had been in North-Africa, in Algeria, as a young sergeant. As he mentioned the town of Sukara, my brain started working, and I said: "Sukara? This is where my father-in-law spent some time as a young man." He asked for the name and when I said Eduard G., he called out: "Oh, Monsieur G.! Of course, I knew him!" It turned out that at the club there not only French officers got together but also civilians, German and French, the people who lived there.

After this, he tried to help me where he could. The transport unit had to bring French soldiers to France for their furlough and bring back those who had to get back to their unit. And it happened that their route ran very close to the village near Landau where Gudrun and Jutta and the whole family clan were living. I was taken along with their next transport, and I was treated with the utmost care and respect.

152

We arrived at 11 pm at the house and Gudrun first thought the French were coming to arrest her (for some unknown reason). But then I called out to her and everything was alright.

Now Manfred was home but he had, of course, no job. At first there was a lot to do on the farm. So much had been neglected. Manfred learned what he needed from other farmers and soon had everything back to where it should be. But he could never feel quite safe. When men were needed to work as lumberjacks in the woods, he went there. He stayed away through the week and only spent some Sundays at home.

After a year or so, it was decreed that members of the Arbeitsdienst could apply for positions as state employees. Manfred entered the postal service and soon rose to become a supervisor to the whole district. And he loved his job.

Manfred also loved the mountains, hiking and all kinds of sports. Skiing was his favorite and he won so many competitions that Gudrun and then later Jutta, did not know where to keep all the trophies. True, some competitions he won because he was the only competitor in his age class. Not many men close to 80 are able and willing to glide down a mountain with skill and elegance.

Manfred died when he was 97 years old. I do not know what experiences and feelings he kept hidden among his memories. I know that all through his life he had managed to get something good out of unfortunate circumstances. He could see the positive everywhere. He was always kind and caring. One thing he kept insisting: "Never waste any food, being the smallest morsel."

Gudrun was an unordinary good cook. She and I had regular telephone conversations over the ocean. Her first question was always what I did plan to cook. She was even interested in my – simples – recipes. Gudrun always helped people when she could and she was always gracious. She lived until her age of 100.

Manfred and Gudrun, were always positive despite many harsh difficulties. Throughout their lives they were full of energy and being exciting about new things to learn.

Leonore and her Children's flight out of East Prussia

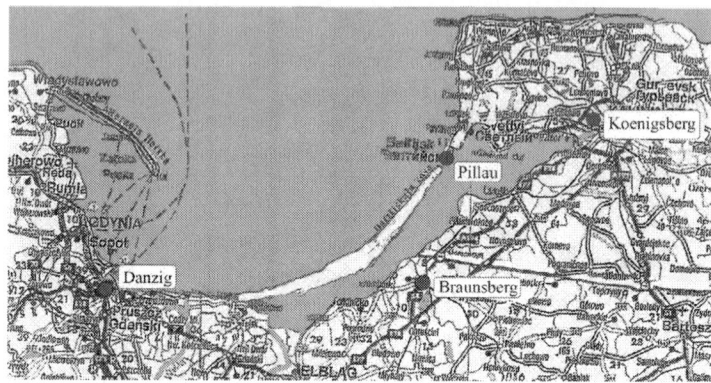

Flight with Children out of East Prussia / Leonore and her Children After the War

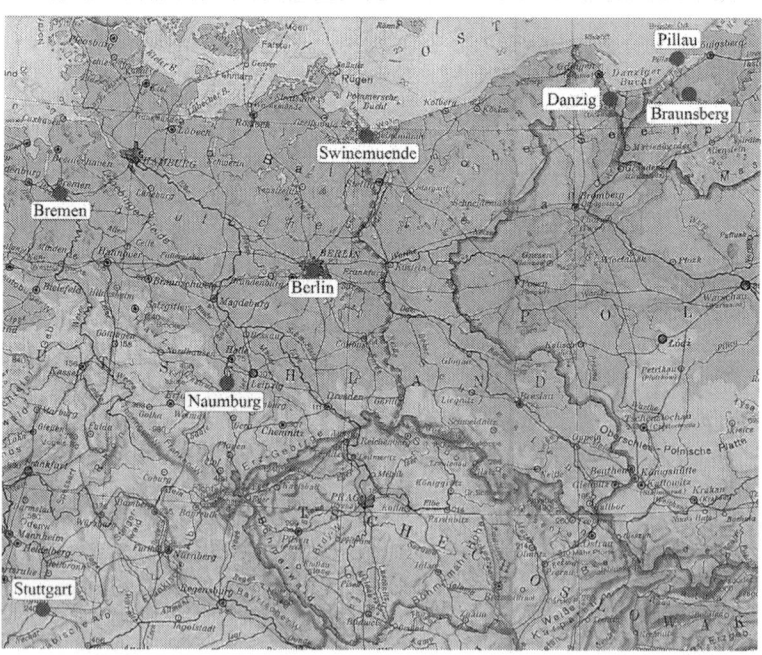

Leonore and her Children's Flight out of East Prussia (probably born 1913)

The province of East Prussia is far in the Northeast the main German but it has been an important part of the German Reich for generations. Prussians had settled there starting about several thousand years ago; Viking artifacts have also been found. During the past several centuries a mostly German population lived together with a Polish minority. Königsberg, (now Kaliningrad) the capital of East Prussia was for a long time the second capital of the whole German Reich, next to Berlin. The famous philosopher Immanuel Kant (1724 – 1804) was born and lived in Königsberg. The university there had been named after him. After WW II all Germans were expelled; the area given partly to Poland, partly to Russia. A few years ago the Russians have again named it "Kant University" and are they even considered giving the whole city back its German name.

Leonore and her three small children lived with about 40 miles southwest of Königsberg and about 10 miles south of the coast (or rather the Haff).*) Toward the end of the war, at the end of January 1945 the Soviet army had advanced close to her hometown of Braunsberg (now Braniewo) and they had to flee. *) The coastline to the Baltic Sea in this area is not open but a "lagoon" about 60 miles long and almost 10 miles wide which is contained by a fifty miles long and very narrow offshore premonitory. Almost at the northeastern end of the premonitory a narrow waterway connects the Haff with the open sea. There on the tip lays the town of Pillau (Baltiysk) with its harbor. To this town and harbor Leonore and her children had to return, from it they were setting out several times.

Clawing one's way through eminently dangerous situations, trying to make the right decisions, coming out alive, is hard enough when one is responsible only for oneself. Having young children to bring through hell, is so much harder in every way.

Leonore and her three young children survived the flight from East Prussia into (Eastern) Germany. About a year later she described their ordeal in a letter to a close friend. This friend had saved the letter and allowed me to use Leonore's story of her experiences here. Leonore wrote:

Easter Sunday 1946 in Naumburg
By the end of January, it was a Monday or Tuesday, I was finally ready to separate myself from our possessions. Before that I had been packing like crazy, thinking it all could be sent to me later.

Now I accepted the inevitable and went to the railway station in order to organize our flight west. I even bought tickets, which a little later one didn't even have to do any more. I am only telling you this to show you how, in my bird brain, I imagined that everything was still working normally like it had been the day before. You may imagine my shock when everything was totally different.

The next evening, with my three children I was standing on the icy cold, drafty platform the whole night, starting at 6pm. The children whimpered. Finally at 4 am we were shoved through a window into a train for soldiers being transported west. There was terrible turmoil around us. We were only taken because I had three children. Women with only two children were left there crying and yelling. This alone was so terrible that I don't like to remember it.

In the train, we were allowed to squeeze ourselves between the soldiers. They even made some kind of hammock for the children out of a piece of a tent. I felt a heavy weight drop from my shoulders that we had made it. The train did start but after half an hour it stopped in the middle of nowhere. We did not sense anything. It stood there the whole day. Finally it started again. I can not describe to you how I felt when it went backward and stopped again in Braunsberg, from where we had started. Only on arrival did we learn that the route was blocked off. The first Russian tanks were already in Elbing.

There are many moments in my memory that I view as the worst but I must say that I felt so very down when I, late at night, walked with my children back to our house from which I had ripped myself apart before. I also did not know if I was the only one who did not manage to get out. Only the next morning I learned that they were all back, the wives of my husband's comrade's with their children. Most of them had not even left.

The ten days or how many they were as we were encircled in Braunsberg, are like a bad dream. The misery of the refugees around us, the poor, hounded people who tried to get across the Haff, first in one then in the other direction and came back totally exhausted and frozen. The snow on the Haff was ½ meter high and the wind was ice cold. The field hospital trucks (Sanker) that came by our house, filled with frozen and exhausted people! All these horrible things that happened there are like a nightmare. And then the ragged appearances of our soldiers! All this looked already like dissolution. Our house stood, as you know, at the end of town toward Frauenburg, and there was constant coming and going. We women among us were like a family and doubly fused together through the misery.

I still see us all together under the light of a small candle stump. There was no electricity, gas and water anymore, water only for one hour early in the morning.

Outside our house were parked masses of military vehicles that had come from the front. A dead horse was lying in front of the door for days. Across the street in the people's garden a field kitchen had been put up and from the small room upstairs the soldiers had erected a communication line.

The Russians came closer every hour. They were already beyond Frauenburg. I don't ever want to suffer again the pain of conscience of what one should do, traveling on foot across the Haff*) *) A "Haff" is this a lagoon, separated by a narrow peninsula (2 miles wide) of the sea. This Haff is over 60 miles long and about 12 miles wide. During winter it will normally freeze. taking the risk that a child would not be able to make it (how many children froze to death there!) or let ourselves fall into the hands of the Russians. A different possibility did not seem to exist, even though one was always abroad and listening to others.

Now that the Russians were ½ hour away, our (political) local boss was still brash enough, to pretend to us that they would be beaten back and flight would be unnecessary. Anyway, he would not make trucks available for our use. While Allied low flying planes were shooting at everybody and everything that moved, one ran around to seek a possibility for flight. It is probably worse to fight for something then if one resigns into the inevitable, at least for one's nerves.

Then, on February 4ᵗʰ there was suddenly a chance for flight. The wife of a comrade with her 3 children (the youngest 6 weeks old) and I with my three, made it together, first with a truck that we finally got (but not from the local boss) to Rosenberg near Heiligenbeil. It was a tingling trip because the planes roared close above our heads, so close that they probably recognized us as refugees and did not shoot. But one could never know. In Rosenberg (near Danzig) we stayed the night with people who were fishermen. The next day we left the children with them and walked to the airport at Heiligenbeil to possibly be able to get out by plane. We should have saved ourselves the trouble. By the way, this was the day of the first heavy attack on Braunsberg, our hometown. At the airport we also had to throw ourselves down to hide ourselves from planes. Of course there was no possibility for us to get out by air.

But early the next morning we managed to get on a freight cutter (equipped with an ice breaker) to Pillau, tightly confined between wounded soldiers who had not even been bandaged yet, sick and refugees.

In Pillau we spent one day and one night in a terrible above-ground bunker because of artillery bombardment. These hours I remember as the most terrible ones of our whole flight. The bunker was crowded to bursting. The miserable wounded soldiers, the small crying children; the worst was the water dripping from the ceiling, the dripping wet walls, and the stink! And as bad luck wanted it, Helmut, my son, got a terrible diarrhea, and probably high fever. The toilets could not be used anymore. Every half hour I had to go down with him over the crowded staircases and he had to do his business in the open and in darkness which, apparently, many others had done too. Unfortunately each time he wanted to let go, a terrible artillery shooting or strike happened that scared him terribly so that he was already afraid of the next trip down. It is a miracle that one did not catch anything worse under these masses of people. Well, I probably got my head flu there, but it only broke out on the ship.

After we had spent one day and one night in the bunker, we could board a small freighter that should have sailed to Swinemünde), maybe even further.*)* Swinemünde is a German town and harbor about 250 miles west along the coast. *The crew was helpful and wonderful; the 1ˢᵗ wireless operator let us have his small cabin in which we 2 women and 6 children could settle. How we 8 could sleep there I can not imagine anymore but we were away from the masses that were tightly crowded on straw. We got to Danzig-Neufahrwasser*),*)*about 50 miles west *and stayed there for one day. Suddenly the boat was ordered not to continue on but to return east to Pillau to load new refugees. Because there was no way for us to get on from Danzig, the captain had thought to do us something good, to take us again to Pillau. We only learned that we were taken back, when we were already on the high seas. I had had this feeling of inevitability before and by now I was almost used to practice patience. In the meantime Helmut's diarrhea had become worse, he also was vomiting. The poor child became more and more emaciated.*

In Pillau we did not go off the boat but stayed in the cabin for one day, which passed relatively quiet, without bombardment. In the evening the freighter was supposed to leave again but as there were no signs that it would do so and no new refugees had been loaded, we could not take it anymore and went over to a large field-hospital ship that we had seen in the harbor. There we begged imploringly to take us on, especially because of the other woman's 6-weeks-old baby who was declining more and more. Helmut too became more and more miserable.

Under these circumstances they took us on. This same evening we moved over to the hospital ship and received a small cabin for ourselves. The ship was, naturally overcrowded. The wounded lay in every corridor on every doorstep. Our cabin had 2 bunk beds and a small table. But the best was that we received warm food and the baby got milk.

We started the next morning and from then on everything went smoothly. Most of the night's sailing between Danzig and Swinemünde still was dangerous because we were followed and so we sailed close to the coast without any lights on and as fast as possible.

One occurrence on the side: Before this night, life vests were given out but there were not enough for us. The 1st officer comforted us with this information: "With a life vest going down and drowning only takes longer and is more painful. Without it one sinks right away." Near Swinemünde part of a submerged ship stuck out of the water. It was the Gustloff.)* *) The Gustloff had been a cruise ship, later commissioned to the military as a transport ship. As the time it had been transporting evacuees from East Prussia, Lithuania, Poland, Estonia and Croatia, also wounded soldiers and military personnel. The ship was built for 1,465 passenger, but it was incredibly crowded. On January 30, 1945 it was sunk by a Soviet submarine. By one estimate 9,400 people died which makes it the largest loss of life in a single ship sinking in history. (Wikipedia)

From Swinemünde we were traveling by train. We were not told where the train was heading. But there would not have been much choice anyway except to Bremen. Some distance before Bremen we were shot at by low flying planes. Since the engineer was seriously wounded and the locomotive destroyed, we had to wait in the train for a whole day until a new locomotive was brought.

From Bremen we could take different trains. Traveling through Hannover, Halberstadt, Halle, we made it to arrive in Naumburg on February 18, 1945. After starting out again after the siege of Braunsberg, our flight had taken 14 days.

In Halle we separated from the woman and her children who had so far gone with us. The baby was taken to a clinic right away. I did not think that he would recover, he was already half dying from total debilitation and pneumonia, but he recovered.

When we arrived at my sister-in-laws in Naumburg, Helmut went to bed right away. He was only skin and bones and apparently now has a chronic intestinal weakness.

He can't get rid of diarrhea. I myself had high fever already on the hospital ship. It got better but then got worse again. The physician said it was head flu. After it was gone I had lost any feeling for balance. For a long time I was embarrassed to walk across large empty spaces because

I never knew if I would arrive at the spot I had planned to.

Well, now all this is behind us. Even if the long train trip with frequent stops and the masses of passengers was not easy (in the compartment next to ours a poor young woman gave birth). This second part of our flight can not be compared with the first and with the experiences that we had during the 10 days of being encircled in Braunsberg. That can not be obliterated from our memory.

Today, more than a year later, I am sitting in a cozy and comfortable attic room with a view of the beautiful park. The children are playing outside and all three are healthy. How happy must I be that it turned out this way. When one has seen how on the hospital ship most seriously wounded children and women were carried by, then I can only be so very grateful that we were spared. The children are very lively. Food is available here as much, or rather as little as everywhere in the Soviet occupied area. One is always hungry. But by doing a lot of walking around in the countryside, we could get by with getting some potatoes and feed turnips. They will be gone soon and there is no chance of getting more now. The potato-bellies are appropriate. But the children really look good because they live in such healthy air.

From my "cathedral-room" – our room that is bedroom, kitchen, dining-room in one – we see all of Naumburg lying at our feet with the beautiful cathedral.

Leonore and her Children after the War

In 1946 Leonore had recounted on her letter the nightmare of her narrow escape, with her 3 young children, from East Prussia to the main part of Germany. Almost 70 years later her daughters told me what followed. Here is their narrative:

My mother was born in 1906. After only 7 years of marriage and three children, she was widowed in 1940. Our father died fighting in France. I only saw him when I was a baby.

After my father was killed, Mother planned to move west to the main part of Germany. As preparation, for four years, Mother sent valuable household goods to her mother-in-law per postal packages west. Grandmother kept these in her attic: silver, dishes, linens and others. Later, during the starving years, Mother could exchange these valuables to farmers for food.

Exchanging food for luxury items was not as easy as it sounds. One would walk, ride one's bike, or maybe even a train to a farmstead where one would offer something valuable for food. Women would bring a beautiful table cloth, a suit from their late husband, silverware, and things that were coveted like skeins of knitting wool. If one had something valuable to offer, one knocked at the farmers' door, and shown the beauty, the monetary value, of the practically of one's item. If the farmers liked it or thought they could utilize it, they would counter offer with maybe a part of ham (if one was very lucky) or a small sack of potatoes or similar. Of course, money-wise the valuables were much more than the food, but one had to eat.

In January 1945 we had fled from Braunsberg/East Prussia and in late February arrived in Naumburg/Saale. Our aunt (Father's sister) took us into her two-room apartment because there was no space for us at our grandmother's. Mother became very ill for 3 weeks. Our aunt took care of Mother, but us children and Aunt's two daughters, helped as much as we could.

When Mother started to recuperate, she could look for a new place for us. We moved into a two room attic place with a beautiful view of the Naumburg cathedral (see Leonore's flight report). We three children slept in an unheated room where we also cooked. During the day we all lived in the other room that could be heated some above freezing. The winter 1945/46 was so bitterly cold that there was mildew on the walls, ice flowers on the windows, and the toilet was frozen.

Mother always sang Schubert's "Spring Dream" from the song cycle "Winter Journey".

After the American invasion most of Germany was briefly under American occupation. But then in May 1945 Germany was divided into four zones and individually occupied and governed by the 4 allies, England, American, France and Russia. To our horror the Russians took the American's place in our region. We had just narrowly escaped from East Prussia to flee from the Russians, and now after the war, we had to live with them in Naumburg, East-Germany.

1945-1947 were the worst hunger years. During the war we had not have much to eat, but always one had just enough food to live. But after the war, we were all starving. There was nothing. Only the farmers were doing better. We all had jaundice as the result of having so little food.

Mother would ride a bicycle about 30km (18 miles) to the country in order trying to exchange anything of value for food. Sometimes I was allowed to accompany her by riding on her luggage carrier. I was 6/7 years old (born 1938). The only times we had a "great feast" when food packages arrived from relatives in the USA.

After the first few years, food slowly became a little more available. But these winters were bitter cold, down to minus 20 Celsius (-4 F). We could heat only one room and there was almost no coal to be gotten. In 1946 some Russian officers forcibly requisitioned the main part of the house, the part that the owners lived in. The owners had to move into the attic, so we had to move out. But then we became lucky. We got two rooms, half of the ground floor of a villa. It had belonged to the former foreign minister (Ribbentrop), and now a chemical company. We all got along with another family, sharing the kitchen and bathroom of the ground floor. The villa was set in a garden and beautifully landscaped similar to a park. There was even space for each family to grow vegetables. We children thought we were in paradise.

The UDSSR police (GPU) had seized the villa across from us. Sometimes the Russians threw us little tea packets. In the evening they sang beautiful songs accompanied by an accordion. They were probably homesick.

In 1947, Mother was given a permit to work. She had been a trade school teacher for sewing. She taught how to take measurements, make patterns and how to cut cloth.

This was a sought after profession during and after the war since no fabric and no pre-made clothing was for sale. Mother's students arrived in our apartment with curtains, bedcovers and old clothing to make dresses for themselves. There also was red fabric. It had to be the old flags. One only had to take away the white circle and the black swastika to get it. If possible one died the fabric to a different color.

Mother held three classes per day with a total of 18 students of varying age groups, one at 9am-12, one 2-6pm and one 7-10pm. To make space for her "school", we put our beds away in the mornings and brought them back out in the evening. At late into the night, Mother would sew clothing for us.

The Russians observed that there was always a light on at night and they suspected that Mother was a spy. Luckily she was able to show that her late night sewing was the cause.

Over the years certain aspects of life had slowly somewhat better if not really normalized. In 1948 a "Currency Conversion Compensation" was instituted. In the Western occupied zones, the old currency (Reichsmark) was exchanged into "Deutsche Mark", but only at 10% of its original value. So for every 100 Reichsmark, one suddenly only had 10 Deutsche Mark. In the Russian zone, the former currency was exchanged into the "Ost Deutsche Mark". (Actually, in 1990 after the unification of the two Germanies, at the East there needed another currency conversion because the East-money's value was lower than the Western.) Now in 1948 everybody only had a little bit of money, but now there was more to buy. In the West almost everything was available. In the former Russian Zone, the range of goods was somehow still scarce. 20 years after the war, most young people in East Germany, had never tasted a banana or orange.

In 1949 the Russian zone became the DDR, "Deutsche Demokratische Republik". About the same time the American, French and English zones together, became the "Bundes Republik Deutschland". They were called "Ost-Deutschland" and "West-Deutschland" respectively.

1949 the two Germanies was given jurisdiction to Germans by vote. West-Germany chose a government built on freedom and capitalism. East-German was given a communistic government. Therefore the situation had stayed basically the same.

Everybody had to go to primary school through 8th grade. Subsequently one could choose to enter a profession-track apprenticeship, or continue until 12th grade, followed by the final high school exam and then go on a university. However this choice was not a given to all children. The government had removed most intellectuals from their positions unless they could demonstrate solid a communist loyalty. Therefore, teachers and other intellectuals, who did not show good communist opinion, were fired. Many of those were then forced to work in the coal mines despite mounting health issues.

Only the students were accepted into high school, when they were good communists and be from a family of laborers and farmers. Even one loyalist communist professor's son was not able to get into high school but had to become a carpenter because the father was an intellectual. The communist regime aimed to create an entirely new type of intellectual, derived from laborers and farmers.

Our *brother was not allowed to continue his schooling after the 8th grade. Firstly because he, as all of us three children, was not members of the heavily indoctrinated communistic "Young Pioneers". Becoming a "Young Pioneer" was the unspoken and unquestioned norm. Also we had gone through religious church confirmation.*

The government prohibited churches not outright. But everything religious was frowned upon, especially church rituals, such as the protestant confirmation at age 14. To counter this, this government had fashioned a "Youth Initiation", the communist ritual for 14 olds. All children were expected to attend.

Another reason not to let my brother get into high school, was that he was not from a farmer or laborer family. Therefore, Mother managed to get our brother to West-Berlin, where he got into a high school boarding school.

In the March of 1953 Stalin died. By the political powers, he was praised, honored, admired, given many paeans and vows of loyalty. At that time nobody foresaw that Khrushchev (Chruschtow) would destroy Stalin's "hallow" in 1965. Some of the former powerful party members were uncertain. Now they were not about talked them anymore. Then at June 17th 1953 the civilians in East Germany upraised against the communist government. Soviet tanks were brutally quelled.

We students of middle-class families had stayed away if possible from the commemoration for Stalin.

The situation became more difficult. We sisters were able to attend high school even though we were members of the "Young Parrish Evangelic Church". However, we and others were interrogated to demonstrate that we were not anti-communists. We were allowed to stay in school and finish our high school exams. Boys were more intensely interrogated. These boys, who did not "pass", were kicked out school and even just shortly before taking their high school exams. They were accused having laughed during the funeral of Stalin.

In 1953 I, the older sister, took my final high school exam (Abitur). After this I went to West-Berlin to attend college. In the East I would have been ordered to study agriculture.

In the West the schools had increased from 12 to 13 grades, so I had to take this last year before finally starting college.

When I arrived in West-Berlin, as a young East refugee, I received government support of 100 Deutsch-Mark per one month. I rented a small room for 45DM. The rest was for me to live on. It was good that the school canteen only charged 75 Pennies for the main meal. An orange was 30 Pennies, which I actually could not afford. Sometimes I was invited for dinner at relatives.

Then the younger sister told her story:

Now I, the youngest sister, stayed still with Mother. But in1954 Mother realized one of her sewing students was spying on her. She had already two of her children in the west, one son, one daughter and mother were under observation. The sewing student had remarked that a picture on the wall was missing. Mother had already mailed it to the West. She indeed was hoping to move to the West.

At this time, before a wall between East and West Berlin (1961), one could travel to the West, if one had to obtain a permit if one had relatives there. To get a permit was a little easier when one was elderly. The East German government probably hoped that the old persons might stay in there, therefore shirking the financial burden of pension and eldercare.

In 1955 Mother and I were able to visit relatives in the West. We had to relinquish our East-German identity cards, and were given a substitute card. We were supposed to get our identity cards back when returned. With our substitute card and a carry-on we were able to board the train to the West.

Naturally, we did not plan to come back East. This was 6 years before the wall was built and the fortified fence erected along the countryside, cutting East-Germany off from West-Germany.

Once in the West, Mother as "immigrant" had to enter a refugee reception camp. This camp served to verify her identity and conduct a background check. There she received new papers and a new identity card and assistance to find a job. Since I was a teenager, I was able to stay with relatives.

Mother had to spend only 3 months in the camp, also because she could prove she had a viable profession and that she was employable. She took a job as teacher at a trade school in Stuttgart, Germany.

We siblings were fortunate to grow up in Germany. I received my degree in book-publishing. After my diploma I first went to England as an Au-Pair to learn English because Russian had been my only foreign language. I worked for 8 years in Stuttgart, Germany. My sister studied to become a librarian. She worked for 10 years in Rome, Italy at the renowned history institute "Bibliothecia Hertziana". My brother studied law and is a jurist in Hannover. We all are married, have children and grandchildren in the free and peacefulness of West-Germany.

Mother was an amazing, relentlessly positive and loving woman. If she had not had these exceptionally strong positive traits, we would not have been made it through these hard times. She passed on at the age of 81 years.

Maarten: The Netherlands

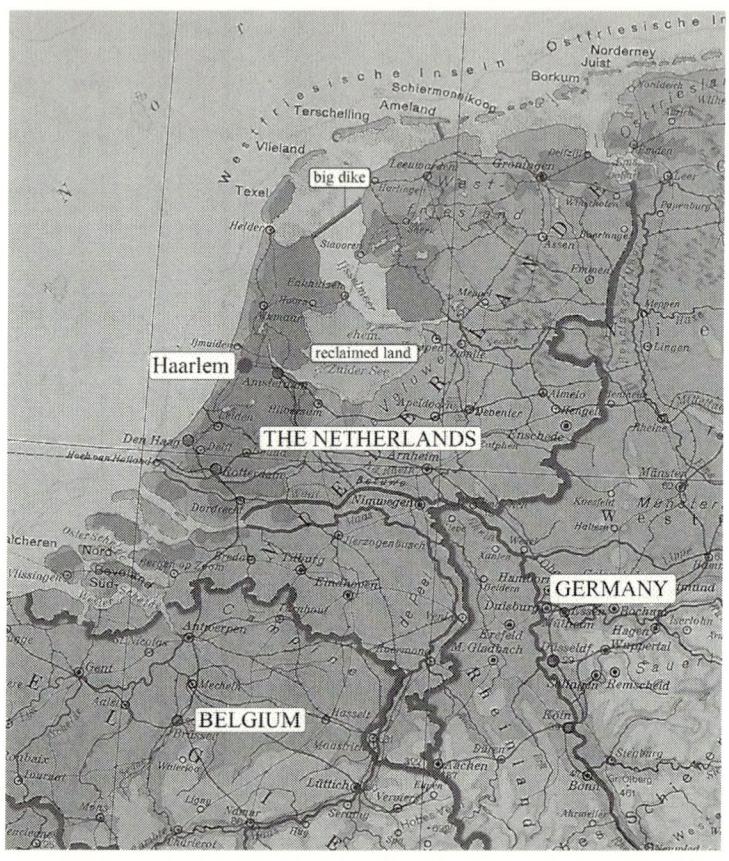

Maarten: The Netherlands in the German Occupation
(born 1934)

Many European countries are thought to carry special characteristics: the Swiss make the best and most precise watches, the Austrians jodel, and French food is the most elegant and tasty. These are mostly superficial generalizations. However, it is a fact that in the Netherlands people are extremely tidy, responsible, caring not only for each other but also for nature. They had to be that way for many centuries.

A large part of the Netherlands*) is just that: nether lands, land that is lower than the sea. *) "Holland" is only the name of two provinces, North Holland and South Holland, but is used for the whole country. The official name is The Netherlands. These low lying areas of the country used to be lakes, marshes, mud flats within the deltas of estuaries, and shallow coastal parts of the North Sea. Over many centuries the Dutch have built dikes around so many of these formerly waterlogged areas, and then drained them, that today they form more than 40% of the whole country.

To drain low lying areas once and then forget about them, will not work because they would promptly become soggy again. The water has to be pumped out continuously into higher lying canals that can then transport it out to a river or the sea. Windmills, these hallmarks of the Dutch countryside, did this pumping for centuries until the arrival of electricity. The saying goes: "God created the world but the Dutch created the Netherlands."

Land reclaiming is still going on. The Zuiderzee, a large bay that extended from the North Sea towards the center of the country, used to cover an area of roughly 2,000 square miles*). It was a relatively shallow body of water, only 22 feet deep at the deepest point. As far back as the 16th century, there were plans to cut the Zuiderzee off from the North Sea, thereby winning more arable land. Finally in 1927 work was begun on the giant dam that now closes most of the bay. *) In comparison, Lake Pontchartrain in Louisiana, which flooded New Orleans in the wake of hurricane Katrina in 2005, only covers 625 square miles, that is less than one third of the Zuiderzee. The most capable engineers, mathematicians, and geologists of the time were called to design this almost 20 miles long dike. It is 275 feet wide and along its top a highway connects the North Holland province with the Friesland province. Two complexes of shipping locks and 25 discharge sluices keep the necessary connection to the sea. The dike took over five years to complete. Four to five thousand people worked on this project every day.

(In this time following the Great Depression, most of them would otherwise have been unemployed.)

More than half of the former Zuiderzee is now dry land, with fields and towns. Further reclamation is planned. With the river IJssel still flowing into what is left of the former Zuiderzee and almost no seawater coming in, the remaining water has slowly turned into fresh water. Its name has now been changed from Zuiderzee to IJsselmeer after the river IJssel that empties into it.

In some areas near the coast and on outlying islets farms have been built in shallow areas of the coast line. Floods and storm surges would cover the pastures but people and livestock were safe.

Throughout the centuries, maintaining the dikes and protecting this hard-won and precious land has played an important role in Dutch life. The dikes had to be checked continuously. The waters of a sudden storm flood could have dug or broken their way through a dike, starting at a weak spot, allegedly even a mouse hole. Legends have taken up the theme too. One tells about a dike warden whose ghost can still be seen on stormy nights, riding his white horse along the dikes, his black cloak flowing behind him. When people spot him, they know that a dangerous storm will soon be whipping the water against their dike and they make extra sure, everything is tight.

This need for constant vigilance and precision might explain why the Dutch as a culture are extremely responsible, exacting, and tidy, and why they view their land as especially precious and defend it fiercely. Only their freedom from foreign rule ranks higher than their land.

In 1573 when the Spanish troops had invaded the country and attacked the city of Leiden, the Dutch were willing to sacrifice some of their hard-gained land in order to be free. They broke down the local dike that held back the sea at this part of the country and sailed their ships over the floodwaters into – or rather over – the city. The few Spanish soldiers that had not drowned, were killed. Freedom was won but at a high price. Many Dutch women and children must have drowned too. It must have taken a long time to build the dike up again and drain the land.

Ship building, seafaring and trading all over the world are part of the Dutch history. Far-away, often exotic, lands were conquered and made into colonies. Trading routes were established early. The Dutch were oriented towards the sea, and some merchant families grew very rich and powerful.

When I was a child, it was fixed firmly in my mind that The Netherlands were the land of hot chocolate. The only packages of cocoa I had ever seen, showed the picture of a comfortable looking Dutch woman in her traditional costume with the winged bonnet, holding a steaming cup of this delicious beverage. Only many years later did I learn that cocoa did not grow in The Netherlands but had been imported from some Dutch colony.

In the early 1600s several provinces joined together. After the 30-year war (1618 to 1648) the Netherlands' independence was officially recognized. Today The Netherlands is a constitutional monarchy. It is part of the former economic union of the Benelux-States (Belgium, Netherlands, Luxemburg) that later served to a large degree as a model for the European Union.

And now, before this rich and intense historic background of The Netherlands, the Second World War unfolded. The Dutch had not expected to be involved in this war, their military was unprepared. The Netherlands had declared neutrality. Hitler broke this neutrality. He planned to use the Dutch coast for launching an attack on England.

In May 1940 (eight months after the war had started) the German army invaded the Netherlands. There was some resistance at first, there was even talk of opening dikes and flood the northern part of the country. But then the city of Rotterdam, a major harbor city, was systematically bombed. The Dutch realized that it was pointless to resist. The ill-prepared military would have been no match for the German army anyway. The country surrendered and the German military began its occupation.

Our Dutch friend Maarten was 6 years old when the war started. He now lives in the US, and he told me about his experiences, his impressions, his feelings.

Maarten's father was a minister in the Dutch Reformed Church, just like his grandfather had been before him. The family lived at first in a small, mostly agricultural, town in the eastern part of the country, near the German border. In November 1939, several months before the German invasion, Maarten's father was transferred to Haarlem west of Amsterdam, where he would serve a larger parish. Maarten recalls:

In Haarlem we lived in the parsonage next to the big church. Across the street was a school that had been confiscated and now housed German troops. The soldiers would always parade past our house.

They would march in typical German fashion, goose-stepping and shouting "Heil Hitler" and raising their arms. One day my two older brothers were on the roof of a wing of the church while the soldiers marched on the street. The boys had armed themselves with small pebbles and threw those down at the soldiers, aiming them in a way that they would click on the soldiers' helmets. The German commander became very angry. He came to our house and wanted to arrest my father. There was a long discussion during which my father pointed out that the children had only been playing. Those were very anxious moments because the soldiers had the power to deport people and frequently they did.

The city of Haarlem, like many Dutch cities in the North, is crisscrossed by canals that often run along the streets. Maarten recounts:

Most of the canals had no barriers or fences between the pavement and the water. At night German soldiers would walk along these canals, and sometimes they were drunk and would fall in, and some would drown even. The Germans accused the Dutch population of pushing the soldiers into the canals. On occasion this might actually have happened when nobody was watching. Who knows. In retaliation, the Dutch citizens who lived near a canal, were ordered to take turns patrolling the canals during the night to make sure that nobody fell in. If it happened in spite of the patrols – one way or an other – the Dutch men (in shifts of five) who had been ordered to patrol the canal where a German had fallen in, were lined up against the wall by a garage and were executed. The Germans did not investigate who might have done it, who might have made a mistake. These five people in this neighborhood were held responsible. "Line'em up and shoot'em!" This was done to set an example.

My father was excused from serving on patrol because he was a clergyman. It is always interesting that in times of war there is still this fear of the clergy, of God's people. Therefore he did not have to patrol the canals but our friends' fathers had to do it.

I asked Maarten if he felt that there was any space for human emotions in this atmosphere of hostility and hatred, and constant danger. He told me of an incident when a German unit was marching by:

The soldiers were always lined up with the tallest people in front and the shortest people at the end. One time a soldier who was marching at the very end handed me an apple. He wanted to be nice. When I think of this in retrospect, considering my age at the time and of our own children now, I suppose he might have had children of his own, and missed them, being so far away from them.

As a child of about nine, I did not realize this, I only felt deep hate toward anything German. I remember – and now I feel bad about it – taking the apple and smashing it against the ground. 'An apple coming from a German soldier is not fit to eat.' I was too young to rationalize those feelings. I am sure the soldier must have felt terrible seeing me do this, but he could not jump on me or do anything else. He had to keep marching.

Food was becoming scarce, especially in the cities. It was also presumed that some of the food was shipped to Germany to feed the civilians there. At the time the German population did not have enough food either. But the farmers usually had a little more. It was difficult for the authorities to calculate exactly how much each field would bring, how many eggs each hen would lay, that is, how much produce the farmers had to hand over to the food distribution centers. This left them with a little more food than the people in the cities got from their miniscule rations. Maarten's family was acquainted with people who owned a farm in the area. Every weekend Maarten and his oldest brother would walk along the dike from Haarlem to this farm where they helped with the chores and were given food as payment.

During those years having some connection to a farm and the little bit of extra food that was to be had there, became a blessing. And the farmers did need help with their work too. Thousands of Dutch older teenage boys had been rounded up and transported to Germany to work in factories there.

In 1942 the family moved from Haarlem to The Hague where Maarten's father would serve in another parish. The coast near The Hague was determined to be a likely location for an attack by the British. A strip of two or three blocks, one half mile inland and parallel to the beach, was declared off-limits to civilians. The houses there were torn down, landmines were laid.

The Germans were building fortifications near The Hague to ward off the British or Allied forces from invading the country. Many bunkers were built and canons set up in case enemy ships should come up onto the beach.

The prohibited area started just two blocks from our home. Our school was actually behind the lines, on the shore side and we could not go to that school.

Right after the war we had to walk through this area again and we saw that the Germans had excavated a deep canal, a moat, with banks so steep that tanks could not cross over it, they would have been submerged completely.

Maarten's parents were still friends with many members of their former congregation in the small town near the German border, and some of them were farmers. Since the children's summer vacations were rather extensive and the food rations too small to feed the whole family of eight sufficiently, the three oldest boys (born 1930, 33, and 34) were sent across the country to their former neighbors to work (and eat!) on those farms. They spent three months there in 1943, 44 and 45*). *) The end of the war had not brought sufficient food right away. There was still hunger in 1945.

Naturally, transportation was a problem. The boys (10, 11, and 14 years old) had to travel the distance of over 120 miles by bike. This was not an easy feat and it was made even harder by the fact that the children were traveling alone, without their parents. Furthermore, the bicycles were in rather poor condition.

There were no inner tubes and no bicycle tires available, so people became very ingenious. Some would ride on the bare rims but they didn't last very long. Others would cut strips of rubber from old car tires and somehow fastened them onto the rims. Some even made wooden tires, beveled pieces of wood that had some cushioning effect. Homemade substitutes were all one had.

Heating was a problem, and electricity was a problem too. There were no electric lights. We had candles and oil lamps. But I remember going to a friend's house and there was a bicycle suspended from the ceiling. We took turns pedaling the bicycle because the little dynamo made the headlight work and the people could read. A truly ingenious use of a bicycle.

The winters were worst when it was so cold and no fuel could be had.

People would cut down trees in town. Streetcar tracks were another source of fuel. The tracks were paved with wooden blocks that had been soaked in creosote or something like it. This process preserved the wood; the blocks were like little bricks. People were ripping them up at night and then burning them in their stoves, just like briquettes.

The summers on the farm brought a lot of work but also plenty to eat. In fact, this posed a problem in 44 and 45 when the boys were very undernourished.

On the first day it was "eat, eat, eat, and overeat". But our stomachs were not used to so much food, and we had to throw it all up again. The farmers had to regulate our food. They told us: "Now, don't eat too much, you have to get used to this."

We three brothers were on different farms. We helped with the harvest, milked the cows, and fed the pigs, and so forth. I really loved doing this.

I have reflected how this did probably start my career as a veterinarian. I am sure that it had a major impact on me. Working with farm animals, taking care of them, stimulated an interest and became my profession ultimately. We are always looking at the bad effects of the war, but a positive result for me was a career in veterinary medicine.

When the Netherlands became occupied, all political parties were dissolved. In their place a Dutch version of the NSDAP*, the NSB* was established, out of which, in turn, the Dutch SS was founded.

*) NSDAP: National Socialistic German Laborers Party; NSB: National Socialistic Bond (Alliance).

But the Dutch people's love for their land and passion for fighting for their freedom expressed itself strongly in the underground movement. I don't know if there was much (if any) sabotage – that was probably soon proved pointless since retaliation was swift and cruel. But giving persecuted people shelter, hiding them from authorities, was done extensively. (Read Corrie Ten Boom's book "The Hiding Place".)

Not only Jews needed places to hide but also young Dutch men because they were rounded up and transported to Germany to work in factories, especially weapons factories. There were even raids during which each house was searched for young men.

My oldest brother was just 15 by the end of the war so he escaped that but I have cousins who were a few years older and they had to go underground. You had to make a decision, do you report or do you hide.

The insidious thing for us was that we had traitors. We had Dutch citizens who sympathized with the Germans and the national socialistic organization, they were the NSBers. This made relations difficult because these people were among us, they were former friends and neighbors, and if you said something bad, they could turn you in. I suppose, they hoped to get "brownie points" with the German soldiers.

I do remember this also from the times I spent at the farm. I knew there was one nearby farm where people were NSBers, and we were told: "Do not make them mad, don't scold them or taunt them in any way. Say nothing because they'll turn you in."

It had become evident very quickly who among the Dutch people were traitors. Especially their neighbors knew because these people would get special privileges with the German occupation forces for helping them and turning in fellow citizens and fugitives.

Many things were done that were not permitted. I am actually proud of the village in which I was born, and where I spent those wartime summers. All this became known in full only after the war. The farmers hid many Jewish people and many young men who were of draft able age who otherwise would have been taken to Germany to work in factories. In Holland more people per capita were being hidden than anywhere else, especially on farms. These fugitives were not visible. They helped in the fields but if a stranger appeared, they would hide. Since I worked in the fields also, I was part of this scheme. I knew these people were there. If a car was approaching or a stranger on foot, they hid under a stack of hay or whatever else was within easy reach. After the war I learned that at one farm the owners had even built a special hiding place, a small room underneath the manure stack. It had a hidden door and if anybody came by, the fugitives could hide in this room. They also slept there. Often, inspections were made; teams came by to see if there were any illegal people around.

As children we did not know much about that because the adults wisely did not inform us so we could not be forced to tell anything if we were asked. But on the farm we were somehow aware of some of these things.

One of my uncles who lived near the town close to the German border, was principal of a school. He had two sons in the age group that was targeted for deportation to Germany He was a small man who had a physical birth defect; he limped and he walked with a cane. He was a wonderful uncle and must have been a great teacher and principal. He was respected by all – and he and his sons were very, very involved in the underground. Probably because of his physical condition he was somehow ignored by the authorities. Had he been a big, tall person he and his activities might not have gone unnoticed.

My father worked with the underground too. He also networked with Corrie ten Boom*). It seems that as a clergyman he was not watched too closely either; he had a little more flexibility than others.

*) Corrie ten Boom (as told in her book "The Hiding Place) and her family were hiding Jewish families in their house until the German officials found out. Corrie was arrested and put in a concentration camp. She survived.

All of this I learned after the war. But I know many places where people were hidden. I visited some after the war. I have also been to the Ann Frank House in Amsterdam and have seen things there.

As far as I know, there was just one concentration camp in Holland, it was in Driebergen. This was a detention type camp.

As the war progressed and the allied bomb raids over Germany became more frequent and more intense, the area along the border with Germany was bombed too, however unintentionally. Allied bomber squadrons, starting from England, would fly over the Netherlands into Germany. In an attempt to prevent these planes and their bombs to actually reach their targets, German FLAK*) units had been positioned close to the Dutch *) FLAK: FLiegerAbwehrKanonen = anti-aircraft canons border, their canons directed towards the airspace over the Netherlands, in order to prevent the planes from ever entering German airspace. When a plane was shot down, it would go down over Dutch territory. American pilots and crew would parachute from their damaged aircraft and many of them would be helped by Dutch people who would hide them and eventually help them to get back to England. (In doing so, the Dutch were, of course, risking their lives.) Now, when an airplane is being hit, it is possible that the bullets will incinerate the bomb load, make it explode in the air and kill the crew either while they are still inside the plane or on their way down while the burning plane crashes onto them. Therefore the crew would drop all the bombs right after the plane was hit, and then parachute down and let the airplane glide a bit further before it crashed. And the bombs would fall on or near Dutch farms and towns.

The Allied planes would enter Germany by way of the Netherlands and the Germans liked to shoot them down over the Netherlands, so they put their anti-aircraft canons close to the Dutch border. The planes would fly over, having lots of bombs on board. Then came the searchlights from the ground, like you sometimes see them here today with promotional signals. The Germans would shine several of these big lights and when they managed to get a plane in the cross beam, they would shoot it down. From the farm we could see the planes catch fire and come to the ground, and we would hope it would not be too close to where we were. I remember definitely going into the bomb shelter. When the planes were caught in the search lights, they would drop their bombs so that they would not explode with the bombs.

They were also carrying a lot of fuel. So they dumped their bombs in the country. Then there were incendiary bombs. They were probably 50 cm long and they were encased in cement so that they would fracture when they hit the ground with the phosphor inside.

Phosphor is terrible stuff, it would devour everything because you could not extinguish it with water. They would drop those. We had some fall near the farm house. They would have to be submerged in water and kept submerged. You could not get anything on your hands, we were not allowed to touch them with our hands, with a shovel was o.k. We were told to tell if we saw any unexploded ones but not to touch.

Hitler kept promising the German people the Miracle Weapon that would turn the tides. It would make Germany win the war over the whole world after all. By 1942 the first two models of the Miracle Weapon were ready. They were called V1*) and V2*) and were guided missils. *) "V" stood for Vergeltungswaffe = revenge weapon. The V1 was about 25 feet long, carried 1,800 pounds of explosives and was driven by a propulsion engine which made it fly at a speed of about 360m/h. The V2 was about 45 feet long, carried 2,200 pounds of explosives and had a jet engine. The range of both missiles was around 200 miles but the speed of the V2 was almost 10 times as much as the V1 and it could fly at heights up to 60 miles. That was more than the speed of sound. Its approach could not be heard beforehand. It could, however, be seen by its fiery tail. 21,500 V1s were started and over 3,000 V2s. But apparently a great number of those did not make it very far. (Wikipedia)

Towards the end of the war the Germans deployed primitive (by today's standards) rockets toward London, England. A launching site was set up on an old, private estate at the edges of The Hague near Scheveningen. It seems that most of these rockets, called V2s were fired off at night. The roar could be heard for quite a distance. They would lift off slowly and go <u>straight</u> up. A fiery tail with smoky plume could be seen. Then, several hundred meters in the air, the rocket would change its trajectory to a horizontal position before it would aim for London. This change in direction was a critical maneuver which would sometimes fail, and then the V2 would fall back on or near its launching pad, i.e. on The Hague, with devastating results. In retrospect, this was early rocket science, literally, not all of it adequately tested.*) *) During the whole of the war 74,172 tons of bombs were dropped on England, 1,350,000 were dropped on Germany. (The Anchor Atlas of World History)

How does hate grow, how does hate find its target, its outlet? In the Netherlands, France, Poland, and other German occupied countries it seemed to be easy to hate the Germans. The soldiers were there every day; many of them behaved badly, committed abominable deeds. They were easy to hate, they stood out from the population, they had faces.

In Germany it was so much harder. Towards whom could you direct your hate? These bomber squadrons that filled the sky like humongous locust swarms, dropping fire and death, they had no faces. We knew, of course, that they were piloted by humans but these humans disappeared behind the machinery. These air-raids were often perceived more in the category of an earthquake or the stream of molten lava flowing out of a volcano. They were terrible, unstoppable, archaic.

The oppression from the inside might have shown itself in human form, the political police, the Gestapo, the small official who felt big and powerful and at the same time was afraid not to follow orders from some "faceless" superior. But the situation was just too complex.

After the war hating was easier. One feared the occupation forces, but one could also somehow hate and especially detest and despise them, hold them in deep contempt. There was, of course, no point in fighting them. The war was over and done with. There was no goal to fight for. The German population was helpless and totally at their mercy. For the Dutch, hating had been easier.

In the Netherlands anything German was hated, the language and the name and the reminders they left behind: the bunkers and the tanks and so forth. Those were not only my personal feelings, my family felt that way, my friends felt that way, the whole country felt that way. This is prejudice but we thought it justified. The Germans, even today, are different from the Dutch in their demeanor. Germans are loud, they speak loud, they like to sing loud; things that are just a little bit offensive. They would come after the war, many years after the war, as tourists, and some people, some of these Germans would say: "Oh, my father was stationed here." That was the wrong thing to say. The German tourists came to the Dutch beaches and they were on the beach and they were loud on the beach, drinking and singing and so forth, and those were echoes that people didn't want to hear. They did not endear themselves even 10, 15, 20 years after the war, coming back and just acting as if nothing had happened, instead of being polite guests, maybe even apologizing a little bit. There was none of that. So that only helped to perpetuate the dislike. I no longer call it hate but rather dislike.

For me personally, I have a German colleague here in the US, who is a close friend. He is younger than I, so I just stopped to think, it is not his fault. We are close friends, we have the same interests within our field, so I have slowly overcome that.

It was therapeutic to have a scapegoat. There has to be a bad guy. The Germans were the bad guys for us, and the Japanese were the bad guys for many years, seen as villains, and they are portrayed in the movies as the bad guys. That is not the individual Japanese person, the family person or anything like that. Somehow we want to blame somebody.

War just doesn't make sense. Armed conflict doesn't solve anything in my opinion. I just as soon have politicians sit around a table and if it takes them years, that's fine with me, but keep talking about it and don't keep destroying.

And then there is the psychological side. New digging into medical files of veterans of the civil war show that the soldiers who saw combat and/or were imprisoned, had a high incidence of physical and psychological/mental ailments that resemble what is today called Post Traumatic Stress Syndrome.*) *) Science News, 2-11-06, page 84

This is a logical psychological and physical response. They never got over it. Maybe this is what makes it difficult to talk about it. Maybe my way to cope with some of the memories is just: that's over and done with, let's move to the future. A blessing for today, but I never had the desire to discuss that with my family. I haven't even discussed these things with my brothers. My brothers are in Canada. I see them once a year or twice a year and we really don't talk about it – except for an isolated thing here and there. I remember this. But we are not sitting down asking: what do you remember, and so forth. We are not interested in doing that. It is history that we don't wish to relive.

Our children have asked, and I have just brushed it off – in their own interest or whatever, because when I say "you wouldn't understand" that's probably a little conceited on my part to assume that.

But I have never given my children any toys, weapons, tanks or guns. I just never did that. I felt not comfortable with that.

Maarten came from the Netherlands to the US as an immigrant in 1955. In 1962, when he had finished going to college he was drafted into the military and served as a captain in the army. But he says:

I was not a very good soldier. I was not comfortable in the army having to learn how to shoot. I remember going out on the rifle range with an automatic weapon and I just pulled the trigger

until it was empty. I didn't try to become proficient. I had done my duty. Those are remnants. I don't believe in guns; they don't solve anything. I have nothing against hunting but even there the risk of using a gun troubles me. I have never been much of a hunter. I have gone along with students in California to go dove hunting. It was wonderful to be out in nature early in the morning with doves and quail but I was not interested in the shooting part.

When with the military I was stationed in Frankfurt Germany. I only wanted to go for a year, so I could not live in on-base-housing. I was married then and we lived on the German economy in a German apartment and it was a very good year. We traveled, we had a car, which the American government shipped over there, a new Pontiac, and we traveled to the Rivièra, and Switzerland and lots of times to the Netherlands to meet my family and all of that. So I lived in Germany, literally, and I have no problems with that. I had to speak German because I made inspections of different places for the army, where the army purchased food that had to be inspected at the source. I made those inspections and because my German was good enough at the time, I did not have to take an interpreter. They were very polite and fine. I had minor arguments, not about the second world war but stubbornness on the part of the Germans. For example, I was in a bakery and they were supposed to have fly screens on the windows and this man argued with me, he said: "But if I have fly screens, how can the flies get out?" Those kinds of things.

But I have good memories too. I had to inspect a trout farm which was in the mountains. I did not think it made sense to inspect live fish, they are healthy. I didn't know much about fish anyway. But the owners were very nice and they gave me a tour and showed me how they do the hatching, and the little fingerlings and all this. It was very interesting. They gave me some lunch afterwards and they acted like friends if you will. So I have positive experiences that way, as these are normal people and it's not a regime we are dealing with.

Like most of the people I had interviewed, Maarten had not talked much of his experiences as a child during the war before he talked to me. He had tried a few times to tell his own children a few events from that time but found that it was just too hard for them to understand the deeper meaning of his stories.

Like, when he told them about the time toward the end of the war when there was so little food that they had to eat tulip bulbs, his children found this funny. They could not know that this had been as desperate an action as for a farmer's family to eat the last of next spring's grain seeds, knowing full well that there was nothing left, no food, no hope for the future.

In The Netherlands tulips were the pride and an important source of income. Tulips have been cultivated for a long, long time. Only in the deepest desperation and to stave off certain starvation can one eat something that has taken generations to produce and that carries hope for the future.

Maarten now lives a very active life with his wife. His hate to Germany has been healed. His working life as a veterinary was spent at a university in Florida. Maarten is content and at peace with the world.

Linde: From Expulsion to a Safe New Home (born 1944)

When we expected our third child, we brought Linde, our au pair, to us from Germany. Linde were perfect. She loved and cared for our children and she did what was needed to be come. She was artistic and was always cheerful and happy and she shared happiness with everybody. After Linde had returned to Germany, we kept a close constant and still do today.

We knew that Linde had been a refugee; there was so many in Germany. We never talked about what had happened. Only later did I realize that Linde had been come from a faraway country and then asked her about it. Many years later I asked her about all this

This is Linde's story:

My parents had been living in Bohemia. This was a large area near the eastern border of Germany where the people spoke German and practiced their German culture. ((28% of Germans had lived in Bohemia and Moravia.)) It was from close to our hometown in Bohemia, going west 100km was Dresden; going south was Prague.

For a long time Bohemia had been part of the Austrian-Yugoslavian empire. After WWI it became Czechoslovakia. Germans and Czechs lived together without any problems. At the beginning of WWII Hitler invaded the whole area. Then after the war the Allied Nations decided to expel all ethnic Germans. There were about 3.3 million.

Towards the end of the war my mother had visited Dresden during the bombardment. She never forgot the burning city. In transit for a couple of days there had been thousands of evacuees in Dresden from Silesia and eastern area. And now everything was burning. After screams could not hears anymore, since Dresden, the city and the people were dead. My mother had not been in the city center and therefore survived.

In 1945, after the war in Bohemia my mother was forced to do hard labor and had to wear a "German Star" similar to the Jewish star. In May 1946 my mother suddenly had to leave within 2 hours. For herself and me together could take one suitcase. I had just turned two years old. We along with other Germans were transported in closed freight cars to the unknown. Nobody knew if the train might go to Siberia.

Decades later I asked my mother about this trip. How many days did it take? Was there space enough to lie down or did everybody have to stand? Did you have something to eat and to drink? My mother did not remember. Like similar survivors she must have put all this out of her mind. But my mother always remembered that when the freight cars finally opened she cried because she heard the people outside speaking German. We were in Germany.

After having gone through an evacuee camp, we were taken to a shack and later to a cellar room. ((During this time in all of Germany live space was scarce because many houses had been destroyed and now so many evacuees needed to live somewhere too.)) I became very sick but a physician managed to find us a dry room and I became healthy again.

My mother worked in the fields for a farmer. In exchange she received a bit of flour, potatoes and eggs. She had nothing but her own strength to work, a baby, two blankets and two pillows.

My mother had no relatives in West-Germany. Her parents and two sisters had been taken to were taken to the Soviet occupation zone to Rostock and Graal Müritz at the Baltic Sea. Her two brothers did not survive the war. My mother never saw her homeland again.

In 1947 my father found us through the" Red Cross' Missings Person Tracing Service". My father was actually a Czech citizen and had not been expelled; therefore, he had not been allowed to go with us. Later he managed to travel through Austria and Bavaria until he finally found us.

My parents never hung onto what had happened. They looked towards the future to build us all a new good life and tried to make a happy childhood for me and my younger sister.

After Linde had been with us, she returned back to Germany. There she worked for many years at a local county office where she cared for Russian-Germans who were allowed to immigrate to Germany. These people had to prove that they were of German descend. They were then given a place to live, they were taught German, and she found them jobs. Many had lost the German language, sometimes even having been forced to communicate in Russian or in Kazakh*) *) The Muslim country Kazakhstan is now the "Kazakh Soviet Republic". Many knew only German lullabies and children's poems that their grandmother had taught them. Linde cared for them, for all they needed. She helped them with personal issues, providing hope and made them finally successful in their new lives.

Even today some of these people still continue the relationships and feel very thankful.

Linde is always cheerful and helping others and happy. We are grateful and happy that she had and still have the close connection with her.

Mariann: a Teacher in Poland

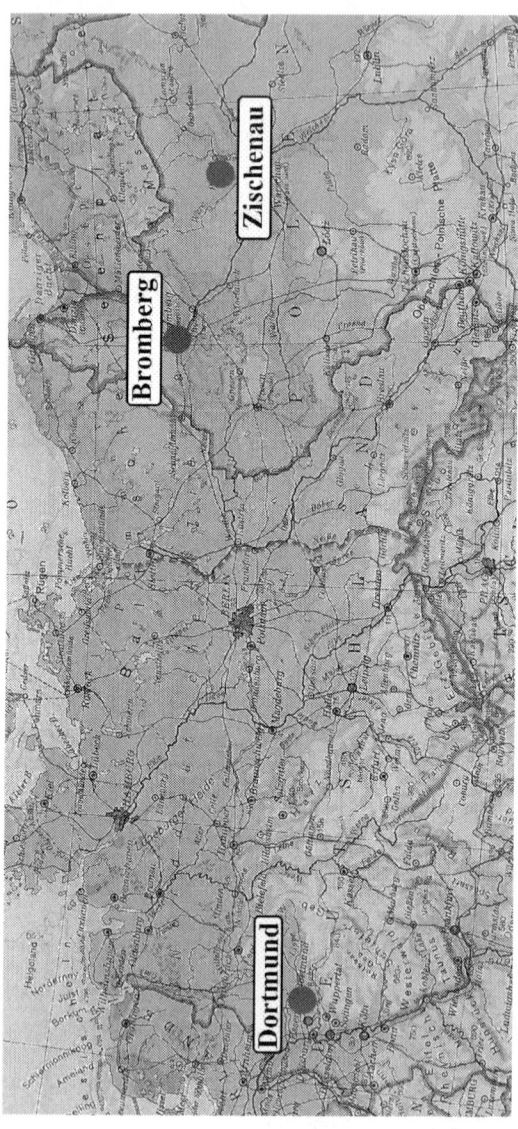

Mariann: a Teacher in Poland (born 1921)

Poland is a rather small country. In size it could compare with Arizona. For centuries Poland has always been squeezed in between Russia and Germany, (or rather Prussia*). *) Prussia had been just one independent German state, each one was ruled by a king or archdukedom, dukedom, etc. Actually Austria had a part of Poland. Through the centuries she had been divided, partially unified and then divided again.

Several centuries ago some German settlers had been called to Poland (and Russia and other eastern countries) to help German farmers and craftsmen to teach the Poles better methods and technology. Over the century the different ethnicities lived peaceably together, however, most of these former German settlers kept there German language and culture.

My friend Mariann is a descendent of these German settlers. Her parents were born in Bromberg. Her father was a very talented violinist, held the post of concertmaster at the Bromberg Theater, a well respected and well paid position.

After World War I the Treaty of Versailles (1919) decreed that Poland be made a totally independent country state. The then German land at its eastern German border area was to become a part of this new Polish state. Now Bromberg was to become Polish and its name was changed to Bydgoszcz. The new Polish government gave the ethnic Germans the choice of staying there and becoming Poles in language and culture or to get out. The newlyweds, who later would become Mariann's parents, chose to move to the west. Since the bride's sister had already moved some time ago to Dortmund in the western part of Germany, their went there too. The young couple had to start with nothing. They could take only one or two suitcases with them. Their possessions and even their bank savings were collected by the new Polish state.

Two years later, in 1921, Mariann was born in Dortmund. The young family was not exactly destitute. The father had found violin students, who wanted to be taught, but money was very tight and the future did not look promising. The reparation payments to France, ordered at the Treaty of Versailles, were a great impediment to the recovery of the German economy. Unemployment was growing, inflation was looming. And Mariann's father did not have a secure job at first.

Mariann tells how things went:

A few years after I was born my father heard that the city orchestra had openings for musicians, especially a violist. Even though my father was a violinist, not a violist, he applied anyway and was asked to play at the audition, as did many others. He must have been very good because he was told that if he could manage to switch from violin to viola in six weeks, he would get the job.* This was very important because it made him a civil servant with a tenured position, the salary guaranteed by the municipality. It still was not much, and money was always scarce. But my parents put some money away all year long so that we could have a little of a summer vacation. Despite everything we were a happy family. My father had a sunny disposition and a great sense of humor and my mother was of a happy nature. *) The viola is slightly larger than a violin and the pitch of the strings are different. On top of this, music for the viola is written in the alto-clef which is different from the treble clef in which violin music is written. To transfer from the violin to the viola, is a formidable task.

On many Sunday afternoons we would pack some bread-cake that my mother had baked and hiked to a café in the country where we would order some coffee and eat our cake. At one such outing, 1932, I must have been 11 years old at the time, my parents looked at the magazines that were laid out for the patrons, and my father took one that had on the cover a large picture of Hitler. He passed it to my mother and said: "Look at this physiognomy! And this wants to be Germany's leader!" At the next election my parents, of course, did not vote for Hitler, but he made it anyway finally.

Mariann was not interested in politics and at age 12 the change in power did not touch her. However, she remembers that, before the Hitler government, beggars had regularly come to their door. Her family lived on the third floor of a modest house in a quiet street.

During the muddled government of Weimar my mother had dreaded opening the door of our apartment when my father was at rehearsals. She had always kept a few coins in her apron pocket because it would not do to tell the beggar to wait a moment for her to get some money and to close the door on him. The beggar would put his foot in the door and that would be even scarier and probably dangerous. But after the Hitler government, now there were no beggars anymore, no men loitering on the streets. Now people were employed by the growing economy and by building the Autobahns. Younger men were working with the Arbeitsdienst*) *) The Arbeitsdienst had actually been founded after WWI and gave young men the opportunity to work at community projects while living in camps. It had been a rather small operation that was not very well financed.

But after 1935 it was taken over by the NSDAP (National Social German Labor Party) and made mandatory for at least one year.

Our own financial situation had not changed. I remember that when I started Upper School, the college preparatory school*).
*) After four years of elementary school the Upper School started for students who planned for a more academic profession. This lasted for more eight years, ended with an examination and let one start at a university. The others stayed for an extra four years in the "Peoples' School" (Volksschule). These students would then start an apprenticeship for a trade.

Many of the girls in my class had these beautiful leather cases with rows of colored pencils, a fountain pen and what not, while I had my wooden pencil box from elementary school. I felt a little ashamed but then my father found his own old, rather simple, leather case from his days as a university student in Berlin. It was red and it had a lot of cracks but I was very happy to get it.

One day two of the girls in my class came to school wearing brown dresses. It was a really ugly brown and I asked my friend what kind of dresses these were. She said these girls were in the BDM, and she explained that this meant "Bund Deutscher Mädchen" (= "Alliance of German Girls", a national-socialist organization). These two girls were not very intelligent and they did not belong to the group of my own special friends. But with time more girls became members of the BDM and then the uniforms changed to dark blue skirts and white shirts, and short brown jackets (an ugly brown that my father called "shit-yellow").

The girls told us about their meetings. They were singing these neat songs and their leader played along on the harmonica or the guitar. Sometimes they marched on the street. After a while it became like a trend in the class, just like today young girls want jeans and other modish outfits. I told my parents that by now eight girls from my class were in the BDM and that I wanted to belong too. My father sighed: "Do you really have to?" and my mother said: "That costs money." The girls had to pay a little bit of a monthly membership fee and then there was the uniform. But I begged and begged and finally my parents conceded. Later it became mandatory to join.

I liked the meetings very well. We sang a lot, all these lively songs that had rhythm. And sometimes we played lining up and marching. When we turned 14 we were transferred into the group for older girls and that was not so nice anymore. I did not know most of the others; they had gone to different schools. And most had already started their apprenticeships and were going to trade school, and they had interests that were very different from mine.

I withdrew a little from that group and then I managed to become part of a sports group within the BDM. It was Called "Glaube und Schönheit" (= Faith and Beauty). *We wore pretty blue skirts and blue slacks and we just did pretty exercises.*

The year 1939, the time before the war, was terrible because we felt that the world was somehow drawing together around us and it looked like war might break out. My father was basically an optimist and he kept saying: "It will be alright, I hope there will be no war." My mother did not think about politics and she would say: "It would be terrible but it probably will not happen." To me it was scary. I was 17, going on 18. All my closest friends had brothers who were a few years older than we were. They were at the age when they would have to go to war and that was for me a terrifying thought.

About one week before the war started, Hitler and Stalin signed a no-aggression pact. The two countries should be neutral. Secret protocols were part of the no-aggression pact that the Soviets should have the right to annex the Eastern countries could include into the USSR. Poland was being divided. Two thirds of Poland was supposed to belong to the Soviets; Germany got the western one third of Poland. Actually the Soviets had already started to invade the Polish area. At September 1st 1939 German military invaded Poland and thus started WWII.

Mariann tells:

And then suddenly there was war. The government told that there had been trouble at the border with Poland, that the Poles had made illegal forays across the border into Germany and that Hitler had to restore order there. Therefore Germany had to march into Poland.

My class should have started the last school of Upper School. We should have taken the college entrance exam (Abitur) in about one year. Now, since war had broken out. It was decreed that we should take the college entrance exam as soon as possible. In our case we were put together with the class above us. Our teachers were desperate. How could they teach us in three months what should have taken a little than a year? A lot of the material was left out and we took the exam.

Around that time, in 1940, the first bombs were dropped on Dortmund. We went to the places where they had fallen to look at the bomb craters, and we were shocked. And then massive bomb raids started in Dortmund. Every night we had to go down into the cellar, most nights even twice, and spend at least two hours there.

All inhabitants of the apartments of the house were sitting in the cellar. This cellar was, of course, not very safe. It had not been built as a bomb shelter but it was better than nothing.

I had wanted to become a librarian but there was no library college in Dortmund. The next one was in Münster in Westfalen at the university some distance north. But my parents did not want to let me go. I was their only child and they wanted to keep me close since nobody knew how the war would develop. My mother suggested that I go to the teacher training college that was only a 15 minute walk from our house. I was very unhappy. I did not want to become a teacher. But finally I gave in. I must admit that I didn't want to go far away either. I wanted to stay close to my parents during this hard time.

A female friend of mine went to the same teacher training college with me. So I was not alone. But the situation there was not nice. We were 400 girls in one class and maybe two or three men who were either cripples or otherwise not fit to serve in the military. None of the teachers knew any of the students. And then the same thing happened as at the Upper School at the teacher training college; it was decreed that we should take the final exam with the class above us. We had had only two years of training.

During the lectures we had to take detailed notes and I did not know shorthand. I wrote everything in longhand but so sloppily – it had to be fast – that I could hardly decipher it later. Therefore I spent all the time that we had to be in the cellar during the bomb raids, transcribing my notes into orderly, legible handwriting. The others slept or conversed but I wrote. That helped me a lot later on.

As soon as I had my diploma as a school teacher, I received an order to report for duty with the government official in the former Poland, in Zischenau (Polish: Zischanov). My parents fetched the atlas, found that it was 80 km (50 miles) north of Warsaw, and calculated that this was 1039 km (645 miles) as the crow flies from home. This meant a trip of one and a half days by train, not counting possible multiple stops in between. One would also have to get out of the train frequently when bombardment and/or shelling occurred.

My parents were devastated. Then, a few days later, I received an order from a different government office, to report to a place rather close to Dortmund for service in the female Arbeitsdienst. We hoped that I could go to the Arbeitsdienst close by and forget about Poland. My father took the letter from the Arbeitsdienst and went to the appropriate office.

The man there asked him why he had come at all. The order I had received, gave all the necessary information.

So why come to him? Then he asked what I was doing at the moment, and my father had to confess that I was a teacher, having just graduated from the teacher training college. And now the man informed him: "Since she has finished her training, she is automatically exempt from serving in the Arbeitsdienst. But she does have to go to Poland and teach there. There is no way around it."

My friend who had attended the teacher training college with me, had received the same order as I, and so we traveled together. My parents came to the railway station with me. I had never before seen my father cry.

We arrived in Zischenau in the evening, after a two day trip. The train station was a good distance from the town and we didn't know where to go from there. Each of us had two suitcases, filled not only with our personal things but also with blankets and featherbeds and sheets because on our draft papers it had said "living quarters on location". We had interpreted this as meaning that we would be assigned a room which we would have to furnish ourselves. Naturally, we could not have taken any furniture with us but we felt that it would be important to have at least something to cover ourselves with at night.

Now we were standing there at the station, both of us rather shy and apprehensive and probably a little scared. Finally we spotted a man standing close by who spoke German. I took all my courage together and asked him where we would find a hotel. We wanted to walk with our suitcases, we were thrifty, but the man told us, it was too far, and we had to hire a Panjewagon. This turned out to be a small conveyance, a kind of a cart pulled by a poor, starved horse between two shafts.

After about 2 km over the bumpy road we arrived at the hotel "Zischenauer Hof". The proprietor was German and I, naïve as I was, asked him right away if there were any vermin in the beds. After all that was part of the picture of Poland with which we had been indoctrinated. He was clearly offended.

We slept well and undisturbed and the next morning we walked to the government building to report there and to ask where our "living quarters on location" were located. Nobody had any idea. But they told us about the principal of the school, Leo Hinz, and that he was very good at organizing.

So we went to his house, a little house at the outskirts of town. He lived with his family that was: his wife, four children and his mother-in-law. The house had actually been condemned but since no new houses were being built, they lived there anyway.

Two other teachers lived there too, a lady of about 30 years and a young man. Leo Hinz's oldest daughter slept in a small, very narrow room at the back of the house. Since we had come, she had to move in with the lady teacher (which neither one of them liked very much) and my friend and I got the narrow room. From somewhere came two old bed frames with some boards fitted in them and the young teacher went to the nearest farm and got two sacks filled with straw. We also got a tiny wardrobe and a little table and this was our "living quarters on location".

And then we had actually a pretty gay time. The principal was very "brown" (=national-socialist) but very nice and easygoing. We danced in the living room on the sagging floor (which must have been rather dangerous) and got along fine with everybody.

Teaching school was a different matter. Our school experience was next to non-existent. During our training we had had a few weeks of watching other teachers in the schoolroom but that did not help much. Most of the children were Volksdeutsche, that is ethnic Germans who had always lived outside the Reich.

When Mariann's parents had left Poland more than 20 years before they wanted to remain German and not become Poles. But many people had stayed in Poland and become Polish because mostly these poor people had nowhere else to go.

They and their ancestors had, alternately, been under German, Polish, and Russian rule. They had, more or less, adapted to their respective rulers. Now Germany, or rather Hitler, wanted to be Poland "Germanized". The ethnic Germans were treated better and got better food ration stamps than the ethnic Poles. The joke went: "Anybody who has ever had a German shepherd, has a right to be German".

This made teaching very difficult. The Volksdeutsche (ethnic German) children spoke Polish at home, their German was not very good but they were very good in mathematics. Then there were the Reichsdeutsche children, the children of the German government officials, physicians, bank people, teachers, etc. After the German invasion these Germans had been either persuaded or ordered to come to this area from Germany (just like Mariann and her friend).

Their children made up about half of the class and they could, of course, speak and write German very well.

There were no schools for the Polish children. They had been closed when the Germans came in and not reopened for the years of the German occupation. The Poles were apparently supposed to stay dumb.

The school where Mariann had to teach in German, was housed in newly built barracks. At first there were four grades, then six and finally eight.

At home in Dortmund Mariann had not real with contact with Jews. There had been a few Jewish girls in her class in elementary school but they belonged to different groups of friends than Mariann's. And Dortmund was apparently one of the places where Jews were not forced to wear the yellow star. Mariann never saw any. But in Zischenau there were many Jews and they were very visible. Mariann remembers:

There were many Jews in Zischenau. We lived on a rather wide street and in the evening the Jews would walk there. They had to walk in the street, they were forbidden to walk on the sidewalks. They walked in rows of three, four, and five. They were Eastern Jews, having beards and curls hanging down at the sides of their faces, and they were always wearing hats or caps. We felt a little scared by these strange looking men because at that time it was the fashion for men to be clean shaven, except maybe for a small mustache (leftover from monarchic times). We did not know at the time that orthodox Jews are not allowed to shave off their beards and that they have to wear certain garb. In my naiveté I thought: 'The Jews know that Hitler does not like them, so why don't they at least shave off their beards?' Also new to me was the fact that these Jews were wearing yellow stars. We had not seen those in Dortmund. Apparently it was up to the city governments to decide.

Two Polish girls came every day to help with the housework and to stoke the large stoves. Once a week a Jewish lady came here to do the nails of all the females in the household. We two girls were sitting there like grand ladies to have our manicures, and we felt a little silly. But we were told that this was necessary to let the Jewish lady make a little money. There was also a Jewish tailor and a seamstress who came to the house. When we had arrived, we had been given ration coupons for a winter coat. I was lucky to get the last one in my size; it was a fake fur coat. I was so proud, even though it turned out later that it was not as warm as my friend's less flashy coat. I bought myself a little green hat to go with it and I felt like a million.

My friend had not gotten a ready-made coat (she was a little more substantial than I) and therefore had bought some heavy fabric to have a coat made. The Jewish tailor came to our house to measure her and pick up the fabric, and later for several fittings.

And then my grandmother sent me fabric for a summer dress. It was green, white and yellow striped and was very stiff because it had served as the awning over her balcony. A Jewish seamstress came to the house and took the fabric and my measurements with her. She was supposed to bring back the finished dress in time for our summer vacation when we were going home. For some reason that I forgot, we were suddenly told that we could leave two days earlier than planned and I had to visit the seamstress to pick up my dress. This was a very depressing experience. She lived in an apartment in a tenement house behind other houses, and it was very crowded. The people there were all Jews. In the corner of the room was a large bed and on that bed lay an old man who was very ill and probably dying. It was terrible for me to see this poverty.

Over the three years that I spent in Poland, alternately in town and in the countryside, I realized that there were less and less Jews and I heard that some had been taken to concentration camps. I asked around what that meant but I could not get real answers. From what I was told and I thought, "concentration" that means to think hard, to focus one's thoughts on one specific thing. The Jews do not like Hitler. It will be made clear to them how much good he has done for us in the beginning and then they will change their thinking. That's what I thought about concentration camps. We probably just pushed this whole issue aside. We were young, we wanted to have fun, and we had this nice living community with other colleagues. We did not have to cook; grandma did this with the help of one of the Polish girls. We could sit down at the table and eat. We were doing well, there were no bomb raids at night; this area was apparently uninteresting for the bombers.

And then I was transferred to the countryside. I had been picked up by an old coach about 40km (24 miles) away. In this place there was a sugar refinery, being used sugar beets. The director, a Reichsdeutscher, had been drafted to the military, as well as the technical manager. I found a room at the manager's house. But it was hard for me because I could not really talk to anybody. The manager's wife was Italian, even spoke German quite well, but she was working each day.

Now I was made to school principal and the only teacher at this village. I had about 17 students. Two of them were Reichsdeutsche.

The Volksdeutsche were somehow good in mathematics, the Reichsdeutsche were of course good at speaking, writing and reading. It was not possible to classify the children into grades because each one knew different things and many spoke little German because they spoke Polish at home. They were all in one room and I had to teach the children at the same time. But I somehow made it.

Then I got a garden where I was supposed to teach the children growing vegetables. I had absolutely no knowledge what to do; I had always lived in the city, so I had to imitate the neighbors. I found radish seeds, for these long, white radishes, and so we sowed all the seeds, rows and rows. It was terrible. Each day at the10 o'clock break I scrapped and grated radishes. It must have grown radishes out of the children's ears and noses.

And then my fiancé got furlough. We had known each other from childhood on and we planned to marry as soon as it was possible with the war situation. My fiancé had asked that I would be free during the same days and he, as a young officer, it was approved. I was so surprised that he had dared to ask at all. We both traveled home where we officially engaged. We wanted to marry at the next furlough but I never saw him again. He was killed in Russia.

Before my fiancé had asked that I would be moved back to Zischenau and it was approved. When I arrived in Zischenau, I was given a class of about 4o boys and girls. Some among were the most outrageous impertinent and nasty boys. By that time the principal had changed to a more than 60 year old and mild man since the former principal had been drafted. Now he would always say: "Dear children, you must not do this!" and made them stay after school, but they always managed to climb out of a window. It was a very bad class. One more than 30 years old female teacher cried and wept each time after having taught just a geography lesson. Now I the youngest teacher and had to teach them. A few of the boys were taller at least half a head than I, and more solid. I was short and slim. But I made it.

Then I was moved to a different village of about 200 residents. All the Poles and the Volksdeutsche lived in small wooden houses, but I had given the only one built of stone and at it was at the very end of the village. Soon I realized how dangerous it was there. Guerrilla bands were in the woods near the village. I was scared and several times I went to the mayor's house to sleep in the barn. The mayor was Volksdeutsch, lived with his wife and many children. I had to eat with the family. It was so dirty and messy, but I ate it anyway.

One morning the mayor's 15 years old Polish hired hand came in, totally distraught, and crying. He had wanted to visit his aunt at a farm that was some distance from the village and had found everybody on the farm murdered. The guerrillas had been there a few days before and had robbed the farm clean of everything edible. They had told the people that they should not report the robbery; otherwise they would all be killed.

But the farm people did not have anything left to eat; they had to get new ration coupons and to obtain these they had to report the robbery because they needed to get food. The guerrillas must have learned about this and so they came and murdered everybody.

After half a year I was moved back to Zischenau. Now I had my friend again. We two girls were convinced that Germany would win the war. We believed in the miracle weapon. Our friend, a government official who kept saying to us: "Look at this map, girls. I always mark the front with these little flags and the front is moving backward. Think about these troop movements. How can you still believe? What can you still have hope? The war is lost." We thought how he can talk that way! He is a defector. And we told him, not to talk too loud so that other people could hear him because then he would be arrested. But we comforted ourselves with the conviction that this man just did not see the facts right, that at the very end the miracle weapon would come and we would win the war.

Mariann and her friend made it out just barely to get home to the West. At home in Dortmund she did not find her neighborhood streets anymore. The houses had been flattened and covered with rubble. Her house had been burned by phosphor incendiary bombs. But her parents had survived. When the schools in Germany were opened again after the war, Mariann was teaching again there with great success, and her students loved her and she loved them. Later many years her former students kept connections with her. It had turned out that she was a born teacher anyway. Mariann lives happily with her physics-professor husband, her children and grandchildren.

I have known Mariann for more than forty years. She is always positive and she helps everyone who does need help. She is active at their church; she loves music and she loves nature. I have never heard Mariann speak negatively of anybody. She takes her age's difficulties with humor. I think that Mariann has given a lot of light and still gives light and warmth to all around her.

Victor: Life Between Four Different Cultures
(Russian, Serbian, German, American)

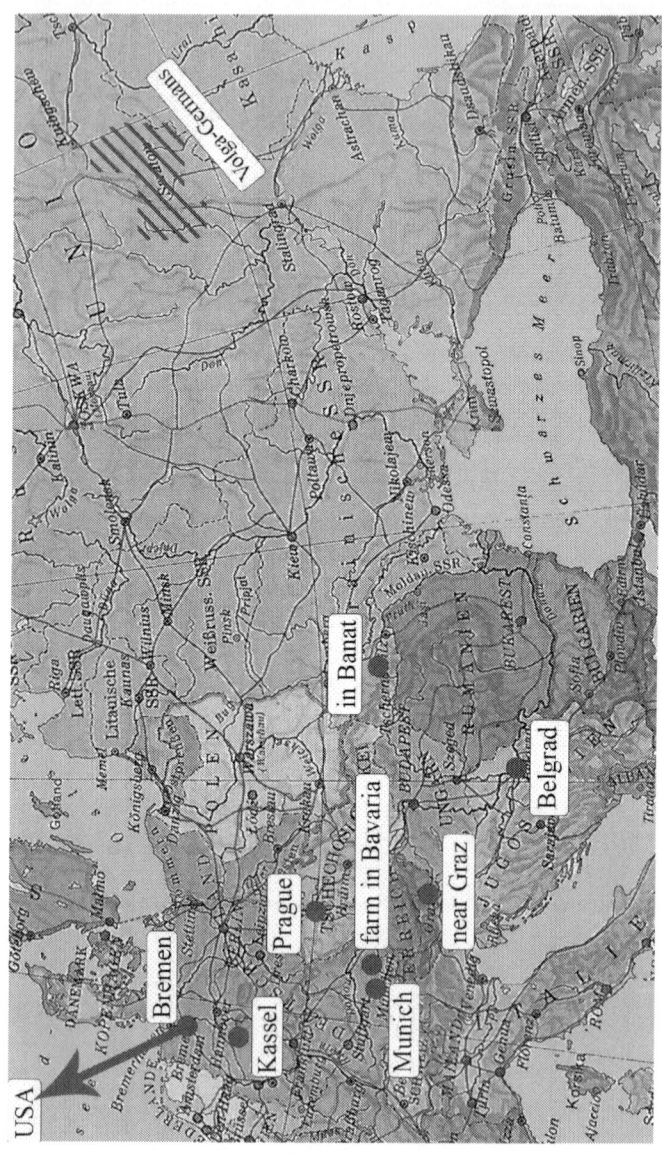

Victor: Life Between Four Different Cultures (born 1934)
(Russian, Serbian, German, American)

Russia and the Soviet Union are often looked upon as being one and the same but they are not the same at all. Russia, this vast and somehow mysterious country, has a long and varied history and a very rich and unique culture. The Soviet Union, however, was founded in 1918/19 by Lenin and Trotzki, after a very brutal and bloody civil war, as a communist federation of states. Russia was the heartland of the Soviet Union but more than 10 other countries were also part of it. The Soviet government built up a huge political apparatus that was supposed to reach every aspect of the lives of its subjects. It also did its best to change Russian culture, life style, and social structure, the people's beliefs and their value systems. When the Soviet Union broke apart in 1991, it left the people, most of who had only lived under its system, confused about values and beliefs and, basically, their culture.

Geographically and economically Russia is divided into a (smaller) European and a (larger) Asian region by the Ural mountain range that runs roughly north-south. Naturally, the European part, with Moscow and St. Petersburg, was always more oriented to the west than the less developed Asian part of the country. Russian royals and nobles had close ties to Europe and the European courts.

Due to larger population density in Western Europe, technological progress went faster there than in the vast spaces of Russia. In 1697 the Tsar decided to travel west himself to see what he could learn there and later apply in his own country. Tsar Peter was 25 years old. For 17 months he toured mostly the Netherlands and England. He brought back with him many western engineers, architects, scientists, and artists.

This royal undertaking must have seemed very romantic at the time. Composers used the story of the traveling Tsar, wildly embellished, as basis for operas. They had him, for example, working, incognito, as a carpenter at a Dutch shipyard. The composer Lortzing's opera "Tsar and Carpenter" is still being played today.

For many centuries royal and noble families had taken young ladies to get married to into other royals and nobles with political reasons. The couple had not met before the marriage.

Tsar Peter the Great (the one who had traveled in Holland and England) wanted more relations with Prussia. Therefore he sent his daughter Anna Petrowna to be married to the Duke of Holstein-Gottorf in, what is today, northern Germany. We do not know if the Russian bride was happy so far away from home. However in 1728 Anna Petrowna and the German Duke had a son who they named Peter, probably after his grandfather. In 1742 when Peter was 14 years old, it turned out that he was the only heir to the Russian throne. He was sent to St. Petersburg, Russia's capital at the time, where his aunt Elisabeth was the reigning empress. When Peter had reached the appropriate age for marriage, the empress Elizabeth chose a bride for him, Katharina, the daughter of a different Prussian duke. The young princess was sent on the long journey into a foreign land to marry a man she had never met. The trip, by carriage and sled, from the bride's new to the Russian royal court in St. Petersburg is supposed to have taken three weeks.

Life at the Russian royal court was full of intrigues and power struggles, especially after the Empress Elizabeth died and young Peter became Tsar Peter III. Peter had always felt more Prussian than Russian. His idol was the Prussian king Frederic the Great. His young wife Katharina, however, embraced Russian culture and language, even though she came from Prussia too.

Katharina felt that she would be much better equipped to rule Russia than her husband. In 1762, two years after Peter had ascended to the throne, he was murdered and Katharina became empress of Russia.

The story of Victor's ancestors begins before these events. When Tsar Peter III came to Russia from his home in northern Germany, he took along several members of his German court, among them a nobleman named Wilhelm, who became Victor's great-great-great-grandfather. Wilhelm served Tsar Peter III very faithfully. When he saved the Tsar's life by carrying him out of his burning bedroom, the Tsar showed his gratitude in a big way. He elevated Wilhelm to the rank of a count and gave him large land holdings east of the river Volga. After Peter's death, Katharina ordered all nobles, loyal to the deceased Tsar, away from the royal court. Also Wilhelm was sent away and from then on, lived on his estates. His family prospered greatly and, through centuries and through many generations, kept their loyalty to the Russian Tsars alive.

This area was rather fertile but thinly populated, and the neighboring Tartars showed no respect for their border with Russia.

When Katharina came to power, she called Germans, especially from southwest Germany, to settle this vast area and serve as a shield to the invading Tartars. Around 1764, two years after Katharina had ascended the throne, about 290,000 Germans had immigrated to the former provinces of Saratov and Samara. Over the next century, colonies extended to the Ural Mountains in the east and the Ukraine in the west. Eventually there were German settlements on the steppes near the Black Sea, in Kazakhstan, Turkistan, and Siberia, among others. These German-settlers kept their language and culture. In 1919 this area was declared to be the autonomy "Volga German Republic" as part of the Soviet Union. However the turbulent years of the Russian Revolution, famine, pogroms, abductions, and war deaths decimated the number of Germans. Victor's family did not stay in Russia.

At the outbreak of the Russian Revolution in 1917, Victor's father, Count Michael, was an officer in the Royal Army. The parts of the military loyal to the Tsar formed the so-called White Army, in contrast to the Bolshevik Red Army. The fighting between the armies was harsh and the White Army fought with great courage and determination, but the Red Army was much larger. The Red Army fought so cruelly, not only against their "enemies" but also by brutalizing civilians. That the White Army had to retreat and Michael with it. From the southern city of Taganrog at the shore of the Sea of Azov (which is connected to the Black Sea) the White Army evacuated large numbers, not only of Russian-Germans but also of Cossack civilians who had lived in these southern areas and who had been persecuted or were in danger from the Bolsheviks because of their loyalty to the Tsar.

Victor tells what happened before his birth and later:

Among the Cossack families that my father Michael's unit helped to evacuate, was also, unbeknown to him at the time, the family of his future wife, Elena. Her family had joined many other officers' families who followed their fathers, brothers, and sons into battle against the Red Army. Elena's mother and older sister helped with the wounded; her older brother took part in guarding the baggage train and was involved in several fire fights. The two youngest, Elena and her brother were busy in the field kitchen or elsewhere in the baggage train. All had witnessed the horrors of fratricidal war, but the most emotionally disturbing were the dead and alive victims of atrocities, according to Elena, by the Bolsheviks. She remembered corpses of cadets, barely 12 or 13 years old, with officer's rank insignia crudely carved on their shoulders, hysterical nurses, bloody from gang rapes, old men in tattered remains of high-ranking officers' uniforms whipped to death with knouts.

For the rest of her life she feared, despised and hated anything and anybody that was even remotely connected with the people, works of art, music, and even the simplified grammar and alphabet instituted by the USSR.

Elena was a girl at the time. After all this her family was evacuated to the Crimean Peninsula, then spent some time in Constantinople (today's Istanbul) and finally settled down in Belgrade, Serbia. There Michael and Elena met, many years later. By this time Elena had become a highly acclaimed and talented prima ballerina and Michael was working for a publishing house. The two fell in love, married, and had a son, Victor, in 1934. They lived near Belgrade for several years, peacefully and in relative comfort.

In the meantime, however, Josip Broz Tito (1892-1980) gained power in Yugoslavia. Since WWI Serbia and other small countries belongs to Yugoslavia. He had become in close contact with Communism during his time as a Russian POW during WWI. When he was released in 1920, he returned home and helped organize the Communist Party in Yugoslavia. In 1945, after WWII he set up a Communist government in Yugoslavia, recognized by the Soviet Union, the US, and Great Britain. Later he made himself president of Yugoslavia for life. He did limit the power of the secret police and allowed some economic and political freedom. But still he kept tight control over his people. Under his rule Yugoslavia (especially the west coast along the Adriatic Sea) became a favorite vacation spot for German tourists. Many Yugoslavians spoke German since large parts of the country had belonged to the Austrian-Hungarian Empire until 1918.

In April 1941, just before Easter, in Belgrad German troops invaded Yugoslavia. Before the soldiers came to Belgrade, it was bombarded from the air. Victor recalls:

I was torn from sleep by a gut wrenching howling that rose to an impossibly high pitch, followed by a millisecond of silence, followed by a whistling that ended in an ear shattering explosion. And again, and again, and yet again. Mom burst into my room, grabbed me from the bed with my blanket, and rushed downstairs into the cellar – which until that moment I did not know existed. Much later we learned that the howling was from sirens purposely installed on the dive bombers to demoralize the enemy, and the whistling was the actual bombs falling to earth.

We stayed in the cellar until finally the horrible noise stopped and it became almost painfully quiet.

When we finally ventured outside, we saw that our neighborhood did not sustain any damage, but I vividly remember that the air smelled strange and there were clouds of smoke over the city. As soon as the bombs stopped falling, Dad left to join his cavalry unit.

Up until then, Easter had always been a happy event. Victor would wake up on the morning of Easter Sunday to the smells of special Easter food and the flowers that covered a long table in the formal room. It was the tradition that guests would arrive from noontime on, for food and exchanging news. The women would stay home to receive the guests; the men (and male children) would go visiting other houses. Victor recollect as former Easter celebrations were.

Dad and I, dressed in our best, left the house a little before noon – it was necessary for us to leave before the guests arrived. We drove from one friend's house to the next, being greeted by the hostesses and daughters with "Khristos voskrese" (Christ is risen) and answering "Voistinu voskrese" (Truly he has risen). The adults would take a small sip of vodka, the children a sip of punch and all would nibble a taste of the endless variety of delicious dishes. My favorites were stuffed eggs, pirozhki with onion and cabbage, and blinchiki with fried ground meat. By late afternoon we would return home, stuffed and happy, full of stories about all the people we visited, the food we ate and the news from friends and family.

But in April 1941, when Victor was eight years old, and Belgrade was bombarded, there were no Easter celebrations. The family lived at one of the suburbs.

The room in its pre-Easter splendor looked unreal. This was the first Easter that Dad was not home, and nobody came to visit.

We watched for several days as people streamed past our house, escaping from the city into the country. The weather was hot and Mom carried a hose out to the street so passers-by could have a drink.

The maid had fled; the cook, who also did the daily shopping, did not come for some time, so there was no fresh food in the house. Victor's grandmother walked from her apartment in the city to be with her daughter and grandson. She must have walked for hours, and she brought some food with her.

Some days later, just as things sort of calmed down, we were again awakened by the strangest sounds I had ever heard.

It is impossible to describe the tremor of the earth and the staccato bursts of high-pitched engine sounds that would then subside into a deep-throated rumble, only to be interrupted by screeching sounds that made my skin prickle with goose bumps. German tanks had arrived on our street and were setting up housekeeping. As the sun rose, I was able to see that the tanks were parking in long rows in the field across the street. While I peeked through the curtains, one of the tanks rolled up to our fence and casually flattened it, swinging the turret back and forth across the width of the yard and house. Of course, this resulted in no response from us, except that Mom yanked me from the window and we ran down into the cellar again. Soon afterwards we heard the front door bell ring and my grandmother went to answer it. She told Mom and me to stay put, reasoning that if they rang the doorbell, they would not harm an old woman. She reappeared at the cellar door with an officer, jaunty in his black and silver uniform and beret. Mom knew some German and the officer knew some Serbian. We were informed that the officer would need the upstairs bedrooms and the attic, and we were welcome to stay at the ground floor. My grandmother explained with much body language that the fence needed to be repaired, to which the officer nodded. The three of us moved what we needed from the upstairs into the maid's room [on the ground floor]. For the next week or so, day and night, there was a soldier in the attic standing in the open skylight, looking through binoculars. I suppose that since our house was the tallest object in the area, it served as an observation post. By midday there was a field kitchen in the yard dishing out wonderful smelling stew and coarse black bread. We were invited to bring our dishes and join the soldiers for dinner.

This benevolent occupation continued for about a week. They fed us. They took off their boots to walk through the house and up the stairs. Not one soul spoke harshly or acted abusively towards any of us. There were frequent attempts to engage Mom in conversation about her ballet pictures or some other object in the house. But they were quickly squashed by the appearance of my grandmother, who treated the conquering warriors like children and was universally respected. By the end of the week they had repaired the fence and were gone. The tracks left by the tanks across the street were monumental. Some were knee-deep on me! – Dad still had not returned.

It turned out that Victor's father, Michael, had been taken prisoner of war by the Germans. On that Easter Sunday (April 7, 1941) he had left his family right after the bombardment of Belgrade had stopped, to join his regiment.

But the military units stationed in and around Belgrade had been totally unprepared to outfit the soldiers with weapons and other necessities. Within the hour Michael, with his platoon at half strength and armed only with carbines and sabers, was on his way northeast. The men were tired, they were all worried about their families that they had left behind, and everyone seemed to think there was no chance of winning this war that had come upon them so totally unexpectedly. At a reconnaissance patrol at night Michael and his men were taken unawares by a German tank unit and taken prisoner. The Germans were surprised to find that their prisoners had no proper weapons on them; Michael had only his saber. "Unbelievable, these people want to go against tanks with swords!" said one officer. The Germans put the prisoners in the basement of the village schoolhouse for the night and drove them to a camp in Germany the next day.

Michael spent three months in a German POW camp for officers. They slept on straw mattresses, ate one meal a day consisting of oatmeal gruel or bean soup with bits of pork back fat, and spent their days bored to tears. Although the Germans had allowed organized sports and even provided some soccer balls, it was inevitable that active men used to being busy at some productive task would be depressed and spiritless, finding themselves locked behind barbed wire and separated from their families. At that time they did not know how lucky they were to at least be treated decently, within the framework established by the Geneva Convention on POWs.

Later the prisoners were given preprinted postcards by the Red Cross to send to their families. The cards said: "I am a prisoner of war in Germany" and the men could mark other preprinted sentences like "I am in good health." Only the signature would prove that this was an authentic message. Michael had not signed with his name but with the nickname given to him by his son Victor, thereby proving to the family that it was indeed him who was alive and well.

My father Michael was released from the camp and shipped home after the German authorities traced his name to the German ancestry and nobility title. When asked about his participation in the Yugoslav cavalry, he had the presence of mind not to mention that he had been a volunteer.

Now Victor's father was home but their problems were not solved. He was unemployed, the publishing firm where he had worked, had been confiscated by German authorities (the owners had been Jews), and money was getting more and more scarce.

But above all he was faced with a personal, moral dilemma. Was he with or against the Germans? His name, his title, his father's ancestry placed him squarely with the Germans. His mother's family, his years of working for a Jewish publishing house, placed him squarely against the Germans.

But then he was employed again at the publishing house where he had worked before. The German who had been put in charge of the firm after its take-over, had, during the short time, mismanaged the company very badly and subsequently was replaced by Michael. But the man now wanted to get revenge. He spread rumors that Michael was not really of German descent but a Russian Jew that he had collaborated with Yugoslavian guerillas, had embezzled German funds, and more. These were life-and-death matters in a German-occupied state, since the German GESTAPO* was known *) GESTAPO: Geheime STAats-POlizei (Secret National Police) to act upon rumors, no matter how ridiculous they were. Now Michael was truly in the middle between two camps. On the one hand, some people despised him for feeling German and working for the German occupation force; on the other hand, he had to prove to the Germans that he was loyal to them. His family seemed in some danger too. In their beautiful house, situated rather isolated in the country, they might be attacked by Yugoslav guerillas who thought them German collaborators or the GESTAPO might suspect them of having contacts with the guerillas. They ended up moving from their country house into an apartment in the city. Michael also told his son to be suspicious of strangers and encouraged him to join the "Hitler Youth". He himself made friends with high-ranking German combat officers and finally joined the Russian Volunteer Corps. This was a branch of the German military, comprised mainly of former Russian, (especially Cossack) soldiers. He knew that becoming a German combat officer, would put any rumors against him and his family to rest, it would also give him the opportunity to fight against the hated communists, fulfilling his pledge to the Tsar and to his commanding general 23 years ago.

The English and American air forces began bombing Belgrade in autumn 1941. Initially these were mostly night raids by small numbers of planes, aimed at military targets such as the bridges across the Danube and Sava rivers and the barracks and warehouses.

The air raid sirens would sound and people would walk down to the cellar to wait for the all-clear sound. These air raids were still relatively harmless compared to the bombardment of Belgrade that started later.

– But before that there were occasions where young Victor experience conflicting feelings about his national identity, his sense of belonging.

I was to discover firsthand what it means to be hated. On a bright and sunny Saturday I had decided to explore the military garage near the park where we did our training. The soldiers on watch knew me and allowed me to walk about the garage and admire such wonders as motorcycles with sidecars with mounted light machineguns, armored cars and huge trucks. I had finished my "inspection" and was thanking the guard at the gate when he suddenly took me and threw me into the wooden guardhouse while he grabbed his rifle and brought it into firing position. A farm wagon drawn by a pair of galloping horses was rolling at breakneck pace past the gate. We were showered with dirt clods thrown by youth in peasant garb who were yelling curses and obscenities as only a Serbian knows how. After they passed, the soldier slung his rifle again and bade me to wait until the wagon was safely away. I hurried home, frightened, excited and confused. The attack could have been made with firearms and hand grenades, not dirt clods. I could have been killed. But the people cursing me were my people, weren't they? They looked and dressed like our cook's husband, and like the milkman! They cursed in the language I spoke. God ... this was not a political discussion by adults using incomprehensible words. This was real. This hurt inside of me, and made me want to cry. I did not understand why I felt the way I did. Needless to say, I did not tell my parents.

During the summer of 1942 Victor spent his vacation with his aunt in the country, among farms. There were no air raid by Allied bombers. Life was peaceful.

Every morning each house would let out their milk cow, to wander down the street with all the other cows headed for the common pasture. They would graze all day and come home in the evening in time for the milking. Since we were the last house before the pasture, our street was thronged with brown, white, black-and-white, crooked-horned, hornless, fat, skinny cows – an unbelievable traffic jam twice daily. In the evening all of them came home, each cow slowly finding her way unerringly into her yard, the owners waiting patiently at their door.

When harvest time came, Victor was invited to go with a neighbor and his people to bring in the wheat and rye. Victor was excited to work in the fields with the others but when mealtime came, something strange happened.

There was little conversation while we were eating, but afterwards, when most were stretched out in the shade, some of the young men (who had met us at the field), asked about life in the capital. I told about the bombing of the harbor, the occasional lack of electricity and water, and living in downtown with all the tall buildings and no grass or trees. They were just curious to hear from someone who had just come from the big city – all except one. He kept asking me questions about my parents and the house where I lived in Belgrade. As he asked and I answered, the people around us grew silent and looked away, avoiding my eyes, and a tension descended on our group. Finally, the man wanted to know where I lived in the village. Before I could answer, the farmer with whom I had come along, interrupted me and said it was time to go back to work. Then turning to me he said: "Please return to the village with the girl that brought the milk." I was crushed but nodded politely and said that I would do so. When we arrived home, my aunt asked her what had happened, but neither the girl nor I could tell her, except that it looked like the farmer was angry at me for an unknown reason. That evening at sunset the farmer came across the street to tell me and my aunt that he had not been angry at me, and actually was proud of my behavior and my attempts at helping. But, he said, it was dangerous for me to be out among the people, because many hated the Germans and might hurt me. My aunt and I did not understand how one could tell that I was friendly towards the Germans, let alone of German descent, but the farmer said that it was easy, and left it at that.

Again I met the specter of hate. This time, instead of hot violence, I felt the coldness of faces turned away, of silence where there had been conversation and laughter, of danger in simply telling someone where I lived.

In late 1943 the allied bombing of Belgrade intensified. The alarms could come anytime, day and night.

The number of the attacking planes increased. There were raids when the deep rumbling sound of engines seemed to encompass the whole sky. Although these planes did not howl like the German Stukas (diving-fighting planes, similar to allied chase-bombers), *they made up for it by the duration of the raids and the sheer volume of the explosions. Civilian areas were hit regularly. Mom's brother was killed during one of the raids. A plane had apparently strayed from the pack and dropped its load in a wide swath of destruction that covered cornfields and a farm, seven kilometers outside of town. The farmhouse, where my uncle lived, was disintegrated; no whole bodies were found.*

These were Allied airplanes. Cities and some rural areas were bombed, just because Serbia was German occupied.

By this time we were quite organized with our air-raid procedures: candles, playing cards, books, blankets and pillows were stored in "our corner of the shelter". At each warning signal we took down a jug of water, a box of sugar cubes, Valerian drops (to be drizzled on a sugar cube to calm the nerves), and a bottle of slivovitz. Sometimes the planes headed away from Belgrade and the all-clear sounded after the early warning. If the planes continued on course for the city, the final alarm signal blew the ululating howl and we trooped down the stairs, Mom clutching the little gray suitcase filled with our family silver and her jewels. I always brought my bear, Mishka. The sound of the alarm sirens became almost as hated as the actual raid. It just wore you down. And then, the sitting and waiting for the first load to drop – Is it coming our way? Will they stay on the river or swing over the town? Oh, yes, they are swinging this way, you can hear the engine drone has changed pitch and is increasing. Wait. Wait. And first the howling, the soul-searing howling as the bombs finally fall. And then the impact, with the trembling earth, the dust sifting down from the cellar ceiling. And the acrid smell if it hit close. Mom and I clutch each other, someone says: "Open your mouth to keep the eardrums from getting ruptured!" Mom prays a hurried, soft-voiced litany "Spasi Gospodi, spasi Gospodi, spasi Gospodi (save us, Lord). Someone is saying the Lord's Prayer. I never could concentrate well enough to put any prayer together. Sometimes there would be a person from another apartment without anyone to be with – he or she would be immediately "adopted" because it is awful to be alone in the shelter without anybody to hug. No more howling. Is the engine drone moving away? Exhale, nibble on the sugar. Take small sips of water. "No, you should not have the Valerian drops unless we have three waves*; it is not healthy to overdo them." *) The bomb attacks would usually come in waves, one large swarm of bomber airplanes after another. *"Yes, I will have a drop of your slivovitz." "Thanks for the cigarette." The engines drone again. Silence in the shelter. No one needs to say "here they come again". This time it's a multi-voiced symphonic scream that dissolves into individual howls – "Phosphorus sticks" somebody whispers. There is no explosion, but we listen for the crackle of fire, the metallic smell of burning phosphorus. It can not be extinguished, they say. The droning of engines diminishes. Exhale. Not us. Someone else. The all clear sounds. I always feel so tired after a raid. We walk stiffly up the stairs. The air is thick with dust. The smoke does not smell like a leaf or wood fire - it smells of garbage and something sweet. My ears feel thick, as if there is water in them. I shake my head to the side and pick with my finger, try to blow my nose gently.*

"Just let it be," says the soldier who guards our house, "it will be gone in a while; it's just the sudden pressure on the eardrums." We walk in the apartment. All our windows are gone this time. Luckily we had opened them and hung heavy drapes in front of them, so the shattered glass is not spread throughout the entire room. Mom begins to sweep the rug. – There are odd shaped pieces of concrete on the back balcony and a lot of gravel-like debris. I start sweeping the balcony and find one of the cats seemingly unhurt, but lifeless, with a tiny trickle of blood from his nose. I cry. He was such a friendly cat.

In 1943 Victor's father had joined the Russian Corps.

The soldiers in the squadron were all Russians, émigrés who had left Russia in the 1920s like Dad and Mom, or members of the Red Army who recently fled the communist regime in their homeland and wished to fight against it, to free Russia from communism.

Victor and his mother were allowed to join his father at his training post in the region of Banat, near the Romanian border. However, the political situation had become such that they did not know if they would ever come back to their apartment in Belgrade. Most of their belongings were either sold or given away: furniture, the precious books, paintings, dishes.

The summer in the little village in Banat was a welcome respite from the tensions, the fear of guerilla attacks, and the air raids of Belgrade. It was safe for them to move around freely since the area was pro-German. Victor's mother could ride her beloved horses and Victor was allowed to watch and even help the unit's veterinarian, a wonderful experience for him which, much later, would become his career and love of his life.

During the fall of 1943 the German military situation changed drastically. Romania was about to join the Soviet Union in its fight against Germany and the possibility of a Soviet invasion of Yugoslavia became very real. In September 1943 all military families were ordered to leave Yugoslavia. Victor's father had arranged for his wife and son to travel to a farm in Bavaria.

There was a train at the station for military dependents.

The train consisted of a giant steam locomotive, a baggage car, a platform car with an antiaircraft gun and two heavy machine guns, five sleeper cars, a dining car, and another platform car with guns. A flatcar, loaded with sandbags was attached in front of the locomotive, to absorb any damage from mines planted on the track.

The going was slow to allow the sandbag-filled flatcars in front of the locomotive to explode any mines that might be on the rail bed. After almost a day of travel the train stopped. No station, no houses, not even farms could be seen. We were surrounded by endless fields of corn. Word was passed to the passengers that

damage was spotted on the rails and the sapper squad that was part of the military guard, was going to investigate and repair the damage. Night was falling; power had been turned off by the engineer to assure blackout, and we were told not to light candles or even cigarettes unless the compartment windows were thoroughly covered with light-proof blankets or regulation blackout paper. Stuck as we were, we did not wish to attract unwelcome attention. The train, loaded with German military families, would make an attractive prize for any roaming guerilla bands. In addition, Romania was on the brink of declaring war against Germany and no one knew whether local Romanian guerillas would be reinforced by anti-German government troops, which could easily outnumber our small security detachment.

It had been an exhausting day. I put my head in Mom's lap and was asleep in minutes. Much later, just at the edge of my hearing, somewhere in the hills, I heard engine sounds, truck engines. Almost simultaneously, I heard our locomotive roar into life, jerking the train alive. Then, blinding light from a flare spilled over the valley and the cannon on the flatcar began firing tracers into the dark mass of the hills. Mom and I huddled on the floor of the compartment, enveloped in the endless, rhythmic, deafening succession of explosions from the cannon. I don't recall what made me turn my head and look at the door of our compartment, but as I did so, I saw a row of holes appear in the wooden frame, splinters flying in all directions, the reading lamp in the corner disintegrating – all without an audible sound, like a silent movie. The train gathered speed. The cannon stopped. Only then could we hear machine gun bursts somewhere behind us and then they also stopped, and it was quiet. Only the wonderful clack-clack of the wheels on the track. We were unharmed. When it became light enough to see, I helped Mom carefully sweep and pick up the splinters and glass shards off the seats.

Soon a chatty conductor appeared with a broom and dustpan, sharing with us tales about the other compartments, as if he were gossiping about the last style in ladies' hats. It seems that the same line of bullets that hit our door frame, had shattered the outside window in the next compartment and several people had suffered cuts from the flying glass. We were lucky to have opened our window, he said, and then announced that breakfast was ready in the dining car. I was starving hungry.

In Budapest Victor and his mother had to change trains to their next stage, Prag. The train station was crowded and, naturally, everybody spoke Hungarian, a language that neither Victor nor his mother understood. Nevertheless, they made it to the train and arrived safely in Prague – where they learned that the farm in Bavaria that should have taken them in, had been bombed. Another place had to be found for them and they had to wait in Prague for confirmation. And then came the first air-raid on Prag.

In retrospect, it seemed that even the air raid warning system was caught napping. There was no alarm given; bombs simply started exploding all over the city. Mom and I were caught on the stairs of the hotel and started running down, following the air raid shelter signs. Just as we reached the doors of the shelter, a giant, invisible hand slammed us into the door, knocking the wind out of me and leaving us side-by-side on the floor, desperately trying to breathe, trying to get up, trying to get to safety. Safety? The stairwell was filled with choking plaster dust and smelled of smoke. I saw Mom's mouth move but I could not hear her. I cried to her that I could not hear and saw that she could not hear me. Blood was dripping from her nose and split lip. Clutching each other's hands, we ran up the stairs of the hotel, snaking our way through the people who were running down to the shelter. I don't know why we ran up, against all logic, but we did. We burst into our room to find all the windows disintegrated; everything that was not in our suitcases torn and covered with glass and dirt, and the shattered chandelier in the middle of our bed. No more bombs fell. After a while, we sorted and packed our things and moved to another room. Mom and I could not hear for several days and had a dry hacking cough that troubled us for some weeks.

Then came the news that another farm had been found, also in Bavaria that would take Victor and his mother in. The farmer had agreed to give them room and board for 80% of Victor's father's salary. They traveled with another train from Prague to München, and from there into the Bavarian countryside.

Victor was fluent in German but the dialect that the Bavarian people spoke sounded to him almost as if it was not German at all. At the farm Victor and his mother were given a room upstairs, a room that could not be heated, just like most of the other rooms, except for the large kitchen where the food was cooked, where the family ate – including the two French POWs who worked as farmhands – , where life happened.

Victor's school was quite a distance away. He would get up at 5 in the morning, walk about three miles to catch the train at 6:30, arrive in the city at 7:30, just in time to catch the street car that would get him to school before 8. School let out at 4 pm which got him home just in time for dinner. In good weather that was o.k. but as winter arrived, his comfort had to be the heated train cars at one end and the heated kitchen at the other.

They had not heard from Victor's father but news of the withdrawal of German troops from portions of Romania and Hungary had become numerous. Then one day in November he appeared at the farm. His unit had been stationed in Austria for a rest after some fierce battles and he had come to see them. He arranged travel permits for Victor and his mother for them to visit him in Austria over the Christmas holidays. But this trip of about 300 miles was not smooth at all and it took them two days.

We were warned by the clerk at the station that travel was badly disrupted by air raids and strafing and that we may have to walk through the bombed-out areas to get to a connecting train. Although he sold us tickets that listed the route, to München – Salzburg – Graz – and then the village, he said we would have to be alert for any trains going in the right direction, because he had no idea which trains worked and which did not. I believe this is the first time I realized that Germany was really hurting. It seemed inconceivable that a German railroad clerk did not know which trains were operable. We made it through München, but had to leave the train somewhere between München and Salzburg and walk for a couple of kilometers to a bus stop. From there, a bus took us to the other side of the bombed-out track to a train. This time we again did not reach Salzburg, because the train stopped to hide in a tunnel while the Salzburg train station was being bombed and strafed. After we detoured around the damaged station, we headed for Graz but had to stay overnight in a beautiful mountain village. The train was crowded but we finally made it to Graz.

The bus that was supposed to take Victor and his mother to their final destination, was supposed to leave a couple of hours after they had arrived at the Graz station.

They settled in the overcrowded waiting room but Victor's mother soon had the strange feeling that waiting at the station was not quite right and decided they should not wait for the bus but walk. It was a long walk; the bus would have taken 45 minutes to cover the distance, and Victor was not happy.

We had been walking for more than an hour when we heard that, oh, so familiar rumble of massed airplane engines followed by the distant thunder of bombs. Graz was getting it, badly. Walking suddenly seemed like an excellent idea.

At this village Victor met many of the Russian-German soldiers he had known in Banat the year before and they talked about his father's bravery and how he had led them out of a Soviet and Romanian encirclement and to safety. It was strange and wonderful for Victor to see how these soldiers worshipped and respected his father.

In 1945, for the first time, I joined Mom and Dad when the New Year's bells rang. We stood at the stroke of midnight, in the middle of the restaurant dance floor, and we hugged each other fiercely and we vowed never to be apart on all the New Year's Eves to come. This was our pledge of survival, our secret shield of love against the terrors of war, and the loneliness of separation, and the fear of losing each other. (Victor was 11 at the time.)

The days with Dad passed quickly, much too quickly. Hours seemed compressed into minutes, and every minute held a warm, happy memory.

I remember the wild beauty of the songs the soldiers sang as they rode in from drill in the evening – old Russian horse soldier songs, of weeping sweethearts and foolhardy, brave men, of the pain of death and separation and of the fierce joy of battle. In vain have I searched for a record that would bring back the soaring, sad, or fierce sound of the tenor lead sung by a round-faced young soldier, the spine-tingling slam of the squadron's voices as they lustily sang the refrain, and the abandon of the whistles at the end of each verse. I have never been able to find a record that recaptured the special feeling of these songs. I suppose, the fault is not in the records. It is simpler than that: just like the Gregorian chant is meant to be heard in the echoing vastness of a Gothic cathedral, the songs of the horse soldier of Russia were meant to be heard while huddling next to a snowy road, watching the columns of riders before you.

The steaming horses and the bundled, armed riders appeared to be a single animal, centaurs, magical beasts enveloped in the wholeness of the warriors' myth, so full of sadness and joy, death and vitality. War is horrible and wasteful and destructive, and it awakens vicious ferocity in humans – and yet, and yet – it makes life so poignant and sweet. After we escape death, there is a fierce joy, a celebration of life, and no nation expresses this dichotomy of feelings quite as wildly and beautifully as the Russians.

Back at the farm in Bavaria, life became harder. Food became scarcer and it became clear that Germany would not be winning this war. From the beginning Victor had helped at the farm because he liked it, now his mother was forced to work too. Then Victor could not go to school anymore because the train tracks were partially destroyed and he himself had even been slightly injured while the train was strafed. Now he was put to work on the fields full time, doing the work of a grown-up farmhand.

It was about the middle of April 1945 when the air strikes on the nearest town became a daily occurrence, and the first strafing attacks on farm workers began. I suppose the strafing of people obviously involved in farm labor was a harassment tactic, or an attempt to interrupt food production. Whichever it was meant to be, it shut down the field work, and Mom and I had to stop our Sunday walks to the forest. The last time we went, she, I and a neighbor's dog were caught in the field between the farm and the forest, by an American plane. It was a twin-engine, twin-tailed airplane with the US white star on its tails. It came swooping out of the sky so low that we could see the pilot clearly behind his transparent canopy. At first we thought he was going to leave us alone, thinking that since we could see him, he would be able to see us, to tell that we were a boy, a woman and a dog. But he turned the plane after the first pass and came back; we could almost physically feel his concentration on us. We knew he was going to shoot.

We were in the open, far from any building or obvious shelter. With the engine roar getting closer, (thank heaven, planes take a long time to turn and line up with the target), we were frantically searching for a place to hide; I actually tried to wave my arms at him. He opened fire way before he needed. The hammering sound of his guns and the little fountains of earth spurting from the ground ahead of him made it clear that he, indeed, was going to shoot us. At the last moment, Mom saw, only a few meters away, a stout bridge over the roadside ditch. It was built of timber and packed earth, solid enough to bear farm machinery entering the fields.

Mom and I crammed ourselves under the bridge just as we heard his bullets slam along the road. He came back twice, blowing by so low that we could feel the wind of his passage under the bridge. He fired his guns as he approached, and again as he swooped up after the pass. The dog had run away from the noise and spraying dirt. We stayed hiding in the mud and weeds for some time before we ventured to run for home. I suppose we were lucky that this hero of the US Air Force did not have any bombs aboard.

The war was drawing to an end. A stream of German soldiers passed by the farm, some orderly, some in un-military looking groups. Finally all was quiet. There were no people walking, no truck picking up milk from the farms, no farm machinery in the fields. *It seemed the whole world held its breath.* Then one morning the sound of tanks was being heard in the distance, American tanks. But before them came a German military Volkswagen*), *) called Kübelwagen, specialty built the military having a heavy machinegun mounted between the front seats, with three teenagers dressed in their Hitler Youth uniforms. They wanted to set up a roadblock at the corner and an ambush right behind the farmhouse.

During these final days of the war some of the local officials all over Germany had the insane idea to follow their government's orders to mobilize every last man, no matter how old or frail, and every boy for the, totally hopeless, defense of the country. The boys in the Volkswagen were of this group. The farmer gave them the gasoline they requested and something to drink but told them that a much better place for an ambush would be about a third of a mile further down the road and no close houses. With that advice he saved his farm from sure destruction and the lives of the people within. The tanks came, the boys fired their machine gun and were, naturally, mowed down by the tanks' cannons. Then the tanks moved on and for this village the war was over.

The armistice had been signed on Mai 8th 1945 but that did not mean that for Victor's father, Michael, everything was over. He and his squadron were moving near the Yugoslavian-Austrian border. Their only hope to survive was to avoid capture by Tito's communist guerillas who would have tortured and killed them, recognizing Michael's unit as Cossack cavalry and part of the Russian Volunteer Corps, that meant, soldiers who fought with the Germans against everything communistic. It would be much better to be captured by the British or the Americans. To reach and cross the bridge over the river Drava could bring them to a British unit stationed on the other side. A mile or so away from the bridge was a German infantry unit who had the same idea, namely to surrender to the British on the other side.

But the bridge itself was occupied by a band of communist guerillas who would not take kindly to being pushed aside, and the British might see a fight on the bridge as directed towards them. But then Michael conceived a plan that the infantry major readily accepted. An armored infantry car with a white flag, driven by two German volunteers was to approach the bridge slowly, making the communist believe that they wanted to surrender to them. When on the bridge, they were to floor the gas pedal and race across the bridge until they reached the British on the other side. Michael reasoned that the communists would not shoot as the car approached because of the white flag and not shoot after the car because of the danger of hitting the British. The plan worked. After a while a British car came back over the bridge, of course undeterred by Tito's guerillas. The British officer could not help the German troops right away but suggested that they, the British, would move their tanks and people back from the vicinity of the bridge so that the Germans could storm the bridge and then come over to surrender to the British. This was to be Michael's very last battle, and it worked. Now Michael was a British POW but his problems were not over. The Soviets had made an agreement with the British that all POWs of Russian origin should be handed over to them. It was rumored that they would all be looked upon as traitors by the Soviets and killed – which later proved to be quite true. Michael (like, probably, many others) tore off all insignia that would have shown that he belonged to the Russian Volunteer Corps. When he was asked for his hometown, he named München (which is only about 80 miles from where his family was) and he was released to go there.

It took until the middle of June for Victor's father to join his family at the farm. He had been lucky because others, especially those who had been captured by the Soviets, spent years and years in captivity. About 1/3 of them never returned from the eastern mines and Siberia.

By July the whole family was on their way north. Life at the farm, or rather with the farmer, had become unbearable. However, they didn't really have any place to go to.

The roads were hopelessly jammed with homeless refugees that had fled from the areas being occupied by the Soviet Army, German soldiers returning home, released political prisoners and freed prisoners of war. Trains ran sporadically, if at all, and there was no public transport other than trains. Mostly, everybody just walked, either carrying their worldly possessions, or pushing a hand cart of some sort. We had too much luggage to carry, and we did not want to abandon such essential things as blankets and winter clothing, or such precious things as Dad's saber and our family silver.

217

It was absolute luck, coincidence, and Dad's ability to recognize an opportunity and to grasp it, that made it possible for us to leave.

We had been packed for weeks when, one day, a pair of ex-cavalrymen appeared, riding a horse-drawn supply wagon with a tent-like cover. They pulled into the yard, Mom and Dad told me later, and asked permission to water the horses. While they took care of the horses, the travelers struck up a conversation with my Dad, who had been working in the hayloft. It turned out that they were on the way home, one to the city of Kassel, the other to a small town near Hannover. Dad asked if they would consider taking on some passengers, the wagon being large and mostly empty. It turned out that they were glad to have extra folk along, particularly a cavalryman whom they could trust, to help care for and protect the horses. The decision to leave was made quickly. I had been out in the fields, tending the hay. By the time I had returned for supper, all our stuff was in the wagon and we left as soon as I had washed in the creek behind the vegetable garden.

Each day we traveled from daybreak till dark. It was July, and the weather was warm and dry. Mom had saved quite a bit of money from Dad's army salary, so we were able to pay to feed us and the horses. At the end of each day, we looked for a convenient place to pull off the road, either in a field along the road or in the yard of a friendly farm. Mom had the privacy of the wagon, while we four men slept on the ground on the thick wool blankets the guys had in the wagon. (Incidentally we carried mine and Dad's blanket with us all the way to the United States.) Supplies and sleeping space were easy while traveling in the country. Farmers were sometimes generous and inexpensive, sometimes stingy and expensive, but they always had food – bread, milk, salt pork, cabbage soup, doughy Knödel (dumpling). We avoided towns because local police were usually not friendly to non-residents, and also because groceries were available only with ration cards. Meat of any kind was hard to find, even with ration cards and, of course, ration cards were issued only to residents.

We traveled essentially without any remarkable incidents. A major concern were the American jeeps and trucks. Generally the drivers completely ignored the existence of the wagon, and roared by within inches of us, trailing a cloud of dust. It was worrisome when they slowed down or even stopped to take a look at us. We were doing nothing illegal, and the guy's discharge papers were in good order, but one never knows about an invader. Humans are human, and the power of a weapon in the hand can be a heady potion. Luckily Americans were not very frequent on the back roads where we traveled.

During this time civilians were, in general, not allowed to travel, even walk, on major roads.

We reached Kassel after about a week. The soldier whose family was in Kassel, guided us through the horribly bomb-damaged city, looking anxiously at block after block of ruined houses and streets blocked with rubble while the smell of smoke and dust still hung in the air. People were digging in the ruins, looking for salvageable belongings and picking out usable bricks for rebuilding. Finally, to our great relief he saw, across three blocks of leveled apartment buildings a nest of undamaged houses – his house was among them. We drove up to the door and the soldier hopped off to run up the steps when the door burst open and a woman screaming his name launched herself at his neck.

The small town near Hannover, where the other soldier's family lived, was virtually undamaged. Victor and his family considered finding a place in this area but it turned out that the whole region was inundated with refugees from Prussia and Northeast Germany who had fled from the advancing Soviet army. The authorities now granted residence only to relatives of the town's citizens. The soldier's mother offered to claim

Victor and his parents as relatives and have them move in with her. Her son was planning to move in with his sister whose husband had been killed, and help her with her tree farm.

We registered with the town police and the mayor's office where we were issued ration cards. We learned to live with the allowable amount of food doled out fairly enough through the ration card system. Shopping was pretty simple. Each shop had the same amount and the same kinds of foods, available to anybody who had the right coupons.

In September Victor started going to school again. The town was bisected by the river Weser, and Victor's house was on one side of the river, his school on the other. The bridge had been blown up by some "patriotic zealot" who wanted to stop the advance of the American troops. It was a truss bridge and the truss had been blown in the center so that the ends of the two halves lay in the water.

Someone had constructed a foot bridge of thick planks, laid end-to-end and secured to the toppled steel girders. The planks were probably a little bit over three feet wide. Two people really had to squeeze by if they met on the bridge. There was a railing on one side.

Both shores were high; the foot bridge first descended along the girders, leveling out about ten feet above the rushing water, and then climbing to the other shore. I never could decide whether it was more frightening to be far from the water and look down from a stomach-gripping height, or to look from only a few feet away at the swirling, gurgling stream that made you feel that the bridge was moving and the river standing still.

When the weather had turned chilly, Victor and his father were taken to the tree farm where the soldier now lived, to help with felling trees for firewood. Victor, twelve by that time, recalls:

I learned to use the two-man logger's saw, where one had to pull-and-give rhythmically to match one's partner's motion all the while keeping pressure downward so that the saw would bite into the wood. I learned to split logs with a maul and wedge, and to swing an axe over my head to get the most power for the least effort.

Victor and his father got to take some of the wood home, and, equally precious, they were given a fifty-pound sack of potatoes for the winter.

As winter progressed, money and food were becoming a concern. Dad had to walk and hitch rides on farm wagons to Hannover, the closest big town, where he sold Mom's jewelry, his silver cigarette case and gold Ruble coins to British officers, (we were in the British-occupied area). Sometimes he traded our valuables for canned meat, sugar or powdered milk. The rations obtainable with ration cards were reduced. In the summer we were issued coupons for about one pat of butter, 100 grams [3½ ounces] of hamburger meat and 200 grams [7oz] of starch (pasta, potato) per person per week; at first vegetables milk and bread were essentially not rationed. In contrast, in November, we had coupons for 50 grams [1.7oz] of meat, 50 dl [a little over 2 cups] of milk and 100 grams of starch, while vegetables were unobtainable, and the bread ration was about one slice per day.

Added to the lack of food was the bitter cold that one could never quite escape, not in school, not in the public library, not at home. After a supper of potato soup and a slice of bread, I would crawl into bed to do my homework, to keep warm and to save our precious firewood. January and February were the worst because then, even the potatoes were used up. I was always cold, and always ravenous. The soldier's sister sent some cherry tree twigs, (no leaves, of course), with which to make a warming and very pleasant tea.

In school the kids also chewed twigs of various fruit trees. I felt like a starving deer, peeling the bark off trees.

Spring came and then summer. We had been working hard at planting and raising vegetables in our hostess' yard. Although there still was very little staple food to be had, our gardening efforts were rewarded with a steady supply of peas, carrots, tomatoes, summer squash, onions and lettuce. I was able to fill my stomach, but the absence of starches and proteins kept me still dreaming of beef stew, sausages, bread and macaroni.

All this time, Dad had been looking for work. Our money situation was grim, and we really did not want to sell off our last precious family treasures. Another major concern was the likelihood that even with money for food we would not be able to survive another winter.

But then they learned about an organization that ran refugee camps for all those who had been displaced from their homes by the war.

The idea was to relieve the struggling German economy of the burden of all the people who were not native Germans, and who had no place to go because of political persecution in their homelands. Large camps were being established by various international organizations and, since the Americans provided the major source of funding, all the camps were in the American zone, in southern Germany. Supposedly the camps offered free lodging, meals and, in some cases, even a chance for employment. It seemed a chance to solve our very pressing problems.

In the late summer of 1946 the rail service, so terribly damaged by allied bombing, had begun to recover. Trains were running on many major routes and baggage car service was available.

From the little town near Hannover they had to travel first into Hannover, then Kassel, München and from there on a local train to the town where the refugee camp was located.

The train from our town to Hannover was moderately full and we boarded comfortably, each with one suitcase. We even found seats for all of us. When the train pulled into Hannover, things looked a bit more grim. The platform for the train to Kassel was very crowded, but since Hannover was the originating station, the cars were completely empty when the train was pulled in for boarding.

After some struggle with crowding passengers, we squeezed ourselves into a compartment, but had to remain standing for our journey to Kassel. Only one train a day went from Kassel to München. It arrived with all the cars loaded with people, and only a few of them struggled to get off, fighting their way through people who were trying to get on.

I had never seen anything so frightening. People were shouting, kids were crying, men used their weight and size to push women and children out of the way, women wedged themselves in front of men using their elbows and suitcases. An argument flared up on my left and someone began beating someone on the head with an umbrella. Holding his own suitcase by the handle, Dad grabbed Mom's and my suitcase under each arm and told us to hang on to his army jacket. Pushing, squeezing, crowding, we moved through the mass of people towards a car that seemed least full. Just as Dad got up the steps of the car and squeezed in, I got stripped off by a sweating, cursing woman who shoved in behind him, effectively leaving me on the platform and blocking Mom and Dad from backing out of the car. I was in a panic. I had never experienced such primeval, hysterical fear. I could see Dad struggling to turn around and get off, I saw Mom being propelled deeper into the car by the crowd. I don't recall what happened at this point. My senses returned when I felt myself being bodily lifted by the back of my jacket and by my arms and being dragged through an open window. God! Mom's frightened face was right in front of me, and a deep, cheerful voice behind me said: "Did I fish out the right boy?" or words to that effect. Mom was hugging me wordlessly, and I turned my head to see a very tall and very thick-chested man in a patched and faded officer's tunic smiling at me. "Thank you," I stuttered, still not recovered from my panic. I saw Dad nodding his head encouragingly from the corridor. We were all on the train together. We were together, all three of us.

By nightfall we had been registered at the camp as war displaced persons (DPs), and were issued two bed sheets, one blanket, one towel and one bar of soap each. We had eaten a delicious stew in a mess hall (with chunks of meat!) and had been assigned bunks in a large barracks with row upon row of beds. Men and women slept in separate buildings, Dad and I in one, Mom by herself in another one. I was dead tired but was able to keep my body moving long enough to enjoy a wonderful hot shower in a giant communal shower building. Ah-hh to sleep with a full stomach and a clean body! True joys are so simple.

We did not stay at this camp very long.

Through his contacts with friends, Dad found a job as a payroll officer with the UNRRA (United Nations Relief and Rehabilitation Agency) administration offices. That job entitled us to move into a totally luxurious two-room apartment in another camp, some 10 km away. Here we stayed for four years.

This camp housed the central administrative offices for, probably, five camps that were run by the UNRRA and later by the IRO (International Refugee Organization).

Camp offices were staffed with a polyglot mixture of local Germans, administrators from France, England, Belgium and Holland, war displaced persons, (Russians, Poles, Baltic peoples, Serbs), and US Army officers and noncoms. The Germans lived in town. The international administrators lived in München, the US Army folks and the DPs (that's us), lived in barracks at the Camp. These were 2-and 3-story quite luxurious buildings, sort of like college dormitories. Most of the people with families had two-room apartments, (no kitchens, of course), all others lived two persons per room. Everybody used communal toilets and showers, one per floor. There was a small recreation room on the ground floor of each barrack. We ate in a mess hall that had a central kitchen, and two eating halls, one for us and the other for the US Army. We were clothed and supplied with toiletries and such from US Army stores.

In this camp everybody worked, some in offices, like my Dad, others in the huge warehouses that supplied all the groceries and sundries for the five camps, still others cooked in the mess hall or were responsible for camp sanitation or security. We were a complete community, independent of the German economy and government. This arrangement created some tension and envy in town, which expressed itself in occasional minor fights between German and Camp youths.

I can't adequately express the comfort brought by the regular, tasty and plentiful food, the clean, well-heated quarters, the feeling of belonging to a location where one did not depend on someone's mercy. Other wonders were the bottomless fountain that spewed sweaters, shoes, fragrant soap, toothpaste, needle and thread, chocolate, cigarettes, coffee, tea ..., and the amazing shrug-the-shoulders attitude shown by Amis about their material wealth. Everything was bigger than life.

To attend the college-prep school, Victor, again, had to get up very early, catch the 6:00 or 6:30 train for the 40-minute trip to München, and there a streetcar for the 20-minute ride to the school.

But München had been heavily bombed and, like in other cities, everybody had to work on removing the rubble.

Two mornings a week, during decent weather, we boarded trucks and were driven from the school to various places in the city. There, we picked good bricks out of the rubble, or shoveled rubble into wheelbarrows, or did other useful jobs that did not require skills with tools or machinery. It was a break from classes, and although none of us ever admitted it, we felt proud that we were contributing to the recovery of our city.

Life in the camp must have been comfortable but it seemed to have no deeper meaning. Victor's father became depressed. Victor recalls:

During one of our chats some years later, he explained to me the depth of his depression at the time for having lost another battle against the red barbarians. The monsters who were destroying all that was good in Russia, his beloved motherland, all in the name of equality and freedom for the peasants and workers. Oh, how he hated the Soviets, and how he mourned for his enslaved people and for his murdered family! In vain will anyone try to understand these feelings who had not suffered the same loss and degradation.

But there came a point in their lives when Victor's father realized that there indeed could be a future and that it was in his power to build this future for his son. They applied for emigration to the USA.

In 1948 the refugee problem in Germany was being resolved by encouraging emigration to various countries. Applicants had to satisfy the entry requirements of the host country and to find a sponsor who would guarantee employment upon arrival. Some of the entry requirements were quite particular: for instance, Australia wanted single women, Venezuela wanted single men who were over six feet tall. The United States accepted all healthy persons who had a sponsor but gave preference to families. An anti-communistic political persuasion was also very important for entry into the USA. We applied in the spring of 1948. The forms were endless, filled with questions that thoroughly covered every aspect of the applicant's life from birth to the present.

Next, we had to locate a sponsor. This was done by way of matching service where sponsors listed their requirements, and refugees listed their education, skills and job record.

A funny mistake, that could have been not so funny, occurred with our family. The clerk matching my Dad's profession (publishing executive) with our sponsor (newspaper publisher) ignored the fact that the sponsor was looking for a typesetter, not an executive. Of course, neither our sponsor nor we knew about this problem until we landed on his doorstep about a year and a half later.

Once our sponsor responded, (that took most of one year), the next requirement was the political and moral screening. Since there was no way to determine the applicant's police record in his home country, US immigration relied on personal interviews of the families by US Army Criminal Investigation Division officers. Each one of us was interviewed separately by a different officer, and then we were visited by yet another officer in our home. After passing all this, the stem-to-stern physical was a breeze.

On the 19th of April 1950 we packed again. We were allowed one large trunk per person that was to be stowed in the freight hold of the ship. In addition, we could bring a medium suitcase into our cabin with changes of clothing, toiletries and valuables. But we all had more stuff than would fit into this limit. The result was that, to save space, we each dressed in most of our clothes. At the time when I boarded the ship, I had on two pairs of socks and underwear, two shirts, two complete suits and an overcoat.

After staying near the port of Bremen for a few days, in the embarkation holding area for those going to the USA and Canada, the ship arrived that was to carry Victor's family and more than a thousand others across the ocean.

But it was a smaller ship than had been scheduled and some of the people would have to wait for the next ship. A groan went up from all of us. To wait, again, to wait, some more?! The transportation officer suggested that he could leave some of the crew if we were willing to work during the passage. Yes, yes! Of course we were willing; we were ready to row his ship across the Atlantic. And so it happened: on 27 April 1950 we boarded the US Troop Transport ship "General C.H. Muir" and sailed for America.

The boarding took forever. We were lined up by boarding card number, which was also our bunk number, on the quay with our carry-on suitcases. Sailors came and led each group of passengers through the bewildering maze of corridors and ladders to their sleeping compartments. Since the compartments were designed for transporting soldiers and housed about 100 bodies each, men were separated from women.

In the compartments there were rows of steel bunks with about 18-inch passageways in between. The bunks were stacked in four tiers with just enough space to slide in between the lower and upper bunk, and between the upper bunk and the ceiling. It was impossible to sit up in a bunk – as I painfully discovered several times during our voyage. Adjacent to each sleeping compartment was the common toilet/shower compartment. It was all very crowded and smelled of human bodies, damp metal and toilet odors. I spent as little time there as possible.

As soon as Dad dropped his suitcase on the bunk, he was called to help organize the passengers into work parties and to ensure an adequate labor force for the ship. We were required to furnish deck crew workers to clean and maintain the outside areas of the ship by swabbing the deck, chipping rust, and painting. Also needed were cook's helpers and food servers, janitors, policemen (Yes, with 1200 bodies on board we needed to keep peace and order), and a variety of other workers. Although everyone had agreed to work while we were on shore, when faced with the actual fact of cleaning latrines or scrubbing pots in the kitchen, some of the people were not very eager to show up for work. After organizing the work crews, Dad had a rather thankless and stressful job of going himself or sending the policemen on "raids" to round up truant workers.

It took eleven days to cross the Atlantic, some of them over very rough seas. How does it feel being in a confined space while the ship plunges and rises from one high wave to the next? Were most people around you are very sick?

Finally, the ship reached New York.

The foghorn, our ship's horn, bellowed a long, drawn-out greeting and just before us we saw the statue that for over 60 years had symbolized the United States of America to the whole world: Liberty, the Lady with the Torch. The deck was silent, completely silent until we passed her.

The ship docked in the early afternoon, but it was dusk until they stepped off the gangplank on to American soil.

We were greeted by a very tired-looking but smiling man, who said "Welcome to the US of A". Were we home?

The friendly man threaded twin wires of a baggage tag through our coat lapels, a regular baggage tag, with our names and destinations stamped on it.

He also gave my Dad a bus pass and an envelope that contained train tickets to Pennsylvania, three $ 5.00 bills, and a note from our sponsor, in which he welcomed us and explained that the money was for food on the train, and that he will be waiting for us in New Castle.

I only remember two things about the bus ride to the railway station: that I never saw the top of a single building, no matter how hard I craned my neck looking up, and that I thought how horrible it would be to be caught in an air raid here.

After some slight problem with the trunks, a wonderfully pleasant and helpful conductor appears and helps us get settled in a compartment. We sprawled in the soft chairs, exhausted, confused, elated – Mom asks: "Are we really here?" looking from Dad to me. We nod wordlessly and I feel tears welling up in my throat. 'We are here! I think, really here.' The words are awe-inspiring, mystical: we are in the United States of America. We came halfway around the world from a shattered land where the major concern was to get food and shelter for today, where one did not dare think about the future, because there was none. We were now in a country where people worked for the future, where there were high schools and colleges that prepared one for a productive career, where there were gleaming giant buses, and vendors with chocolate bars, and where trains moved smoothly and silently so that I did not realize we were leaving New York until I saw a parking lot jammed with cars, sparkling in the huge lights, glide by our window. My thoughts tumbled over each other: I remembered another train ride and another night when the darkness was lit up by tracer bullets, and I shivered. But then I met Dad's eyes and we smiled at each other. I need not ever fear again, I thought. Never again.

At that time Victor was 17.

Life in the United States did not move quite as smoothly as the train had. The family ended up in California where, for lack of a better job, Victor's father, the count and highly respected and decorated officer, worked for years in a rivet factory, as later did his mother, a descendent of Cossack nobility, countess, and acclaimed prima ballerina. Victor worked many different jobs after school. None of them ever complained. They were alive, they were free and they were working not just for food and shelter, but for building a future.

Victor studied veterinary medicine and, after some time in private practice, became a professor at a prestigious university. By now his parents have passed on and his children are grown. Today he lives with his wife and loyal dog in Florida amidst large trees and flowering bushes. In the house one can feel a strong presence of the Russian culture that was his family's. He muses:

Although our family contains a mixture of ethnic and national origins (Holstein German, Baltic German, Serbian, and Russian Don Cossack), our family's soul was shaped by Mother Russia, her land and her people. Russia, a land of vast forests and limitless grass lands, where everything is bigger than life. Russia, as delicate as the lacy frost on the window pane, as lyrical as the midnight song of the nightingale, Russia, as relentless as the gray-green waters of the Volga and as cruel as the bitter arctic snowstorms. Our mother Russia, who teaches her children to laugh one moment, and to weep the next.

The Two Unholy Kings

During WW II and especially at the end of the war, large numbers of German soldiers were taken prisoner by the Soviets and held for years and years – many in Siberia – under incredibly bad and, in most cases, inhumane conditions. The work was extremely hard, the food minimal. More than half of them died from starvation, from exhaustion, torture, "accidents" at work, and being shot or otherwise killed by guards.

But there were still miraculous happenings when humanity shone through the harshness of life.

Several years after the war a prisoner was discharged and came home. He wrote down what had happened to him. The story of "The Two Unholy Kings" is about one such miracle.

But we should not see these events as big, showy things with lots of fanfare. No, miracles like this were embedded in the everyday drudgery and hardship. They didn't actually change anything. They were just a ray of light in a dark and scary night.

The Russians in this story did not analyze or make conscious decisions to act in a certain way. They just lived. They all were in a precarious situation anyway. Under Stalinist rule anybody could find themselves imprisoned and worse without warning. Furthermore, practicing religion in any form was strictly forbidden.

Under all these circumstances it is understandable that this story, told by a German soldier who had been imprisoned in Siberia, has an almost surreal quality.

The Two Unholy Kings

Under a Russian Christmas Sky / by Wolfgang Schwarz

It was, of course, the craziest thing in the world, to just get up and run away, without having prepared anything: no flight route, nothing to help me make it through the time it would take through and this impossible distances of this endless country. But out of desperation one does the craziest things.

I was away from the construction site the moment our guard went off for a minute to warm his feet. I ran over the snow into a valley where I could feel myself hidden from sight, and I turned myself over the heavens, clouded as they were.

The heaven that was a heavy, wintry Russian Christmas sky, like a kind old man, who did not yet breathe February's sharp, icy breath. I confided to him that I was a poor, tormented man. I was sure would understand me.

And he understood me very well, for, just as I had slipped into the valley, I was called through the open doorway of a little house, to come on inside. It was a house, lovingly protected by a thick straw roof, where a colorful company had assembled around a child being baptized.

There was great joy over my arrival. A peasant woman put her arms around me, an old man kissed me, others slapped me on the shoulders. Who I was, seemed totally unimportant to them as well as the fact that I was not one of them but a German, and even one of those who were closely guarded. All that was of no importance to them. The only thing that mattered was that I was here. And immediately I was given a full glass of Vodka.

What I saw first were things that I had not seen for a long time: clean clothes, linen that shone with embroidery, a table covered with the most beautiful and best food to satisfy any hunger, pillows arranged pleasingly, and especially: people who had a different look on their faces than the ones I normally saw around me. These faces were not pinched but round; they looked like apples. There was also an old priest with a shaggy head who looked like Saint Peter. One could have been afraid of him. But his hands were as soft as wax. They dripped on a cradle in which lay a little boy. And that was the reason for the colorful company and allthis festivity and cleanliness: A baptism was being celebrated, and furthermore one during the time of winter and Christmas. It was a very special baptism.

"The baptism of a Christ child", whispered a toothless crone into my ear. And with that she slipped a few rubles into my pocket. "Do you know what this is?" asked the priest. But the others laughed and said: "all of them know it."

But this was not all. Now the priest turned away from the child. He came toward me, put his hands on my shoulders and said: "You are the King from the Orient." Someone stood next to me with a bed sheet in his hands. He draped it around me, suddenly transforming me into a king; me who had until now been the lowest of his servants, standing in an icy hole, trying to break a frozen lump off the ground with my hoe. Suddenly I was a king. And a circlet of golden cardboard was glued to my forehead.

"That's how it is." said the priest. "At such a baptism during winter and a Christmas time the door stays open. Then the kings come, the first, the second, the third. The third usually is late. He comes the next day. But the first and the second, they come."

I let everything happen to me - that they kissed and embraced me again, that they gave me more Vodka and put pickled tomatoes and cucumbers into my mouth, and finally asked me to sing a song for them: "because the kings sing", said the priest, "they do not speak".

At once my heart was heavy. Singing? What should I sing? Had I not unlearned singing? When had I sung the last time? But then I remembered that I had indeed sung a few weeks ago. That was when I had pushed my cart, loaded with a few dried-out corpses, to the cemetery. Actually it was not quite a cemetery, just a spared-out spot between two potato fields.

And so I sang what I had sung then, the song of the good comrade*). I sang it and I cried. And all the others cried with me, and they all thought it was very beautiful.   *) Text of the song is on the next page.

But then the second king came. He was greeted like me, with Vodka, kisses and hugs. He did not want to be greeted in this way but then somebody said to him: "Aren't you from the area of Rostow too?" And he really was from the area of Rostow, he was from the lagoons of the river Don. His father was a Cossack*) and his mother had secretly celebrated the birth of the Holy Child. *) Cossacks were originally peasant soldiers from the area of the Don and Dnepr rivers in Russia. They had their own ethnic identity, and they were fierce fighters. During WWII many Cossacks sought on the side of the Germans against the Soviets.

So he let it happen that he too was made a king – just like me. Even though he had already seen me and had threatened me with something dark, but the others might not have noticed. So I just closed my eyes and prayed, the first time in many months I prayed: that he may not shoot me, that he may show mercy towards me, that some light from the baptism in this dark little house may illuminate him too.

Because the second king was the guard from whom I had run away. He was still holding his rifle in his hand.

"But brother, whenever has a king be seen carrying a gun?" said the priest and took it away from him. And he let him.

Then we both stood side by side. He did not look at me. But then the others said: "Two kings! What a miracle! We have two kings and the kings must love each other."

But the guard was still not looking at me. He was a square fellow who did not talk much but he could handle the butt of his rifle with great force, however, he had a mother who had secretly celebrated Christmas. And so he knew about it and sang – just like me – when he was asked to do so. He sang the legend of the twelve robbers. The first verse he sang alone. Then the others joined in. And since I had heard this song and had remembered it, I sang with the others.

That's when he looked at me for the first time: 'Not too bad, this one, even though he ran anyway. He knows the legend of the twelve robbers. Maybe he knows other things too.' But then his eyes turned cold again. He probably remembered that he had to catch me and look me into the cage.

Finally we were urged to eat as much as we wanted, everything in odd order, as it is common with the Russians: bacon and pierogges, hash browns and baked cabbage, milk cakes and pancakes. And we had to drink too.

And then we were real drunk. I don't remember how we got back to the camp, we two kings with the sheets and the cardboard circles on our foreheads.

I only know that the guard had his arm around me, that I carried his rifle, and that he kept saying: "My name is Nikolai and your name must be Michael, do you understand? That was my brother."

But when we arrived at the guardroom, he acted as if he had never embraced me and had never told me about his brother. He pushed me across the room with the butt of the rifle and raved and cursed as if I was the worst criminal he had ever taken to the cage.

And he did indeed put me into the cage. But he arranged for the cage to be heated, and from his pocked he pulled some bread and pierogges to keep me from starving. And after two days he came back and said: "I have heard that for you it is Christmas today. On such a day you can't stay in here.

And then he said: "One king has to help another king, isn't that so?"

*) The song of the good comrade is an old soldiers' song telling about a soldier's grief in remembering his best comrade and how he saw him fall and die next to him on the battlefield. It has a somber and stately melody and it used to performed whenever there was a memorial service for soldiers.

Text (by Ludwig Uhland) and melody (after a folksong 1829)

Ich hatt' einen Kameraden,	I had a comrade in arms,
einen bessern findst du nit.	a better one you won't find.
Die Trommel schlug zum Streite,	The drum roared for battle,
er ging an meiner Seite	he marched at my side
in gleichem Schritt und Tritt,	in step with me,
in gleichem Schritt und Tritt.	in step with me.
Eine Kugel kam geflogen	A bullet came flying,
gilt's mir oder gilt es dir?	is it meant for me or for you?
Ihn hat es weggerissen,	It tore him away,
er liegt mir vor den Füßen	he is lying at my feet
als wär's ein Stück von mir,	as if he were a piece of me,
als wär's ein Stück von mir.	as if he were a piece of me.
Weil mir die Hand noch reichen more	He wants to take my hand once more
derweil ich eben lad'.	while I am just loading.
"Kann dir die Hand nicht reichen	„I cannot give you my hand;
bleib du im ew'gen Leben	but in the eternal life
mein guter Kamerad,	stay my good comrade,
mein guter Kamerad!"	stay my good comrade."

Lucas: a Life Across Continents

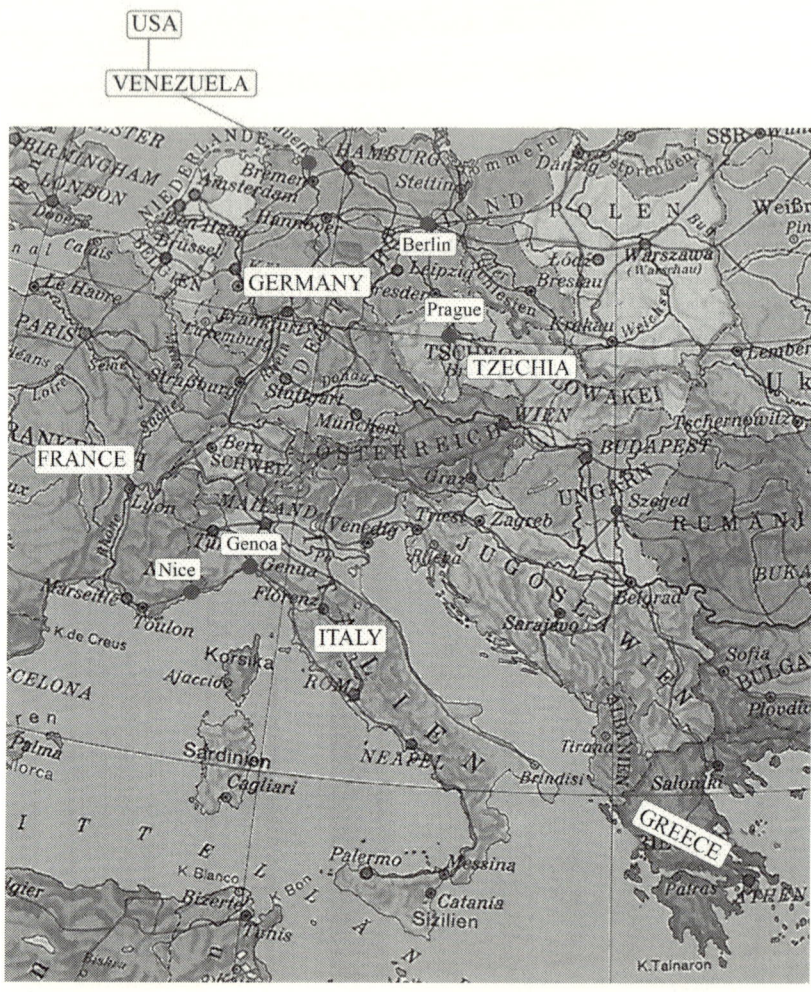

Lucas: A Life Across Continents (born 1926)

Lucas' father was Greek, his mother had been Czech, Lucas was born in Czechoslovakia (in 1926), and the family lived in Germany. This background could be taken as a prelude to a life that stretched over much of Europe and then the Americas. He recalls the many stations of his life:

My father had a factory in Berlin that produced dietary products for diabetics. But soon after Hitler's government had come to power, Jewish businesses (and their owners) were not really safe anymore. It did not make any difference that my father was Greek. Jew is Jew. My parents felt it was better to get out of Germany before it became too late. Around 1936 my father gave up the factory and we went to Karlsbad (Karlori Vary) in the Sudetenland part of Czechoslovakia. My grandmother, my mother's mother, lived there. We had spent summers there, so it was not a dramatic change for my sister and I. The main difference was to move from a large city, namely Berlin, to a smaller, slower place.

But in 1937 Germany re-annexed the Sudetenland, of which Karlsbad was a part, and we went to Prague which, at the time, was still in a sovereign state. In March 1939 Germany invaded Czechoslovakia and occupied Prague, and three weeks later we had to leave because we were foreigners. We went to Greece. I was 13 years old at the time.

Moving to Greece was a very big change for us, the culture, the food, the language; everything was strange. I did not speak Greek but, naturally, had to go to a Greek school. I sat in class, listening but not understanding very much. The director seemed sympathetic to my plight. He had to go to the market two or three times a week to buy provisions for the school (which was a boarding school) and he used to ask me to come along and carry the bags. I liked this much better than sitting in class.

We stayed only three or four months in Greece. My father had not come with us; he had gone to southern France to build up an existence there. When things just did not work out for us in Greece – we were all unhappy there – my father suggested that we move to southern France too. I went first. I went by boat, traveling alone for the first time in my life. My father met me in Marseille and then took me to Nice.

Rumors about the war became more pronounced and my father wanted my mother and sister also out of Greece and be in France. They arrived in Nice two days before the war started.

It had been a 24-hour train ride for them. This was in the fall of 1939. Soon German troops occupied the northern part of France, but Nice and the southern part were occupied by Italians. They did not bother anybody, not us, not the other people. Nevertheless we were in a precarious situation there. We had never been able to obtain work permits in France where we only had limited visas expiring every six months. This would have given the police the opportunity to arrest us whenever we had to apply for an extension.

In 1943 The Allies landed in southern Italy and the Italians withdrew their troops from France. The Germans now came to occupy all of France and we had to flee again. In June of 1943 my father (as all other Jewish men) was forced to leave Nice and move to a small town in the French Alps called St.Martin-Vésubie, the so-called "residence forcée", under police surveillance. We followed our father there as he was our only means of support and because of the town's vicinity to the border with Italy which was just two miles away.

Similar to Hitler in Germany, Benito Mussolini had developed fascism in Italy. In 1922 King Victor Emanuel III, under pressure, made Mussolini chief of government. By 1928 Mussolini had dissolved all parties except for his own National Fascist Party. His government was practically a one-man dictatorship. Personal liberties of citizens were restricted; the economy was controlled by the state. Mussolini had supported Hitler in his war efforts but after extensive defeats and losses of the Italian military, he tried to get out of the treaty with Hitler. When he was not successful, the king had him arrested on July 25, 1943, and Pietro Badoglio was made in charge of the government. Badoglio immediately dissolved the National Fascist Party. Even though he could not get out of the treaty with Hitler, either, he started secret contacts with the Allies. When Italy's truce with the Allies was finalized in September 1943, Italian troops in southern France, Italy, and in the Balkans were taken prisoner by the German military. King Victor Emanuel and the whole Italian government fled to Bari in southeastern Italy where the national continuity was preserved at least for the very southern part of the country. (Meyer's Neues Lexikon)

In August 1943 we heard that Mussolini had been arrested and replaced by Marshal Badoglio as head of the Italian government. Then Nice were occupied by the Germans and the occupation of St. Martin-Vésubie seemed imminent. There were many "forced residents" and one night we all left. We were about 80 people but soon broke up into smaller groups. My mother, my sister and I were left with a group of seven people. It was very cold.

We hiked up a high mountain and found barracks there of an Italian garrison. Many of the troops and officers were also leaving. They said: "The Germans are coming; we are going. We are not fighting for them." They went with us and helped us in many ways. We went down into the valley and stayed at a farm in a place called Entraque (in the Piedmont region). A few days later there was an announcement: "The Germans are here and want to meet all the refugees in the central plaza of the village for an important message."

In our group was a gentleman who said: "Never on your life! Let's pack and go to the mountains. This is a trap." And he was so right. The people who went to the village plaza were loaded up on trucks and never seen or heard of again.

- - - - -

In 1990 I went to Europe with my son and I wanted to show him the places from which I had escaped, "Otherwise you would not be here and I would not be here." We went into this village. It was still the same village with the water fountain in the center, very, very picturesque, even though a little touristy now. It was a hot day in June and we went into a bar to get some coffee. An old man was standing there, and I said to him: "You probably would not believe this, but I was here 47 years ago." And I asked him: "Do you remember when the Germans were here and there was a group of refugees?" "Oh yes", he said, "sure, sure. Oh, they took all of them, you know. They took all of them." I said: "No, they did not take me and my mother and my sister." He could not believe it. "You are a survivor of that! Oh, it was so terrible. They took everybody, loaded them on trucks and left." So he remembered. My son could not believe his eyes. I had told him the story, of course, and now he could see the reality.

- - - - -

Back in 1943 we had escaped from the village into the mountains but it was cold and wet and we were hungry. For about two weeks a farmer let us sleep in his stable but one night he came and said: "I am sorry, you have to go. The Germans are coming." So we went again up into the mountains. Some people must have told the Germans that there were refugees up there because they came on their motorcycles. They did not find us because where we went, there was no road. We later met some nice Italian woodcutters. They advised us that we should stay in one of the hunting cabins. It was September, the hunting season was over and the men assured us that the Germans would not look for refugees there.

In the cabin we had shelter from the rain and the cold, and there was even water. The woodcutters brought us some food too. We stayed there for several weeks but then it became too cold and we went down into another, larger village. There it happened like before that some people realized that refugees lived in a certain house and we had to go into the mountains again. The Italian peasants were kind and compassionate, despite the fact that they ran great risks. The Germans were in control in the cities and were patrolling the countryside. If they had found us, not only would they have taken us away, but they would also have burned down the farms of the people giving us shelter.

During that time we subsisted mainly on potatoes, chestnuts, and sometimes polenta (corn meal pudding). We slept in barns at night, next to the cows, but had to hide somewhere else during the day. As winter was approaching, we were told that the heavy snowfall and cold would soon make it impossible for us to stay any longer.

We were in five different places before we ended up in Genoa. For most of the time a man had been with us but at the end he found somebody who would smuggle him into Switzerland on the promise of being paid there out of the man's Swiss bank account.

Before we came to Genoa, we had been in Piedmont, the region of Italy which is adjacent to France. When it was no longer possible for us to stay in that area, we took the risk of going to the nearest town from where my mother made a phone call to an acquaintance who, she hoped, could help her locate my father's stepbrothers who had been living in Trieste. Luckily she was told them that we were now hiding in Genoa under a fictitious name. Our relatives took us to Genoa by train where we moved into a small unheated apartment on Via Assarotti. We lived in constant fear of being questioned by the janitor and the neighbors, and being turned in to the police. I remember that we lived on the 8th floor, without elevator, and often had to rush to the air-raid bomb shelter in the middle of the night.

One of my uncles and another lady helped us to get so-called postal identity cards so that we would be safe there. At the time you could get such cards if two people swore as witnesses to your identity. We kept our first names because they sounded Italian but changed our last name. My mother spoke Italian well because she had lived in Italy for some time before her marriage. Mine and my sister's Italian was not so good. But we explained that we had lived in France.

My uncle had given us some money as a start but then we were pretty much on our own. Having learned that the Catholic Church was helping Jews, we got in touch with them and we were given some money.

Since I had attended hotel school and graduated from that school, I decided to get a job as a waiter in a restaurant. My mother and sister knitted little baby shoes which a lady bought from them. It was pittance but it was still enough to buy food.

In Italy, like in Germany, most able-bodied men had been drafted into the military. Many jobs that had been traditionally male were now filled by women but there was still heavy work, in factories and elsewhere, where men were needed. In occupied Netherlans the German Military Police would search houses and round up all young men that could be found, to be transported to Germany to work there. In Italy it seems that only those young men were taken into labor camps that could not prove that they had a stable job.

One night I walked home after I had finished work at the restaurant. It was dark and a mixed patrol stopped me on the street. A mixed patrol consisted of an Italian policeman, a German military policeman, and a third man. On some impulse I started running. I ran and tried to hide in the dark entrance of a house. Unfortunately there was a couple standing in there, kissing, and I bumped into them. They screamed and the policemen came and arrested me. But I think the Almighty up there protected me. At the police station was an officer who was a regular patron of the restaurant where I worked and he recognized me. He said: "Why, I know him. He is a waiter at the restaurant 'Da Ettore'. Let him go." They let me go but now I was scared because I had to give them my address and all the other information. We immediately looked for another apartment and moved there, to the Piazza Paolo da Novi, the next day, just in case they would come and check if I had told them a true story. It had become dangerous for a young man of 17, 18, or 19 to be out on the streets. Therefore, I decided to stay home. My mother and sister could still go out. Women were not bothered and they looked Italian anyway. My sister had brown hair, my mother black, and they were both rather petite, not Nordic.

I used this time when I had to stay indoors to learn English. I got myself a thick book and dictionaries and reading matter. I think that was where I learned most of my English. This happened in 1944. I spent seven months in hiding until May 1945 when the American 8th Army came and liberated Genoa. Being confined to the apartment was one of the worst ordeals of that period for me.

After the liberation my English came in handy because I soon found a job as a waiter in one of the military canteens. The Americans had gone on to Germany but the British stayed.

We then found out about and made contact with a committee that helped refugees to repatriate. We told them that we were from France but had come to Italy illegally when the Germans occupied southern France. They took down our names, looked at all our papers, and after four or five weeks we were notified that there were now transport facilities to take us to France. We were loaded onto a truck and driven to Nice. At the border we were given the de-lousing treatment, we were sprayed with this horrible smelling stuff, so that we would bring no bacteria or lice into France.

In Nice we felt safe. The Americans had a recreation center there for soldiers who were serving in Germany and could come here for two weeks R + R, rest and recreation. It was run by the Army but the actual work, like taking care of the bicycles that were rented out to civilians, was done by civilians. I found a job there and was glad for my knowledge of English. It was an interesting job, also, because the checking in and checking out of bicycles meant cigarettes and chocolate. In postwar France things were very difficult. Everything was still rationed and the food situation was very bad. We as young people, I was 19 at the time, got larger rations than the adults. But it was still difficult to get the basics like sugar, oil, flour, rice. I had a good friend, a former school mate, who worked in a pharmacy. He used to get us condensed milk, but on the black market, which meant at special, high prices. Sometimes I would even resell it and with the profits buy my own condensed milk. I had many different jobs just to get ahead. Many people were unemployed. I could not have a real job because as a foreigner I had no work permit. Entering France, we had become Greek again.

Between 1945 and 1947 we had contacted the American Consulate to see if we could immigrate to the US. I had a cousin in New York and I was sure she would give us an affidavit and all that was needed. She did that but we could not go to the US because there was no transportation available. So many people wanted to go to the US that the ships were booked out for years ahead and we could not afford to go by plane. We would have gotten visas if we could have proven that we had transportation.

At that point a former schoolmate of my mother wrote from Venezuela that it would probably be easy for us to immigrate to Venezuela. He had established himself there as a doctor; he had a clinic there. He wrote that it was a very hospitable country that even subsidized new immigrants for two or three months.

And he thought once we were in Venezuela it would be easy to get to the US from there.

We went to the Venezuelan Consulate in Paris, received our visas and boarded the boat to Venezuela. This was in 1947. The trip took more than two weeks and we used the time to learn Spanish. Since we already spoke Italian and French, we picked up Spanish pretty fast. It was just another romance language. It is not like if somebody speaks only Russian and Czech; then it would be difficult to learn Spanish.

Coming to Venezuela was, at first, even worse than coming to Greece years before. The heat was hard to bear, the people were very different and for my sister, at 23, the men were a problem. But we managed to get jobs almost immediately. My sister worked at the reception of a hotel and I got a job at an office as secretary-correspondent. Food was not scarce at all in Venezuela, we had some income and, despite the culture shock, things got better little by little.

My sister got married to a man whose uncle had been a prominent lawyer in Germany. Through him we learned that in Germany a restitution law had been instituted. If we would put in a claim right away (because time was running out) we would get some restitution. We filled out all the forms but I only received a lousy sum, probably in the neighborhood of one thousand dollars. This was called compensation for lost opportunity to study. But people, who had actually been in concentration camps or lost their family in a camp, naturally received more. We could, of course, not compare ourselves to the people who had suffered so much. But my sister and I had lost several years of our lives by hiding, running from place to place, being in constant danger.

In Venezuela I studied some more, I took courses in business and management, and in 1958 I started working for the oil industry. I did very well and did rise up rapidly. Then, in 1975 Venezuela nationalized the oil industry. Foreign companies were kicked out. From then on things went downhill. There were cliques, and foreigners like me were not very welcome. Yes, in Venezuela one was still looked upon as a foreigner even after 25 years.

Around 1980 I had had enough. A friend of mine, whose wife was also Venezuelan, had retired in Florida. He told me about the advantages of the university town where they had settled: the children could attend the university, the quality of life was very good and the real estate prices were lower than elsewhere. I went to Florida, looked around with my friend, and I liked it very much.

Later I came back with my wife and we bought a piece of land in a nice subdivision, close to the university and to shopping, but quiet and pretty with lots of trees. But now we had to get visas, which was very difficult. Finally I got a visa for three years as an intra-company transferee, a sort of purchasing manager for the company. We moved to Florida but six months later the bottom fell out of the Venezuelan currency, the Bolivar. Export and import restrictions were installed; there was no foreign currency available. I could not do anything. As the end of the three years approached we faced having to go back to Venezuela. But then we learned that there was a visa lottery and that I would have preference because I was born in Europe. People born at Colombia, Venezuela, Argentina, and Asia were excluded. And this was probably the 6th time that somebody up there really had us in his heart because we made it, we got our visas. Later I learned that for 25,000 available visas there had been over one million applicants. I could hardly believe that we were among the lucky ones. I can still see it myself, it was in 1987 when I went to our letterbox in the front yard and the letter from the Immigration and Naturalization Service was in there. I opened it and it said: 'You have been accepted. Send us all the data and all the forms.' My wife had gone shopping so I jumped into my car, drove after her and found her in the grocery store and said: "Look, look, look! We got it, we got it, we got it." It was such a happy moment. Then, of course, came all the red tape. But three months later we flew to Caracas to pick up our visas at the American embassy. I was 61 years old. From now on I could work officially, translating and interpreting.

It is fantastic. When I think about all the mishaps, I also think about all the breaks I got. One has to count both. I have to be grateful for many things. I have passed many bad moments and I have missed an education but on the other hand, I am in very good health, I have two wonderful sons who have no problems in life. I have been spared many illnesses that others had to go through. I am so lucky. Of course, everything is not perfect. But what is perfect?

My Family

The war can have impacts on families that are not as obvious as others. This was the case for my family.

My father, as a journalist, obviously had special insight into the political situation before Hitler came to power. He had been the politics editor of a daily newspaper in northern Germany. The owners of the newspaper were followers and supporters of Hitler. Sometime in 1932 they told my father to either write his articles in the National-Socialist view or leave the newspaper – which he did.

My father had met my mother some time before and the two decided to marry despite his poor financial situation. His hobby was photography and he was good at it and could "keep his head above water" by taking portraits of people and developing the film himself.*) *) At the time was only black-and-white photography. Developing and printing of photos was relatively easy.

After a year or so, already well into Hitler's chancellorship, the young couple got a job managing a youth hostel on a mountain near the French border. This was actually not an easy job. There were frequent meetings where large groups of "Hitler-Youth" young men stayed at the hostel for a few weeks, mostly in tents. My mother had to work with a large number of girls in the kitchen, who worked for the (probably very hungry) boys. My father put together lectures about history, geography, literature, culture, combined with the maintenance, pictures he had taken, and care of the hostel, and fixing what needed to be fixed.

In the autumn of 1933 one late evening, a longtime friend of my father came to the backdoor asking for help. He was a Jew and he needed to flee the country. Of course my parents took him in, fed him, gave him what he needed, money and maps, and let him go again. The next day a police officer came, asking if this friend had been with them. Both my parents said no. But later they thought about it and felt it was not worth lying and that their friend surely was safe across the border by then anyway. So my father and my very pregnant mother went down to the town's police station to report that, indeed, they had seen the friend, and my father said something like: "This is my home country. And what kind of government is this when a citizen can not live in freedom but has to flee the country!" My parents went back home undisturbed. I was born a few weeks later. Maybe the local official wanted to be considerate towards my mother or maybe it took them some time to get advice from their combined with supervisors.

Anyway, I must have been already about four months old when my parents were fired from their job. My father was declared as not being "politically acceptable", especially around young people.

What can an unemployed young family with a four months old baby do in the middle of the winter? My Aunt Lisa, my mother's sister and a teacher, had some, rather small, savings. With this and their own my parents made a down payment on a house in the Black Forest which seemed to be suited to be made into a guest house. It proved to be alright. Soon guests came to enjoy the beautiful landscape and the clean and fresh air.

It must have been hard work for both my parents. Some guests came who had been ill and wanted special nursing, by of course, my mother. Aunt Lisa came whenever there were school vacations to help.

And then some local regional government office apparently found or been reported that my father was not a good National-Socialist and kept him under surveillance. Where better to do this in prison. I have never understood the principle behind this. He had to report at certain intervals to be incarcerated for a certain amount of time. In between these jail times he could come home.*) *) I learned much later that it was the practice of the Nazi regime to put people in prison from time to time, who were not politically acceptable but not considered dangerous.

When I was three years old my mother became ill with pneumonia. Her immune system must have been weakened by too much work and too much worry about my father. Antibiotics had not been discovered yet (or it was not available there) and it was the depth of winter. When the snow was finally passable the physician came. But it was too late. My mother passed away in early March of 1937. Aunt Lisa took me to live with her, and my father took a job as a clerk in a factory a few towns away. I never knew when he had to spend time in jail.

In 1943 my father was working in a city in the Black Forest and Aunt Lisa and I traveled there because we had planned to spend the summer vacation with friends not too far away from where he worked. The three of us rode a cable car up to a mountain and up there we said goodbye to each other. My father went back to the city and Aunt Lisa and I hiked through the mountains to where our friends lived. I can still see my father turned around and walked away. This was the last time I saw him.

At home again a couple of months later I was allowed to spend several days at my grandparents' house in the next village from where we lived. These were always good days because both my grandparents, Opa and Oma, were wonderful people and behind their house was a large garden with flowers and vegetables and berries and fruit trees and rabbits and chickens. When Aunt Lisa came back, she took me out into the garden and said to me: "Papa's heart has stopped beating." The reality of this pronouncement did first not fully register with me. Maybe it was because that summer I had taken leave of him and had sensed deep down that we would not see each other again. I don't know. I was nine years old. It was war. Men died all the time somewhere far away. Many fathers of my school friends would never come home again.

Only many years later did I learn what had happened. Papa had been in prison again. There were always interrogations about something. But one day he was told that two of his friends from years back had been brought to the same prison and that they had admitted to having had homosexual relations to him. My father at first said that this was not true, which of course it was not. But then the person interrogating him said that if he admitted to homosexual relations with his friends, the friends would be freed. My father believed the interrogator and, wanting to save his friends, said yes. Whereupon the man laughed and told him that they had executed the two friends already the day before. At the time being homosexual was a crime in Germany (as it was in many other countries and still is in some). Now that the officials had my father's "admission" – no matter how false it was – they could put him in a concentration camp. Aunt Lisa had visited him shortly in prison, after this interrogation had happened and he had told her about it. The next day in prison, while she was still in the city, the transfer to the concentration camp was to be performed. A day or two later she was informed that he had died. She never learned how it had happened. I myself have wondered for some time but then decided that I would never know and I did not even want to know. (Many years later, already in the US, I told this story to a friend who was about my father's age. His first question was: "Was your father Catholic?" Upon my affirmation, he told me that the Nazis declared all Catholics as homosexuals, who they wanted to get rid of.)

When Aunt Lisa had picked up Papa's few belongings from the prison, she had asked a prison guard if her brother-in-law had been tortured. He said: "Oh, never! He was so much better than everyone." I accept this also. Maybe the guard said this because Aunt Lisa was an attractive young woman (just 40 at the time). But I accept it as the truth because I know that my father was a very, very special person. He was highly intelligent, he was warm and caring, he could do anything he set his mind to, no matter if it was something practical or mental.

In this wartime when one could get essentially nothing, he found little things to make people happy. Aunt Lisa once said to me: "I have never known anybody who could give presents like your father." People liked and respected him and he liked and respected people.

Years later Aunt Lisa gave me the journals that Papa had written for me. He had written about books he had read and what he thought and felt about the ideas expressed in them. He also had written about his own ideas about life and death and how he thought I should how I should live to be happy. He had put together a very large book for me, in which he had glued pieces of music and stories that I might like and that I would I find interesting and as samples of our culture.

After the war, the French occupation forces took all books of some people, and especially from teachers. Our landlady saw how a neighbor's books were being loaded (in potato sacks!) onto a military truck. She ran to us and asked what which books she should save by hiding them underneath her large apron. Aunt Lisa gave her to save this big book that my father had put together and the small books he had written for me. The lady saved these and now I still have everything. I think that my father somehow had a premonition that he might not be around by the time I would be old enough to discuss his ideas with him.

Papa was also a wonderful musician. As a young man he had taught himself to play the piano and the violin and he played both very well. Music must have been his refuge. Whenever he came to visit us, he would bring some new songs that he had composed. He tried them out on our piano and then had Aunt Lisa sing them, while he accompanied her. Only later did I learn that he had composed and written them down in prison where naturally there was no piano. He was hearing his songs for the first time on our piano at home. I have a stack of books filled with his songs. Some are in the style of folksongs, others like "Lieder" but all are warm and melodious and very precious.

I have asked myself at times if I ever grieved for him and I must admit that I have not really. I think that his death has never been quite real to me. I know in my head that he died in 1943 but that had not kept me from secretly expecting to meet him somewhere. Especially when I came to America in 1964, I would catch myself, looking into men's faces in the absolutely unreasonable hope to see him again. Maybe, just maybe, he had escaped from Germany (because I know the government often lied). In the last 30 years or so, I have not done this anymore. He was born in 1895. He could not possibly be alive anymore. But I sometimes dream that I find him and get to spend precious times with him.

As a child I sometimes imagined my mother coming to me but not as a person but rather as an angel. My parents are always real and loving to me. I feel their good light around me.

Nicole: The Pianist and French Resistance Member (born 1920)

My French friend, Nicole, was born in 1920. She was 19 when the war started and 24 at the war ended at 1944 *). *) for France, especially for Paris, the war ended one year before Germany. She spoke German fluently but only a smattering of English. At her marriage to an American officer, her sister had to translate forms for the newlyweds between French to English. In America Nicole learned English very fast.

I met Nicole when she and her family moved to a town in Florida with a distinguish university.

A couple of university women had founded an "International Club", whose purpose to give foreign and American women an opportunity to meet. This is where Nicole and I got to know each other. She had learned Germany fluently, and a little bit of English. I had taken French at school for nine years but my English was still rather rough; so it was natural that we could spoke in our own languages. We found so many similarities in Europe's cultures, literature and especially music. Nicole was a talented pianist and teacher for advanced students. My piano playing was only basic but I knew much of music and loved classical music. We became close friends and stayed it for her life.

However, when I asked her to tell me about her life before, during and after the war, her own experiences and totally different feelings came out. Nicole told me:

When I was 15 years old (1935), I went to Germany for 3 months to improve my German. At school I had learned and practiced German for 3 years. Now I lived with a very nice family in Köln (Cologne). I met several nice German students. When I complained that in France in school I had too much reading, French, Latin and Greek and so on. The Germans told me I was so lucky: I could read whatever I wanted to while they could only read what was not on a forbidden list.

I saw men working in the streets. They were not wearing uniforms but had armbands with swastikas on. I think they were members of the Arbeitsdienst. They were to build and repair streets, and work on rivers, and so on. I had no contact with them.

One day I was out canoeing with a group of students and it got late. One student (17 years old) asked me to call his mother because it was late and she would worry.

251

I told him to call her himself. But he said he could not and showed me the telephone booth where was a sign "Juden verboten" ("Jews prohibited"). In the city were Jewish stars marked at some stores that belonged to Jews. There was no vandalizing – yet – only the signs.

I learned the word "Ersatz". There was Ersatz-coffee and there was margarine instead of butter. And this was in 1935, four years before the war even started.

Back in France a family friend from Prague visited us. She was crying and said to my father "Please don't let Germany invade Czechoslovakia, my country." In 1939 Poland was invaded and the war started.

I was in Paris, studying music. My brother was here too, studying medicine. My family lived in Lorraine which was some distance to the Maginot Line, the defense between France to Germany.*) *)France had built the Maginot Line during WWI and strengthened it in WWII. *People living close to the Maginot Line were evacuated, moved to central France. I saw so many refugees and it was absolutely horrible: horse-drawn carts with people crying, children and babies. They could not save their houses and farms and had to leave all behind.*

In 1939 at the beginning of the war there was first the so-called "drole de guerre" ("the funny war"). There was absolutely nothing happening, no shooting, nothing. Of course we had to observe black-outs. We could not have Christmas lights, only a cradle in the crypt of a church, black curtains and everything. Well, it was quiet till May 1940. At the time I was in Paris studying music with my brother who was a medical student. My mother would come from Lorraine regularly to check on us. When she came, we picked her up at the "gare de l'est"(the east station). One day she came off the train and said: "I don't know what's going on. We had some funny airplanes all over." They were gliders. The Germans had started their invasion of France. My mother never went back to Lorraine. Later my younger sister came by train; my father had sent her to Paris. Her train had been bombed by the Germans in several places. In Paris we had to be very careful not to make loud noises, not slam doors because she would jump at everything. She was still reliving the bombings she had been through. My father was still in Lorraine and then the Germans came.

I remember that in Paris the French burned their resources of petrol and of oil. Paris was penetrated by thick smoke. It was just awful. All this thick smoke; and we can not breathe.

With the Germans coming closer and closer we decided to
leave Paris. Luckily my mother, sister and I could go to Orleans by
train where we had friends waiting for us. My brother left on his
bicycle. We didn't know what happened to my father. In Orleans
the Germans kept coming closer, so we left Orleans to go to
Richilieu (near Anger; about 400km, 250 miles, from Paris) First we
traveled by a horse-drawn cart. There were so many people. I don't
remember why we later abandoned the cart and continued on foot.
At one point I became separated from my mother and sister. I had
to hide in a ditch because I was machine gunned by an Italian
plane. They missed. I wished I could have spit at them but of course
I couldn't do so. Finally we found each other again and kept going
on foot. We slept in a field but then were picked up by an
ambulance. They took us to Richelieu where our relatives were
waiting for us. Back in 1938, we had been afraid that war would
come. W e had sent our relatives important papers, jewelry, silver
and valuables to be buried in their yard. After some time my father
joined us there by car. He hadn't come anything from our Paris
apartment. He had taken his car with as many people as possible -
it was more important to save lives than possessions. Then my
brother came on his bicycle. He had also been machine gunned on
the road.

Then the Germans came to Richelieu. I remember that one
morning I had gone to mass with my cousin. We came out of the
church and there were Germans marching in the street. They were
all good-looking soldiers, very disciplined and they sang beautifully.

At home we were all crying. My father and our relative,
both WWI veterans, listened to the BBC. They heard de Gaulle
saying "Français, Français!" and then Churchill came on.

We still had the car and some gasoline and so can we were
returning to Paris by car. When we drove through Chartres we
stopped at my grandmother's and my aunt's. There were lots of
Germans in their large gardens. When we got to Paris we couldn't
believe it: there was no food. The stores were empty. We had never
seen a store without milk, butter, everything.

In 1940 the German occupation of France had started.
Armistice Day was November 11, when WWI had ended. The
Germans had put a swastika on the tomb of the Unknown Soldier.
My brother was really involved in a lot of activities that I don't
know too much about. He told me to get my bike and bring some
flowers to cover the swastika with flowers, and he said to do this
really early or otherwise because the Germans might catch me. So I
had a small bouquet of violets. I put them in the pocket of my
raincoat; I still remember that.

The stems stuck out and a French policeman said: "Mademoiselle, the stems are sticking out. You better push them back into your coat pocket." After I put the flowers there, I went back home. At the Metro station several students were arrested. I don't know what happened to them.

In 1941 the occupation slapped a curfew on us. One evening my brother and I came home just in time and were still able to push the electric button to open the door to our house. Our apartment was on the 6th floor and we went out on the balcony to watch what was going on in the street below. We lay down on the balcony so we wouldn't be seen. I think I will never forget this enjoyed seeing this. A German patrol unit was marching by and you could hear their heavy boots; they were very precise in their marching. And there was also a young French woman, wearing wooden shoes. (At the time we had wooden shoes because we didn't have leather for soles.)*) *) It was long before soles were made of rubber and other synthetic made material. *The woman walked in her clogs in exactly the same rhythm as the soldiers, so they would not hear her. We on the balcony kept whispering: "I hope she's going to make it, I hope she's going to make it!" And she actually did it. We saw her reach her door, push the button and slip inside. This was a really very happy sight.*

Later in 1941, I think, the curfew was lifted again. We had actually enjoyed the curfew: We did invite friends, stay at somebody's home and have a good time. We French don't live to work; no, we work to live and enjoy life. So they lifted the curfew because it just did not do much good.

In 1940/41 my friend's father was shot by the Germans. He was like a martyr. He was a physicist and probably had politically unfavorable opinions. One day my friend sent got me a note, saying to check the newspaper. There was a notice with a black border around stated it, listing the names of all the people who had been killed. Her father's name was on it. There was no information about why, where it had happened, where they were buried. After this my friend joined to the French Resistance, helping people where help was needed. She was arrested by the Germans in 1944 but was liberated by the Americans. So she was saved.

We were all starving. We were the lucky ones because my parents could afford to buy on the black market. We were not completely starving but were always hungry. And I remember: it was so cold, terribly cold. We had no heat. We had pants for heat and even with them, I still remember, we slept with scarves and hats, gloves and socks. Oh, it was terribly cold.

If we left a little bit of water in a bowl, in the morning it was totally frozen. It could easily have been 28° F in our apartment. And the cold and the hunger stayed with me.

At some point I started to distribute this clandestine newspaper published by the Resistance or whatever. I remember I was given to carry them in bags on my bicycle. I could not leave any distributed because they were too precious not to be distributed. In 1944 my brother was arrested for the first time but only for one day. He told me: "Stop distributing the newspaper, because they will get you too". So I stopped.

I kept taking my music course but we couldn't pay my teacher because he was a Jew. When the war started between Germany and Russia, we couldn't buy Russian music. In 1943 I remember giving a recital and toward the end of the recital a raid started from English bombers came but I kept playing. The lights went out and the sirens sounded. But I kept on playing. I was not to give in the bombs.

My memories of America and Pearl Harbor: I was in class and the professor said something about it that we didn't understand. Later someone said that Japanese had attacked Pearl Harbor, and America had now joined the war. When we got home my mother was listening to the BBC. She spoke English really well, she was bilingual, and told us about the attack. We didn't really know what had happened, but for us it was a happy day.

One day in 1943 the Germans were searching our place. We had a beautiful ham, bought on the black market, of course. We were never about to give this to them. My grandmother was there, sitting up in bed, having tea or something. We hid the ham under Grandmother's pillows. The German officer opened the door and saluted to her. But he never discovered the ham under her pillow. After he left we all enjoyed our ham. So you see once in a while we had a few laughs too.

Until 1944 traveling was very difficult because of the bombs. The English and the Americans were bombing roads, trains, bridges, everything.

I was in Chartres then giving a piano recital. I remember there were Germans in the audience, of course I didn't look but then I played Chopin's the Revolutionary Etude. It was understood that Chopin had written it as a revolution when Warsaw was taken. So I used this as my encore, my own little protest.

Once my brother was riding the Metro, standing close to a soldier. He had a scalpel with him, because he was a medical student. He quietly got out his scalped and started to cut the soldier's tunic, open wider and wider. Some people left the train and nobody saw. My brother often had papers with him, false identification papers for Jews. He hid the papers inside his gloves. Many times passengers were checked on the Metro and we too were frisked. They frisked him but never thought of checking his gloves. I must say, I was scared stiff.

The Germans tried to brainwash us, saying they we were saving us from Jews and Masons. But we tried to make them as uncomfortable as possible. For example we always directed soldiers to go south when they should have been going north, and go west instead of east. After they realized what we did, they were not so nice anymore.

My grandmother and aunt lived in a large and beautiful house in Chartres. One German also lived at the house but he was a civilian. He tried to help out as much as he could and gave them some little food, a little bit of coal. One day some Germans came to check the house and I was there. I had to show them the whole house, from the attic to the basement. My grandmother was in her eighties and my aunt had cancer. But then I did something real stupid: As the Germans were leaving, I told them I had understood every word they said. My German was fluent by then. Three days later they threw my grandmother and aunt out of the house and took it over. The German civilian said he could not believe that anyone and can do such a thing. He tried as much as he could to help my grandmother and aunt. I don't know what happened to him later. He had a wife and child.

In 1942/43 the rations were very small, especially for young children and older people. Clothes and shoes were also rationed but they were almost impossible to find anyway. So we wore wooden shoes. But they were so elegant that later the Americans would to buy them for their wives. In fact, when I came to the United States, my husband insisted I bring my wooden shoes. They were not very comfortable but they were elegant. Each summer we would unravel the sweaters we had worn the winter before, wash the wool and then knit new sweaters for the coming winter. It was so cold, we needed to do that. We had no new clothes. One of the best Christmases was when my grandmother managed to have a blouse sewn for me from a nice white tablecloth.

In 1944 the bombing intensified, especially by the American ones. I remember one incident while I was teaching in Chartres.

The Americans bombed a train station where the trains but were not very accurate so sometimes they destroyed houses too. The Resistance had also blown up a bridge and there was a break in the bombing while it was blown up. We were hiding in the cellar and afterwards I came out and saw something is very sad because it shows what war does to people. You know me, I am not a mean person. But I saw a young German soldier being carried by on a stretcher, a young guy, mainly 19 or 18. He was laying helpless stretcher, his brain oozing out, and I laughed I remember that. I laughed loud and clear; I was so happy to see that. My brother had just been arrested so I was happy to see the dead soldier I know that he had probably a mother, father, brother or sister. And to this day I think it is terrible what war can do people. But I honestly was happy to see that.

My brother was arrested in 1944. He had not come home one night so we thought he had been arrested. But then he came back the next day. Then I never understood this. He told me: "Stop distributing the newspaper; they're watching you." Then later (it was between the 20th of May and the 6th of June) there was a phone call from a man saying he wanted to talk to the lady of the house. My mother was there, but he said he wanted to talk to me. He said: A young Frenchman had been arrested by the Germans and this was my brother. I was told he had been taken to the penitentiary. What could I do now? I took my bicycle and went to the penitentiary and asked what had happened. That was a crazy thing to do.

I walked directly to the soldiers at the office and talked to a sergeant. I called him "lieutenant", and the lieutenant I called "major". I did not call the colonel "general". I knew how the Germans are with titles and they're important to them. I asked him: "Why did you arrest my brother?" I was furious. Remember I spoke German fluently went on and on. Finally one of them, a lieutenant probably, took me outside and said: "You'd better go now." He said to meet him at 10 o'clock tomorrow because they'd send the prisoners out by bus. I did as he had told me. He said my brother will be taken out at 3 o'clock by bus to the train station. What could I do? Well, I followed the bus! You know me; I just followed the bus. The back of the bus was open and there were Germans with machine guns. I followed the bus anyway. I was a girl and brazen, so I just followed it. I went all the way inside the station to the train where they'd put my brother. Of course I never saw him again. But my brother had asked a German soldier to tell my sister: "I will not try to escape because if I do they will take my family. I want my family to feel safe. I will not try to escape." This was the last thing he said.

I walked along the train, closed and locked, with a piece of paper in my hand, and wrote down phone numbers of those arrested. I could hear people tapping. Of course I called all their relatives. I kept the paper and made a duplicate for the children to have as a remembrance.

What did we do after that? Well, the Americans landed, D-day came I remember. I was teaching a lesson to a girl at her house and the mother said: "Do you know what happened? They are here, they are here!" I asked "Who?" She answered: "The Americans! They landed!" And we thought of all the sacrifice that had entailed. But we were so happy! We put out flags; we had colored paper, red, white and blue. The bells started ringing. And the Germans began to leave Paris. They left Paris in cars and horse-drawn wagons, carrying their wounded. And of course they were stealing everything. I still remember cars with paintings and everything. They were looting en masse. We were waiting, of course, for the Americans to come. This was in 1944.

My sister and I were there. The Americans came, and they liked the French. However some Americans were bitter because they were not the first to enter Paris; Eisenhower let de Gaulle come in first. So the French tanks came first. We got up on the tanks we talked to them. One of the French soldiers gave me a and number to call his mother to tell her where he was. He had been with de Gaulle in England. Of course I called.

Then the Americans came. Of course we jumped on their tanks too. You have no idea what it meant to be free from the Germans. We walked under the Arch of Triumph; it was incredible. I still have the signatures of some of the Americans that came in. It was just crazy. Some Germans were still shooting from the roofs. My sister was caught in the subway because of that and could not get back. I had my bicycle and made it home. I still remember being at home hearing the noise of the Germans shooting from the roof. It did not last long. This was the end of the war for us, in 1944. Of course it was not the finished for the Americans because they still had the Battle of the Bulge.

Nicole and I met in Florida almost 20 years after the war. Wonderfully, we could be great friends despite what happened during the German occupation of France and after the war the French occupation of Germany. It was as if what happened was in a different life time. Now we could start to live again.

Nicole lived in Florida for the rest of her life. Music had always been her greatest most love.

We could talk always about everything, and we understood each other. Nicole was a "great soul", recognizing others' thoughts and needs. Once she told me that every night she prayed for everyone who needed it. I think she was helped by her faith through every part of her life.

While telling me her experiences, she said:

"I had to go through bad times. I would not want to have gone through all this. But I am glad also because it has grown me through it and it has made what I am. I am grateful for living and I enjoy it."

Friends (My friend Nicole is French, I am German)

She had asked her: How could she be my friend?
The armies of our respective countries
had fought each other through a long and brutal war.
We both had lost family in this war.
Our friends and neighbors might have shot at each other.
How could she be friends with a woman like you?

When she told me this,
she laughed
because this question was so utterly ridiculous.
And I laughed with her.
But deep inside it made me feel small, helpless
and then very angry,
the type of anger that has to stay inside and boil there
because it has no target it could hit,
causing burns that will never quite heal.

I had laughed with my friend about this dumb and ridiculous question.
How could we not be friends?
We shared so much:
Growing up in fear and feeling the very real hatred all around,
having so little to eat that a few slices of bread was special
and a few ounces of horse-meat were a rare treasure.
Living in constant fear.
Having nothing to feed the fire in winter
but the sacks of pine cones and twigs that had been collected,
and suffering through the bitter cold.

Living in constant fears.
Going to sleep in the cellar and not knowing
if we would be able to crawl out of it again
or if we would be pinned under the rubble.
Living in constant fear.
Waiting for loved ones and neighbors who never came
because they had been burned by phosphor to the size of little children
or had been shot or tortured to death.
Living in constant fear.

And we remember how, out of there dreadful, darken years,
we squeezed so many tiny, precious specs of light,

how we lived in these close-knit and very pragmatic communities
that grow among people facing danger together.
How sometimes our frail little words
were made to feel safer, a little more comfortable, and almost happy
by little acts of kindness and care,
by lucky coincidences,
by the joy in the immaterial treasures of our own cultures
which bombs and brutalities could not reach.
During these times we did not keep secrets and surprises from others,
but celebrated birthdays and Christmases the night before
because we might not be alive the next day to celebrate.
We found pride and delight in being inventive with nothing.

Later we realized in wonder
that during these dark years of our childhood and youth
we had not examined, judged, or evaluated this darkness;
we had not even examined, judged, our pain and our fears.
And neither had the people around us done so.
There had been no time for that. We were busy just to live and to survive.
Only years later did our experiences slowly start to come into focus.

. . .

An old story is being told about a man
riding on a dark and foggy night
for miles over an empty, snow covered plain.
When he finally found a light and people with it,
he learned that he had not been crossing a plain,
but had been riding across the largest and deepest lake on the continent,
frozen over for the first time in a century.
The realization of the danger he had been in it, killed him on the spot.

. . .

The realization of the severity of our experiences did not kill us.
We would even have mocked anybody who would have whined and complained
and claimed emotional or other "damages" from these years.
Life at the time had been like this and that was just it.
We had been lucky to survive.

We two friends from opposite sides of a terrible war
can't help but feel close to each other
in the knowledge of our experiences.
We don't care what did what to whom.

We don't talk about
what I saw her countrymen do
and what I didn't see but know they did.
We don't talk about
what she must have seen my countrymen do
and what she didn't see but knew anyway.

Many years after the war we met for the first time in this new country.
We had come as strangers into a strange culture,
looking forward to new experiences,
ready to offer the gifts of our own cultures
and to receive the gifts of our new country's culture.

How could we not have become friends after all this?
We share so much.
We share so much with each other
and so little with the woman who posed that ridiculous question
out of her own poor, narrow, safe and regulated life.
But then how can we dare to judge her judgment?
how can we dare to judge her life?
We have our own world of experiences
that is secret and hidden from so many others,
no matter how wide open it seems.
What can we know about this other woman's secret world?

The anger inside me has cooled.
Old pains and fears don't hurt anymore.
I am holding the sum of these years in my hands
like a large rounded jewel,
dark and shimmery with countless little flecks of light,
a jewel that is very, very precious.
I am content.

Author

Waldtraut Wanninger was born in Germany, where she lived during the time before the war, during the war, and the aftermath. She received a Masters Degree in Business.

In 1964 she came to the U.S. with her husband, who has a PhD in Physics, who had been invited to do research and teaching at a university in Florida to further the U.S. space program.

Waldtraut has translated many American children's books into German for family and friends.

She and her husband still live in Florida today.

Explanation of Terms

- **Arbeitsdienst**: "work service". In 1931, when the economy was poor, and unemployment high, the government founded a service where young and unemployed men were housed in barracks or camps and were fed. They worked on civic and land improvement projects; they drained swamps and built or improved roads.

  This was first called "Freier Arbeitsdienst" (free work service). 1935 Hitler changed this to "Reichs-Arbeitsdienst" and mandatory for all young men.

  Later the Arbeitsdienst was also mandatory for young women. They mostly worked at farms since the men were at the military. They also worked in families where young children needed to be taken care of.

- **Cossacks**: Russian folk that had their own culture and dependent political views, living in the south Russia. Mostly of them were against the Soviets. During WWII many Cossacks fought on Germany's side against the Soviet Union.

- **DP**s: (**D**isplaced **P**ersons) Evacuees from eastern countries.

- **Ersatz**: substitute

- **Flak:** **Fl**ugzeug-**A**bwehr-**K**anone (anti-aircraft canon)

- **Gestapo** (**Ge**heime **Sta**ats-**Po**lizei), the Secret State Police, was feared everywhere because it hunted down the slightest political deviations. In 1944 (right before the end of WWII) 32,000 Gestapo agents were working in Germany and all of the occupied Europe countries. The Gestapo agents often wore uniform but also sometimes civilian clothes. If someone had spoken about any political deviations, friends, neighbors and others did not report it to the Gestapo.

  After the war in the German Russian occupied zone the Stasi started. Stasi meant **Sta**ats**si**cherheitsdienst (State Security Service). It worked similar as it had worked the Gestapo before, except now one could not say anything about communism. The Stasi had about 90,000 full-time employees, who were assisted by 170,000.

A funny note: After Germany was reunited, the Stasi was dissolved. It was said that so all of the Stasi agents were now unemployed and became taxi drivers. Apparently in east-Berlin a passenger had to give the taxi driver only the name of one's wanted destination, and would be taken to the place. It said that these former Stasi agents knew everybody's addresses.

- **Freicorps:** "Free Corps" first used for voluntary armies in Germany. After WWI the term was used for paramilitary units. The Free Corps got famous at the term of the Weimar Republic to fight in some towns against the Communism.

- **Hitlerjugend**: (Hitler Youth) It was mandatory that all boys and girls starting at age 10 and had to attend meetings each week. Uniforms should be worn. The Hitlerjugend were meant to be taught the NSDAP philosophy, but only a few leaders did this. Most leaders managed his/her groups somewhat like Boys/Girls Scouts.

- **NSDAP**, **N**ational **S**ozialistische **D**eutsche **A**rbeiter **P**artei (National Socialistic German Working People Party). This means: National Socialistic was to declare this party was only "national" not international, in contrary to the large Socialistic Party that was working at least in all of Europe. This Worker Party had to draw the unemployed. After 1933 the only Party in Germany was allowed, no other ones.

- **NS** was abbreviated for NSDAP. All kinds of organizations were written before them, like the (mandatory) "NS teacher association", the "NS women organization" who were supposed to train women politically but usually help and teach about practical matter. There was even a "NS Club for small gardener".

- **Ortsgruppenleiter**: is the political mayor of a town or city.

- **Panjewagons:** Panjes are small but very strong and tough horses. They are especially used to pull special smallish wagons in Russia and all in west Asia.

- **Reich** is an area that is a combination of kingdoms, dukedoms, etc. and ruled by an emperor. The 1st Reich was founded at 800 AD by Emperor Charles (actually the Holy Roman Empire at 962). The 2nd Reich started 1871 and ended 1918 with WWI. Hitler called Germany the 3rd Reich (from 1933 to 1945).

- **Reichsdeutsche and Volksdeutsche**: During the 3ʳᵈ Reich people living inside the borders of Germany when it existed at 1933, was called Reichsdeutsche (Reichs-Germans).

- **Volksdeutsche** (People-Germans), people who were all ethnically Germans but lived in different European countries.

- **Russia Soviet Union**: According to the story teller, I have interchangeably used "Russia" and sometimes "Soviet Union". The Soviet Union existed from 1918/1919 until 1991.

- **USSR:** The Soviet Union consisted the annexed all smallish republics in the region under the order of Russia.

- **SA:** (**S**turm **A**bteilung), "Storm Department", started as being paramilitary. The SA had to protect and supervise the official meetings of the NSDAP.

- **SS:** The "**S**chutz **S**taffel" was already started at 1925 as a Protection Squadron. About 300 men were excited about the plans that Hitler showed them which was to build a new respected, safe and prosperous country. In reality this paramilitary organization was to protect Hitler and to fight members of other parties.

  In 1933 Hitler made Heinrich Himmler the chief of the SS. Later became SS the elite guard of the Nazi Reich and Hitler. It was executive forces prepared to carry on all security-related duties, without regard for legal restrain. Himmler was the most cruel and brutal person that one can be.

- **Spartakus-Revolte (1919)**: "Spartacist Revolt" was a left-wing uprising designed to establish a Communist state in Germany and destroy the Weimar Republic. The Spartacist league was a group within the Communist Party.

- **School System:** Children started 1ˢᵗ grade at 6 years old at the "people's school". Children who wanted to learn a trade stayed for 9 years. After this a child started his/her 3 years apprenticeship either with a master or at a factory's training department. During these 3 years the student had to go to the "Berufschule" (trade school) once a week where they were taught the theoretic basics of their trade and business areas. School is still mandatory until 16. When children have not decided what they want to be or they do not want to work later, they have to go to trade school anyway. These girls have to attend the basics of housework.

- Children who want to prepare for an academic profession or a higher position take an examination after 4th or 5th grade and move to the "Höhere Schule" (higher school) for 9 school more years. After passing the final examination, "Abitur", one can then apply to a university.

- **Stuka**: (**Stu**rz-**Ka**mpf-Fluzeug). Named as the mostly Allied **dive bombers,** these planes could kill people via on board machine gun carried one or two bombs.

- **Weimar Republik**: Weimar Republic was the German government from 1919 to 1933. It was founded after the Monarchy (after WWI) and lasted through Hitler's ruling of Germany. The Weimar Republic got its name from the German town, Weimar.

Bibliography

Von Bismark zu Hitler
Sebastian Haffner
Kindler Verlag GmbH, München, 1987

Anmerkungen zu Hitler
Sebastian Haffner
Kindler Verlag GmbH, München, 1978

Deutschland, Deutschland über alles
Joachim Fernau
F.A. Herbig Verlagsbuchhandlung GmbH, München, 1972

Der SS-Staat (English as *The SS-State*)
Eugen Kogon
Kindler Verlag GmbH, München, 1974

Blick durchs Prisma
Wilhelm zur Linden
Vittorio Klostermann, Frankfurt am Main, 1964

Der Untergang
Joachim Fest
Alexander Fest Verlag, München

Staatsstreich, Der lange Weg zum 20. Juli
Joachim Fest
Goldmann Verlag / Jobst Siedler Verlag, Berlin, 1973

Der rote Faden
Wolfgang Heintzeler
Seewald Verlag, Stuttgart, 1983

The Hiding Place
Corrie Ten Boom
Baker Publish Group, Grand Rapids, MI, 1071

Weimar 1918 – 1933
Heinrich August Winkler
Verlag C.H. Beck, München, 1993

Schwäbische Spuren im Kaukasus
Peter Haigis / Gert Hummel

Sternberg-Verlag, Metzingen, Württemberg, 2002

The Two Unholy Kings
Wolfgang Schwartz
Die Rheinpfalz, local newspaper, 1948

Atlas zur Erdkunde
Hermann Lautensach
Keysersche Verlagsbuchlandlung, Heidelberg, 1954

Meyers New Lexicon
Meyers Lexiconverlag, Mannheim, Leipzig, Wien, Zürich, 1993

The New Encyclopedia Britannica
Helen Hemingway Bento, Publisher, 1973-1974
Auckland, Geneva, London, Manila, Paris, Rome, Seoul, Sydney, Tokyo, Toronto

Der Spiegel (weekly German political magazine)
Spiegelverlag Rudolf Augstein GmbH, Hamburg

Wikipedia
Google

Made in the USA
Middletown, DE
12 July 2022